Material discourses of health and illness

Material Discourses of Health and Illness explores the way in which the meaning, context and consequences of bodily phenomena, ranging from sex to heart disease, are created and transformed by human activity. It introduces a range of theoretical perspectives which can contribute to an understanding of the meaning and context of embodied experience, drawing on phenomenology, ecological psychology, post-structuralism and social constructionism. A critical overview of the methods and rationale of qualitative research and discourse analysis is given, and key issues confronting discursive researchers are addressed. These include the status of physical 'reality', the problem of relativism, and the question of how the validity of qualitative research can be established.

This book provides practical examples of how these approaches can be applied to the field of health psychology with a collection of sophisticated discursive analyses of health-related topics, ranging from eating behaviour and childbirth to dialysis, deafness and AIDS. Each chapter explains and justifies a different approach, reflecting on its practical utility as well as its limitations.

This imaginative and timely reconciliation of discursive and materialist perspectives will interest a wide readership of health and social psychologists, sociologists, feminists and anthropologists.

Lucy Yardley is Senior Lecturer in Psychology, University College London, and author of *Vertigo and Dizziness* (Routledge, 1994).

Material discourses of health and illness

Edited by Lucy Yardley

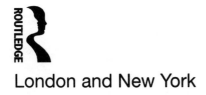

London and New York

First published 1997
by Routledge
11 New Fetter Lane, London EC4P 4EE

Simultaneously published in the USA and Canada
by Routledge
29 West 35th Street, New York, NY 10001

Typeset in Times by Routledge
Printed and bound in Great Britain by Mackays of Chatham PLC, Chatham, Kent

British Library Cataloguing in Publication Data
A catalogue record for this book is available from the British Library

Library of Congress Cataloguing in Publication Data
A catalogue record for this book has been requested

ISBN 0–415–13823–X (hbk)
ISBN 0–415–13824–8 (pbk)

Contents

List of contributors   vii

Preface and acknowledgements   ix

1 **Introducing material–discursive approaches to health
   and illness**
   Lucy Yardley   1

2 **Introducing discursive methods**
   Lucy Yardley   25

3 **What role does the body have in illness?**
   Alan Radley   50

4 **Interpretative phenomenological analysis and the
   psychology of health and illness**
   Jonathan A. Smith, Paul Flowers and Mike Osborn   68

5 **Social and material ecologies for hearing impairment**
   William Noble   92

6 **Disorientation in the (post) modern world**
   Lucy Yardley   109

7 **The relationship between representational and materialist
   perspectives: AIDS and 'the other'**
   Hélène Joffe   132

8 **Discourses and sexual health: providing for young people**
   Roger Ingham and Denise Kirkland   150

9 **Discourses of pregnancy and childbirth**
   Anne Woollett and Harriette Marshall   176

10 Diet as a vehicle for self-control
    Jane Ogden   199

11 Speaking the decorated body
    John Soyland   217

    Index   232

Contributors

Paul Flowers is a researcher at the Medical Research Council's Medical Sociology Unit, University of Glasgow. His research interests include multi-method approaches to the study of sexual health, sexual behaviour and sexuality.

Roger Ingham is Reader in Health and Community Psychology at the University of Southampton, and Director of the Centre for Sexual Health Research. He has published widely in the field of sexual health research, and has been Consultant for the World Health Organisation's Global Programme on AIDS. Previous research interests include accident risk and young drivers, and football 'hooliganism'.

Hélène Joffe is a lecturer in psychology at University College London. Her primary areas of interest are social representations theory, with specific emphasis on epidemics, and individualism; her recent (1996) publications can be found in *Journal for the Theory of Social Behaviour* and *British Journal of Medical Psychology*.

Denise Kirkland is a postgraduate student in the Department of Psychology at the University of Southampton. Her thesis topic is 'Strategies for risk-reduction in sexual conduct'. She is also a part-time lecturer at King Alfred's College, Winchester.

Harriette Marshall is a Principal Lecturer in the Psychology Division at Staffordshire University. She is a member of the editorial group for the journal *Feminism and Psychology*. Her main research interests include identity, issues around gender, ethnicity and the role of psychology in relation to inequalities.

William Noble is an Associate Professor in the Psychology Department at the University of New England, Australia. He is author of *Assessment of Impaired Hearing*, and (with Iain Davidson) *Human Evolution, Language and Mind*. Forms of communication and artifice are his particular interests.

Jane Ogden is a Senior Lecturer in Health Psychology at the University of London, where she teaches both psychology and medical students. She is currently conducting research into women's health, and her publications include *Fat Chance* and *Health Psychology: A Textbook*, as well as numerous papers on eating behaviour, smoking and risk.

Mike Osborn is a clinical psychologist employed by the Doncaster Royal Infirmary and Montagu Hospital NHS Trust to work with patients with chronic pain, trauma and genito-urinary problems and in the occupational health department. His research interests are in the psychology and phenomenology of illness and trauma.

Alan Radley is Reader in Health and Social Relations in the Department of Social Sciences at Loughborough University. He is the author of several books, including *Prospects of Heart Surgery* (1988), *The Body and Social Psychology* (1991) and *Making Sense of Illness* (1994), and is editor of *Health: An Interdisciplinary Journal for the Social Study of Health, Illness and Medicine*.

Jonathan A. Smith is a lecturer in psychology at the University of Sheffield. His research interests are in the psychology of health and illness, self and identity, life transitions, and qualitative approaches to psychology. He is co-editor of *Rethinking Psychology* and *Rethinking Methods in Psychology*.

John Soyland was Lecturer in Culture and Communication in Psychology, at Lancaster University, where the present research was carried out; he currently lectures on history and philosophy of psychology in the Psychology Department, University of Sydney. He is author of *Psychology as Metaphor* (1994), and *The Body in Culture: An Introduction* (1997).

Anne Woollett is Reader in Developmental Psychology at the University of East London. With Ann Phoenix and Eva Lloyd she edited *Motherhood: Meanings, Practices and Ideologies* (Sage) and with David White she wrote *Families: A Context for Development* (Falmer). Her research interests are in families, children's development and women's experiences of childbirth and parenting.

Lucy Yardley is Senior Lecturer in the psychology department at University College London. Author of *Vertigo and Dizziness* (1994), she has an enduring obsession with the (strangely neglected) topic of (dis)orientation and (im)balance, and uses mixed methods to study the mind–body in health and illness.

Preface and acknowledgements

This book originated in a series of seminars instigated by Jane Ussher within the psychology department at University College London, which ultimately led to the establishment of the Women's Health Research Unit. The relationship between the material and discursive dimensions of human lives continually resurfaced as a central and problematic topic in a series of discussions of issues pertaining to sex and gender, health and illness. I am grateful to Jane not only for initiating these discussions, but also for suggesting that we should (separately) edit what eventually emerged as parallel and complementary books on this subject. This volume illustrates material-discursive approaches to topics which fall within the traditional province of health psychology, while the book edited by Jane Ussher, entitled *Body Talk: The Material and Discursive Regulation of Sexuality, Madness and Reproduction*, is more concerned with feminist issues and mental health.

The purpose of *Material Discourses of Health and Illness* is twofold. One objective is to explore and illustrate at a theoretical and practical level the diverse ways in which analysis of the socio-linguistically mediated nature of our lives might be combined with an appreciation of the material, embodied nature of human existence. The relationship between the material and discursive dimensions is currently a prominent concern within many disciplines, including sociology, anthropology, philosophy and feminism, but until very recently there has been relatively little debate on this topic within the field of health psychology. Indeed, it is only in the past few years that the relevance of discursive theory and methods has begun to be appreciated, and outlets for discursive health psychology research (such as the *Journal of Health Psychology* and *Health*) have appeared. A second objective of this book is therefore to introduce health psychologists who have limited familiarity with discursive approaches to the philosophy and rationale of discursive analysis, and to show how it can be applied to the subject of health. Discursive language and methodology can sometimes seem alien and obscure to those more accustomed to experimental psychology, and I have consequently endeavoured to clarify, explain and justify material–discursive approaches in a manner which will contribute to a progressive convergence and collaboration between researchers who employ traditional methods, those who espouse discursive methods, and the growing numbers of health psychologists who (like myself) combine both.

I would like to thank the anonymous book reviewers for their constructive and encouraging comments on the initial proposal, Roger Ingham for his helpful advice and support, and I am grateful to Sandra Beech, Natalie Owen, Emily Phibbs, Jonathan Smith, Janet Stoppard and Jane Ussher for their comments on earlier drafts of my chapters. I am indebted to all the authors in this volume for their excellent contributions, for their positive responses to editorial comments, and for their active collaboration in the production of what we intend as a collection of analyses that are diverse and imaginative, but also harmonious and pragmatic.

Chapter 1

Introducing material–discursive approaches to health and illness

Lucy Yardley

The aim of this book is to explore a variety of ways in which a 'material–discursive' approach to health and illness can be implemented. The word 'discursive' is used here in a very broad sense to designate a range of approaches which recognise the socially and linguistically mediated nature of human experience. The term 'material' simply signals attention to the physical features of human lives, including not only our bodies and corporeal activities, but also our environment, institutions, technology and artefacts.

Discursive approaches[1] have been rapidly gaining acceptance and exerting increasing influence across a number of disciplines, especially in the social sciences and humanities, and are now becoming increasingly popular within health psychology. These approaches are actually multiple, disparate and constantly evolving, but nevertheless share a central assumption: namely, that human activities and social practices have a profound influence on the nature of reality – both subjectively experienced and scientifically observed reality. It is simply impossible for humans to transcend their own capabilities and context; ultimately, we can *only* perceive the world around us by means of human senses (even when their investigative capacities are vastly extended by human technology) and in relation to human desires and activities, and we *must* explain it to ourselves and others using human cultural concepts and language. If it is meaningless to conceptualise an 'objective' reality which is somehow independent of our activities and understanding, this means that the neutral perspective to which science claims to aspire can never be attained. Consequently, rather than striving for the illusory goal of objectivity, it is more productive to examine the way in which our reality – including the particular version of reality portrayed by scientists – is shaped by the purposes and conventions, aspirations and assumptions, which form an intrinsic part of human life.

While some psychologists have welcomed the opportunities that discursive approaches offer to re-examine our conceptions of health and illness, others have viewed discursive ideas and methods as challenging, or even threatening, the fundamental principles of psychological theory and research. Some fear that abandoning the goal of scientific objectivity leads inevitably to 'radical relativism' – a situation of intellectual anarchy in which all beliefs and values are treated as equally valid or invalid. This legitimate concern is addressed in Chapter 2, which discusses the alternative methods and standards employed by discursive analysts, and the complex and un-resolved problems pertaining to the assertion or negotiation of intellectual authority. Although discursive writers are careful not to assert that their own (or any other) beliefs and values are universal and timeless truths, very few adopt the extreme relativist position that no comparative evaluations are permissible; rather, they seek to debate and elaborate the criteria for decid-ing the merit and utility of an analysis.

A second objection to discursive approaches is that they privilege the socio-linguistic dimension to such a degree that the material dimension of human lives is denied or overlooked. It is certainly the case that the new appreciation of the importance of culture and language understandably led many discursive analysts interested in health issues to focus initially on the implications of social and communicative aspects of these topics. For exam-ple, discursive writers have examined how illness can be accommodated and assimilated by the sufferer by means of narratives (e.g. illness as a turning-point in life, or illness as an enemy to be fought and ultimately vanquished) which are used to create a viable new identity (Frank 1993; Riessman 1990). Discursive methods have been used to study the impact of dominant repre-sentations of health and illness in modern Western society, such as those which characterise people with disabilities as 'damaged goods', irreparably defective and unfit for display (Phillips 1990). In order to show how 'reality' is created by linguistic and social practices, others have analysed the way in which medical diagnostic practices are used to recast certain behaviours as 'symptoms' of mental 'disorder' (Harper 1992; Pilgrim 1992; Soyland 1994).

However, there is now a growing awareness of the need – which is particularly acute in the field of health and illness – to consider how the socio-linguistic aspects of experience relate to our material existence. To give just one example: in what way do the practical consequences of visual impairment (e.g. the inability to recognise and greet friends in the street or corridor) feed into the identity and social relationships of blind people?[2] Conversely, how do beliefs about the material aspects of blindness (e.g. that visual aids eliminate visual impairment, or alternatively that someone who carries a white stick is unable to see anything) influence the activities and opportunities of those with visual impairments? As soon as questions such as these are posed, it seems obvious that the socio-cultural and material aspects of human experience are intimately linked and that, while each *can* be studied separately, it is also useful to explore their reciprocal influence.

It is clearly important for health psychologists to include the material dimension of human lives in their theory and investigations, but how this can best be combined with socio-linguistic analysis remains a difficult ques-tion. One solution is to retain traditional methods of researching the physical and behavioural aspects of health and illness, but to also consider the impact of cultural and communicative factors, using discursive techniques. But for many discursive analysts, it is not enough simply to add a socio-linguistic angle to a traditional biopsychosocial analysis if this entails treating certain health-related phenomena as real (e.g. clinical test results) and others as socially constructed (e.g. illness perceptions). The problem is that, in practice, life cannot be simply dichotomised in this way. For example, an 'illness perception' may draw on embodied self-knowledge, such as an awareness of serious disease prior to medical diagnosis. Conversely, medical students soon discover that convention and interpretation are involved in determining the significance of even an X-ray (see Radley 1994), and that X-rays can serve a primarily symbolic function by reassuring the patient or affirming the expertise of the doctor. It is for this reason that a 'material–discursive' approach is adopted in this book, presenting a range of illustrations of the varied and complex manner in which the socio-linguistic and physical dimensions of health and illness are intertwined.

The second half of Chapter 2 outlines some theoretical perspectives that appear compatible with a material–discursive approach, and then considers the diverse ways in which the chapters following apply these perspectives to health- and illness-related topics. However, as a prelude to discussion of the possibilities for *material*–discursive approaches, it is useful to consider first the nature and origins of existing discursive approaches to health and illness. The next section sketches a brief outline and history, therefore, of biomedical, biopsychosocial and discursive perspectives on health and illness.

CHANGING PERSPECTIVES ON HEALTH AND ILLNESS

Development of the biomedical model

Over the past three centuries during which modern medicine has developed, its success has been attributed (at least by the historians of the medical profession) almost entirely to advances in the understanding and control of biological processes. Improvements in health and longevity are credited to the victory of medical science over nature: the conquest of invasive disease, the correction of physical malfunction, the repair of accidental damage, and the management of risky events such as childbirth. These triumphs are in turn attributed to ever-expanding scientific knowledge about the mysteries of anatomy, physiology, biochemistry, and (most recently) molecular genetics, together with increasing technological capabilities relating to procedures such as diagnostic testing and surgery.

In this biomedical account of how ill-health is conquered, the achievements of biomedicine are typically somewhat overestimated. Despite the undeniable, and often wonderful, power of modern medicine to cure, prevent or alleviate many physical ills, reduced morbidity and mortality rates in Western populations are actually due in large part to socio-economic and life-style factors such as improved diet, housing, hygiene and safety (Lewontin 1993; Fitzpatrick 1991). But the rhetoric of biomedical supremacy seems persuasive because it forms part of a larger discourse which has dominated Western thinking since the birth of the industrial era (Gordon 1988) – a discourse which asserts that by means of accurate observation and rational deduction human beings can attain an objective knowledge of the nature of reality that will enable us to predict and control nature (including our own bodies).

One of the fundamental premises of this 'realist' or 'objectivist' view is that facts about the world can be empirically ascertained by an objective observer (ideally, a trained scientist), and that these facts are independent of the socio-cultural context in which they are determined and untainted by the assumptions, goals, activities or previous experience of the observer. Subjective phenomena such as attitudes, beliefs, values and emotions are considered to be potential nuisance factors which can obscure or misrepresent the true state of affairs. From a realist perspective, biological phenomena, which are regarded as objective facts, therefore tend to be seen as more reliable and fundamental (and also more controllable and commercially useful) than the psychosocial context and meaning of these phenomena (Benton 1991). The result has been the emergence of a dominant biomedical model of health and illness which is based on 'biological reductionism' – in other words, a belief that bodily events are best explained exclusively in terms of objective physical processes, and that these must be distinguished from the psychological and social factors which might bias or distort how physiological events are perceived. Consequently, whereas physicians and healers in previous and non-Western cultures might see the social, subjective or spiritual significance of illness as an intrinsic and significant part of the phenomenon (a view often shared by the afflicted person and his or her associates), modern Western diagnostic practices are designed to exclude, or at least isolate, these aspects of illness in order to focus more clearly on the biological processes, which are regarded as of primary importance.

Development of the biopsychosocial model

The dominance of the scientific biomedical approach has never been total. One alternative model of the way health should be understood and promoted is the parallel tradition of 'social medicine', which in the last century took the form of large-scale interventions to improve public health through measures which ameliorated living and working conditions (Turner 1992). In the early part of the twentieth century, psychoanalytic and psychosomatic theories and research helped to foster an awareness of the contribution of the psyche to ill-health. And during the latter part of this century, as acute contagious disease has given way to chronic illness and disability, and the costs and limitations of scientific medicine have become increasingly apparent, there has been a growing appreciation of the need to consider psychosocial influences on health.

In the 1970s, the application of behavioural principles to health problems gave rise to the interdisciplinary field known as 'behavioural medicine', while 'health psychology' emerged as a new discipline. At the same time, a psychiatrist named Engel proposed the 'biopsychosocial model' as a framework for integrating knowledge about the biological, psychological and social aspects of illness (Engel 1977). Based on systems theory, the model was intended to foster the analysis of developmental processes and the reciprocal interactions between different levels of the human 'system', from the biochemical to the socio-cultural (Engel 1982; Schwartz 1982). The model was warmly welcomed by social scientists because it affirmed the importance of psychosocial factors and over the past two decades there has been a vast expansion in 'biopsychosocial' research.

As recommended by Engel, most of this research has produced quantitative measures of psychosocial variables such as behaviour, beliefs or perceptions, and then correlated these with signs of the presence, severity or progression of disease. These descriptive studies have been complemented by analysis of the physiological and medical consequences of experimentally or therapeutically induced changes in reported beliefs or behaviour. One major advantage of this approach has been that it has enabled psychological research to win acceptance from medical clinicians and researchers who are familiar with the language and procedures of scientific investigation. Employing methodologies such as laboratory-based experiments, quantitative questionnaire data and statistical analysis, it has been possible to achieve widespread recognition in medical circles that psychosocial factors significantly influence health status. The consequence is that psychology now forms a (relatively small) part of the medical school curriculum, and clinical and health psychologists have been given an increasingly substantial role to play in the promotion of health and care of the sick.

Development of discursive analyses of health and illness

Health psychology has always drawn inspiration from mainstream psychological theory, and especially from social and clinical psychology. While these disciplines were dominated by the behavioural and cognitive paradigms, there was relatively little difficulty in combining psychological and biomedical data; both were considered to have a similar epistemological status as scientifically verifiable facts, amenable to objective and quantitative measurement and analysis. However, the rise of discursive theory and methods in social psychology (e.g. Gergen 1985; Hollway 1989; Potter and Wetherell 1987) and constructivist approaches in clinical psychology (e.g.

Mahoney 1993; McNamee and Gergen 1992) has led some critics to question both the objective reality of biomedical and psychosocial 'variables', and the suitability of the traditional biopsychosocial model as a framework for understanding and researching human experiences of health and illness (Armstrong 1987; Stainton-Rogers 1991, 1996; Stam 1988).

A key problem identified by these critics is that the biopsychosocial model seeks to assimilate and incorporate non-medical aspects of health and illness while retaining an essentially biomedical perspective. For example, Engel advocated adopting a 'rational scientific approach to behavioural and psychosocial data' (Engel 1977: 132), in order to create psychosocial variables comparable to biomedical measures. This implies that standardised measures of such entities as 'personality' or 'cognitions' should be regarded as objective indices of underlying psychological realities. But from a discursive viewpoint, it is a mistake to 'reify' such psychosocial phenomena by treating them as if they were objective facts, since this limits our understanding of how and why these phenomena come to be construed by our language and society in one way rather than another (Henriques et al. 1984; Shotter 1993). Instead, discursive analysts view psychosocial phenomena such as personality or cognitions as changeable concepts which are created and maintained by roles and relationships, cultural conventions and social practices – including the activities of research psychologists who promote particular ideas about the 'underlying' causes of what people say and do. Hence, rather than allowing the psychosocial realm to be analysed in biomedical terms, discursive critics of the biopsychosocial model argue that we should reinterpret the biomedical realm from a psychological and socio-cultural viewpoint.

This enterprise inevitably raises some potentially sensitive issues relating to ideology and power relations. Whereas the image of science as objective and value-free allows traditional researchers to regard these issues as separate from the process of determining the truth, the discursive view is that not only the objects of study but also the process of research are deeply influenced by social relations, conventions and objectives. The socio-political implications of specific ways of depicting health and illness are therefore relevant to understanding their function and meaning. For example, Waitzkin (1991) has described how the social background, role and training of doctors can lead them to unconsciously reinforce dominant ideologies such as the importance of being economically productive or 'fit for work', and to define expressions of distress (which may indicate real psychosocial conflict) as symptoms which can be soothed (or suppressed) by medical treatment. Clearly, health psychologists are not immune from this form of critique; for instance, Stam (1988) has suggested that the lack of a distinctive theoretical framework for health psychology may be attributable to the need of the profession to secure funding by establishing its utility in a domain dominated by the medical profession. Since exposure of the implicit functions of particular approaches to health and illness can be discomfiting, it is important to appreciate that contemporary sociological theory does not suggest that power is a matter of deliberate oppression by individuals or groups. Rather, power relations are embedded in our systems of linguistic meaning and social organisation, and are therefore constantly renewed in social interactions (Foucault 1988). The role of the doctor is thus maintained by the expectations and behaviour of patients as much as by the interests of the medical profession or the government (Silverman 1987).

Recent critics of health psychology have also suggested that insufficient attention has been paid to the socio-cultural context of health and illness (Marks 1996; Stainton-Rogers 1996). Modern Western culture portrays people as private and bounded; consequently, illness is seen as principally a problem of the individual, and psychological variables such as depression or locus of control are viewed as essentially personal characteristics. In contrast, discursive theory posits that the identity, behaviour and expressed beliefs of individuals are largely engendered by their cultural history and social position (Shotter and Gergen 1989). The origin, meaning, purpose and implications of individual attitudes and actions can therefore only be understood in the wider context of the socio-linguistic customs and constraints which produce (and are in turn reproduced by) the discourse and activities of individuals (Harré and Gillett 1994). Any investigation into the psychology of health-related beliefs and behaviour must consequently consider their socio-cultural functions and connotations, and the way in which these may be influenced by class, age, gender or ethnic background, by macro-level social policies or micro-level patterns of social interaction, and by representations of health in the media, in medical discourse, or in casual conversation.

The qualities of discursive analysis can be most easily conveyed by concrete example, and so although the whole of this book is intended as an illustration of discursive approaches to health and illness, two brief samples of discursive analyses are given below.

Illustration 1: discursive analyses of coping

There has been a great deal of biopsychosocial research into how individuals can best cope with actual or potential health problems, either by adhering to a life-style or regimen which maximises physical health or by adopting attitudes and strategies which minimise the negative emotional and social consequences of illness or disability. This research has considered whether approach or avoidant styles of coping are most successful in the short-term and long-term, how coping styles may relate to the individual's degree of optimism, hardiness or resourcefulness, and how coping can be encouraged and supported by provision of information or training in skills. Focusing on the individual, relatively few of these studies have considered the way in which the material and social environment influence how people attempt to cope (although some have considered the impact of limited environmental interventions, or the effect of interactions with family or friends). More significantly, none have reflected on the social origins and implications of the *concept* of 'coping', to which this literature itself contributes.

The latter is a crucial omission, since discursive analyses have suggested that, for the healthy majority, the concept helps to maintain a sense of control over the dangerous, irrational and inferior forces of nature represented by our bodies (Kirmayer 1988). The consequences for the sick, therefore, can be far from benevolent; in order to preserve the illusion that control can be attained, those who fail to 'cope' must be condemned as either weak, defective, or culpably lacking in motivation or effort (Pollock 1993). Encouragement to cope, therefore, may be experienced as pressure to conform to society's ideals of normality, whether by concealing and 'overcoming' physical disabilities (Ville et al. 1994) or by stoically enduring pain (Jackson 1992).

In a similar vein, Lupton (1993) has pointed out that the well-intentioned health promotion literature nevertheless ignores the way in which discourse about the 'risky' behaviour of individuals serves the social function of justifying an increasing degree of surveillance and control over the behaviour of employees (even during leisure hours). Public health initiatives can thus be a means of policing behaviour considered deviant or undesirable; for example, recreational drug use and sexual promiscuity are strongly discouraged, while risky behaviours such as horse-riding and overwork are not. At the same time, the rhetoric about the need for self-care provides a way of seeming to tackle a health problem without actually addressing factors which contribute to it, such as poverty and stress.

Illustration 2: discursive analyses of the diagnostic process

Discursive analyses have shown how biomedical conditions can be considered, in one sense, to be *created* by consultation with the doctor (e.g. Barrett 1988; Taussig 1980; Waitzkin 1991). Initially, the doctor elicits and interprets a variety of forms of information (e.g. reported symptoms, medical history, test results). A highly selective diagnostic process determines what information is deemed relevant and reliable, and the diagnostic significance of each of these types of information is partly ambiguous. Even the interpretation of scientific data is heavily influenced by social conventions concerning what is 'normal', 'acceptable' or 'healthy'. For example, decisions about the clinical status of an individual's weight or emotional state – and even their blood pressure or blood sugar level – are affected by cultural and contextual factors, as well as subjective judgements (Mishler 1981; Ogden, 1994). Nevertheless, from this assortment of equivocal information the doctor generates a diagnosis which is treated thereafter as an unambiguous objective entity physically embodied in the patient. The authenticity of this diagnostic entity is then reinforced by constant repetition of words such as 'disease', 'patient', 'cure', and is regulated by the professional practice of enshrining 'legitimate' knowledge in medical journals (Stainton-Rogers 1991).

A common realist reaction to this kind of analysis is to object that if doctors' statements about disease were no more than a set of socio-linguistic practices agreed within a particular professional community, how could material accomplishments such as dialysis or kidney transplants ever have been achieved? However, the discursive analysis does not deny the scientific analysis of physiological functioning – it simply emphasises that biomedical entities are not simple facts, since the definition, character, meaning, and implications of these phenomena are fundamentally shaped by socio-cultural practices and preoccupations. The interpretations of doctors are not generated in a vacuum; their meaning is defined in relation to the relevant socio-cultural context – in this case a well-defined set of medical practices. Hence, a statement by a doctor that a patient has a disorder will typically imply examination or test results which other doctors would concur indicated disease, as well as the promise of a programme of treatment which the biomedical community considers beneficial.

If a *material*–discursive perspective is adopted, this argument can be extended by acknowledging that our embodied existence forms an intrinsic and vital part of the shared socio-cultural experience upon which our systems of language and meaning are based (Shotter 1993). Scientific assertions are thus 'discourses contextualized by the formations of culture, including the construct called *nature*, in which they are generated and by which they are constrained' (White and Wang 1995: 392). In other words, neither doctors, scientists, nor anyone else can easily justify statements that are obviously inconsistent with the shared experience which constitutes our 'reality'. But this reality is not the fixed, objective, physical world of the realists, but a world which is simultaneously material and (psycho)social, and which is constantly shaped and reshaped by the perceptions, intentions and activities of the members of society. This material–discursive view is elaborated in the second part of this chapter, which describes in more detail some of the theories on which it draws.

MATERIAL–DISCURSIVE APPROACHES TO HEALTH AND ILLNESS

Discursive writers have themselves become increasingly aware in recent times that discursive analyses of health and illness may have focused too exclusively on the socio-cultural aspects of illness, thus relegating the body to a passive, subsidiary role (Fox 1993; Turner 1992). The physical dimension of health and illness seems strangely absent from many discursive explorations of the personal and social meaning of symptoms, and the discourse and medical practices associated with illness. This emphasis on the primacy of the discursive dimension was in part a reaction against the reductionist materialism of the biomedical model, whereby social and psychological interpretations of biological events were assigned a secondary importance to the underlying 'reality' of disease. But insistence on the primacy of the socio-linguistic aspects of health and illness simply reproduces, in inverted form, the previous dualism of the biomedical model, and reinforces the mistaken idea that material existence can only be studied by physical scientists. If social scientists concern themselves solely with the personal, social and linguistic context and meaning of health-related issues, they risk seeming to implicitly acknowledge both that meaning can be divorced from concrete reality, and that the physical realm is beyond the scope of social science. This restrictive view will be countered below by introducing some of the theoretical perspectives upon which the contributors to this book have drawn for their material–discursive analyses.[3]

Meaningful materiality and the communicative body

Any approach to material being which could be readily reconciled with discursive analysis would need to incorporate an understanding that activity and context profoundly affect not only socio-linguistic meaning but also the material aspects of our existence. This entails an appreciation that the material dimension of living organisms is not an objective realm of neutral physical matter and mechanical processes, but is itself imbued with purpose and continuously shaped and reshaped by dynamic interaction with the environment.

A number of writers have suggested that phenomenology provides a suitable framework for studying the meaning of embodied experience in health and illness (Freund 1990; Radley 1995; Smith 1996; Yardley 1996). Early phenomenologists such as Kant, Hegel and Husserl provided an alternative to the realist tradition by drawing attention to the way in which our consciousness of the world is mediated and transformed by subjective processes. In this century, philosophers such as Heidegger and Merleau-Ponty extended the analysis to highlight the intrinsically meaningful and intentional nature of embodied 'being-in-the-world'. Whereas the traditional dualist view of the body characterises it almost as a physical machine, animated by a controlling mind which directs its activities and responses, the phenomenologists depict the embodied self as a dynamic state of purposeful engagement with an environment to which we are pre-attuned. Indeed, Merleau-Ponty (1962) stands realism on its head by asserting that our physical being is an embodiment of our will to exist, and that embodied selfhood is an accomplishment actively maintained by processes which range from the biological to the psycho-social.[4]

If embodied existence is itself meaningful and purposive, then there is no need to draw a sharp distinction between a subjective, intentional mind and an objective, value-free body. The way in which the phenomenological self transcends the mind–body dichotomy can be illustrated by the example of pain, which is not a neutral bodily sensation given meaning only by conscious reflection, but is rather a pre-conscious reaction of physical and psychological distress, protest and repulsion (Coulter 1979; Jackson 1994). The phenomenological integration of self and world also transcends body boundaries; changes in climate are experienced as changes in the self (for example, sweating and languor, or a dread of exposure to the elements), while states such as fatigue or anxiety can transform previously comfortable and safe surroundings into an exhausting or threatening environment (Gallagher 1995; Van den Berg 1987; Sartre 1948).

An understanding of the intrinsic meaning of the symbiotic relationship between self and environment also underpins the 'ecological psychology' of James Gibson (1966, 1986), and in particular his concept of an 'affordance', a term he used to designate the ecological properties of things and events. These ecological properties are created by the relationship between active beings and their environment, and so cannot be reduced either to objective physical attributes or to subjective intentions or beliefs.[5] For example, water 'affords' drink to a thirsty mammal, respiration to a fish, buoyant support to a competent swimmer, but immersion and death to a non-swimmer. An ecological analysis not only emphasises that many properties commonly attributed to the individual or environment actually exist at the interface between the individual and their environment, but also reveals how mutable this interface can be. For example, physical disability may be seen by observers as a stable personal performance deficit (e.g. a limited capacity for walking), but for the individual concerned it is experienced equally as a characteristic of specific physical circumstances (e.g. the need to traverse long distances or climb stairs). Moreover, the disability may vanish once either element of the person–environment interface has been appropriately modified, whether the mobility of the individual is extended by a motorised wheelchair, or the accessibility of a building is enhanced by the provision of ramps and lifts.

From a discursive standpoint a limitation of ecological psychology, and to a lesser extent phenomenology, is that although it provides a framework for analysing dynamic and meaningful self–environment relations, these seem to be conceived in predominantly asocial and pre-linguistic terms. However, although the introspective methodological tradition of phenomenology (see Chapter 2 for a description) is associated with a close attention to apparently private, individual experience, the meaning of this experience is embedded in the context of an environment which is both social and physical, as Merleau-Ponty explains:

Our relationship with the social is, like our relationship to the world, deeper than any express perception or any judgement. . . . We must return to the social with which we are in contact by the mere fact of existing, and which we carry about inseparably with us before any objectification.

(Merleau-Ponty 1962: 362)

'Objectification' is the process whereby the meaning of our lives is partly shaped by linguistic representation and social relations; for example, a body which is experienced at the phenomenological level as a site of pain or desire, or as the capacity to run or to eat, might in addition be objectified as a desirable female form or as a defective physiological system. Merleau-Ponty is hence emphasising the point that it is possible to understand human experience as being social and meaningful even at a pre-reflective, pre-linguistic level of analysis. But, in practice, it is difficult to dissociate the phenomenology of embodied experience from its communicative and symbolic functions and implications. Just as we are born into a pre-existent physical environment, we are born into an established social milieu in which the cultural meaning of our incarnation (represented, for example, in the attitudes and aspirations of our parents and grandparents) predates our physical conception (Lings 1994). Moreover, just as our biological and perceptual–motor capacities are adapted to the potentialities of the physical world, our communicative and symbolic propensities are attuned to the possibilities of the socio-linguistic world (Levin 1985). From the first, our bodily existence is hence a social, symbolic and communicative medium. We communicate directly through our bodies; as infants by touching or smiling, screaming or imitating (Meltzoff and Moore 1995) and as adults by posture and gesture, costume and dance (Mauss 1979). Our culture and social position are manifested in our bodily dispositions and tastes – a feminine way of walking, a middle-class 'ear' for classical music, or a regional predilection for pickled cabbage (Bourdieu and Wacquant 1992). Our embodied lives may even provide a primary source of metaphor and foundation for language (see following section: Material discourse and the embodied society).

It is clear that the phenomenological perspective is able to encompass the prominent and active role of embodied being in the construction of the meaning of health and illness. Indeed, one of the phenomenological effects of any body change, whether caused by ageing, weight gain, pregnancy or illness, is to draw attention to the body, which is ordinarily the taken-for-granted background to intentional activity and selfhood (Csordas 1994). In her autobiographical phenomenological analysis of multiple sclerosis, Toombs (1992) observes how the malfunctioning body becomes the unfamiliar 'Other' – a mysterious, inept, even malevolent entity which frustrates rather than expedites her endeavours. At the same time, illness transforms her world, altering space and time itself; places which were 'near' become 'far', the pace of life slows but, paradoxically, the future dwindles and disappears. Moreover, the alteration in identity which accompanies a change in body–world functioning is not a private affair. For example, people prone to attacks of dizziness when they make sudden movements notice how their stiff and cautious demeanour conveys the impression of premature ageing and lack of spontaneity, while their inability to turn their head to a speaker may unintentionally communicate a lack of interest or respect (Yardley 1994).

But while the analytical approaches outlined above acknowledge the relational and communicative meaning of embodied being, they do not fully address the unique and pervasive influence of language on human experience and activity. In order to do so, it may be useful to extend and complement the phenomenological perspective with some form of discursive analysis. For example, Ricoeur (1991) has argued that the open-ended, constantly elaborated description of conscious being attempted by phenomenologists is a form of 'hermeneutics', i.e. textual interpretation. He proposes that interpretation of world and text can be combined if our understanding of the world is conceived as an internal dialogue, a way of explaining life to ourselves, while narrative is viewed as a virtual space in which possible actions and perspectives can be imaginatively experienced. In a similar vein, Csordas (1994: 12) suggests that 'embodiment offers textuality a dialectical partner', while Turner (1992) has attempted to analyse the body as both a system of representation and the sensual basis for lived experience. The attempt to reconcile ecological–phenomenological with discursive perspectives may be facilitated by combining an awareness of the meaningful, social and communicative character of material being with a recognition of the material nature of discourse and society. In the following section, therefore, I will outline some of the key elements of discursive theory and then explain why language and society are not as abstract and insubstantial as is sometimes assumed.

Material discourse and the embodied society

The realist view of the world is generally associated with a 'representationalist' theory of language, which asserts that words derive their meaning from their relationship with the 'real' thing that they represent. But during this century philosophers and linguists have come to realise that words can gain their meaning from the social context in which they are used and from their relationship to other words. Structuralist and post-structuralist analyses of language have shown that words form part of a complex web or chain of meaning which has many levels. Meaning is partly created by linguistic opposition ('illness' implies the concept 'health') and partly by a radiating network of metaphoric imagery; for example, in the previous sentence the analogy of a 'web' might convey a sense of how we are trapped in linguistic meaning systems, while the notion of 'levels' could be linked to the idea of hierarchies and value systems and/or the concept of accumulating strata of meaning. The meaning of a word cannot therefore be adequately contained in a restrictive dictionary-style definition; meaning is not fixed but ambiguous, and so is created by the word's context and usage, including the intentions and understanding of the speaker–writer *and* the listener–reader (for further explanation, see Hollway 1989; Potter and Wetherell 1987; Manning and Cullum-Swan 1994).

This can be illustrated by considering the apparently simple and concrete example of the meaning of a blood pressure of 160/95. A denotative meaning of this technical term is that it signifies hypertension; this is the interpretation that might be required in a multiple-choice exam on cardiovascular pathology. The connotative meaning could be that medication is required or, alternatively, that the patient might suffer a stroke. Which of these implications was intended would be clear from the context. For example, in the first instance the reference to high blood pressure might occur in a consultation in which medication was prescribed, while in the second case it might be mentioned to a nurse taking over the patient's care. In both cases the full meaning can only be realised by a listener who can interpret the sense of the word using culturally shared knowledge; in the consultation the patient understands that the measure of blood pressure should be taken as a diagnosis, which in turn will typically imply treatment, while in the second example the nurse's training will have provided the information necessary to appreciate the significance of high blood pressure for prognosis and hence nursing care. But in a different context an allegorical meaning might be intended. Perhaps the high blood pressure may be mentioned to a demanding relative as an indication that the individual is unduly 'pressured' – a metaphorical concept which can in turn evoke a host of other symbols ranging from the idea of an unnaturally fast pace of life to the image of an overheated boiler about to explode.

Analysis of how words acquire their meaning from what Wittgenstein (1953) has called 'language games' reveals that language is primarily *functional* rather than descriptive. For instance, the mention of high blood pressure to a relative will seldom be simply a bland announcement of physiological status, but might instead serve as a plea or threat to a relative who is perceived to be adding to the individual's stress levels, or as a justification for retiring from arduous activities. Similarly, in his analysis of the meaning of statements about pain, Wittgenstein concluded that they are not intended as descriptions of internal sensations but are social performances demanding sympathy, protection or attention; adult expressions of pain are elaborated from the primitive cries of a distressed infant and serve a similar purpose, but are shaped by cultural conventions concerning the appropriate mode of communication of someone in pain (see also Harré 1991).

Rather than treating accounts or texts as more or less accurate reflections of some underlying concrete reality, discursive writers suggest therefore that we should ask what kind of meaning is being created by a certain use of language, and for what purpose. Since 'discourses delimit what can be said, whilst providing the spaces – the concepts, metaphors, models, analogies – for making new statements' (Henriques et al. 1984: 106), it is important to study the way in which language produces or constructs particular versions of what we think of as reality. For example, Herzlich (1973) and Pierret (1993) have drawn on social representations theory to show how concepts of health are linked to wider discourses. These include the idea of health as prosperity, with its connotations of a capital reserve of health which only profligate (hence blameworthy) individuals would exhaust, or the equation of healthy with natural, which implies a quite different view of health as threatened by an aberrant society which disturbs the harmonic balance of nature. Another example is provided by Haraway (1991), who highlights the recent trend towards using metaphors derived from the discourse of information-processing technology to characterise the self–environment relationship; the brain is depicted as a decision-making system, activity as a form of robotics, while DNA is portrayed as the machine code of life.

It is this interest in the way in which language generates its own worlds of meaning that can give rise to the impression that discursive theory disregards the material dimension. But discourse does not exist in a vacuum; indeed, a key concern of post-structuralist analysis is to expose the ideological interests and power relations in which particular discourses are embedded, and to which they contribute. And as Foucault (1980: 57–58) has remarked, 'nothing is more material, physical, corporeal than the exercise of power'. Because we are intrinsically social *and* embodied beings, the material dimension of human lives is always socialised – mediated by language and consciousness and modified by social activity – while the discursive dimension is inevitably physically manifested, in our speech and behaviour, institutions and technology. This can be exemplified by returning to the information-processing metaphor in the previous paragraph. Our understanding of the world in terms of information flow, drawing on analogies with computers, has given rise to a biogenetic technology which now allows us to reprogramme organisms. At the same time, society itself has been transformed into a sophisticated information-processing system in which the movements, communications and activities of individuals are indeed increasingly monitored and controlled. Hence information technology is at one level a discursive symbol – but one with material derivations and consequences as well as extensive ideological implications.

One way of approaching the dual nature of our existence is suggested by the early social constructionist theory of Berger and Luckmann (1966), who noted that the nature and lives of individuals are delimited by a combination of physical and social constraints and potentialities. These are subjectively experienced as equally 'real', in the sense that they have an existence which is partly independent of any single person's consciousness of them. For example, social structures such as working and housing conditions, and practices such as dietary habits and health-care customs, have as real and inevitable an impact on the health of many working-class people as do physical entities such as viruses, genes, or environmental pollutants. Berger and Luckmann portray the relation between biological and cultural factors as a continuous dialectic between 'being a body', which refers to our phenomenological experience of embodied life as the basis for intentional activity, and 'having a body', which is a more detached, reflective, socialised awareness of the body as an object.

More subtle and intimate links between the discursive and material are revealed in the work of Foucault, who has examined how changes in the way we perceive and talk about things are embedded in changes in 'practice', i.e. activities and social relations. For example, in *The Birth of the Clinic* (1989) he described how the development of the 'clinical gaze' – the impersonal attitude to the body which is characteristic of modern Western medicine – was related to the introduction of the physical practice of dissecting corpses. In his analyses of how the individualised bodies of members of modern society have been 'constituted' by what he terms the 'technologies of the self', he notes how discourses about the healthy body or body beautiful are accompanied by the practices of exercising, regulating eating habits or wearing fashionable clothes. Similarly, discourses about the body as a sexual object are associated with the production of pornographic material and the practice of attempting to control the sexual activity of certain groups in society; moreover, these discourses and practices intensify particular forms of body awareness and hence contribute to the creation of the sensations and desires on which they focus (Foucault 1980).

Once the material manifestations of society and culture are taken into consideration, not only speech and texts, but also architecture and agriculture, weapons and clothes, even bodies and babies, can be regarded as 'discursive materials' (Ibanez 1994). This conception of the relation between the discursive and material is epitomised in the popular postmodern image of people as 'cyborgs', a combination of living beings and constructed machines (Featherstone and Burrows 1995; Haraway 1991). Since the cyborg's body is acknowledged as a product of society, the notion of a cyborg transcends the distinctions between the natural (which is often conflated with physical) and the cultural (often equated with abstract). Humans are cyborgs in many senses. We transform our capacities by linking ourselves to machines: plugging our bodies into cars, our eyes into telescopes or microscopes, our mouths into telephones, and our brains into computers. Increasingly, we employ technology to modify ourselves, whether by means of the material technology of implantation or genetic selection, or through the cultural technology of education and self-regulation. And we can also be considered as part of a variety of technological systems – pre-eminently the various forms of the socio-economic system of production and consumption (Deleuze and Guattari 1984). Awareness of the way in which our physical existence forms part of a larger material–cultural system provides a counterpart to the discursive understanding of subjective experience as embedded in social relations and discourse.

Language is linked to practice, not only at the superordinate level of ideology and social relations, but also at the level of fundamental meaning. When Wittgenstein introduced the idea that meaning is derived from functional language games, he suggested that these in turn take their meaning from the shared 'forms of life' into which they are woven (Jost 1995; Van der Merwe and Voestermans 1995). Shotter (1990, 1993) develops this line of thought, arguing that language and practice are mutually constitutive; we share a practical, intersubjective, lived reality in which our language games are grounded, but this shared reality is shaped and sustained by the linguistic rules and common cultural experience which allow us to convey a meaningful understanding of events to each other and to ourselves. Lakoff and Johnson (1980) also trace the origin of linguistic meaning to a form of 'embodied understanding' (Johnson 1987) or 'experiential realism' (Lakoff 1987). They maintain that metaphors provide the basis for thought, and that metaphors are neither logical propositions or representations of an objective reality (the cognitivist view), nor part of a system of abstract, arbitrary relations between symbols (the structuralist view), but derive their flexible connotations from context-dependent, intentional activity. Thus the socio-linguistic realm is rooted in the material realm, which it in turn modifies through social practice. For example, mechanistic conceptions of illness derive from our familiarity with machines, and also constrain the way in which we respond to health problems, channelling our efforts towards functional repair rather than holistic healing.

Derrida provides a final argument against the dualism which begets an opposition between mind and body, nature and culture, material reality and discursive constructions. In his analysis of language, Derrida (1974) has shown that these distinctions can be seen as an illusion produced by language that creates dichotomies, which are nevertheless intimately connected since their meaning depends on their linguistic opposite. For example, it is by naming 'nature' that we distance ourselves from it, and thus create 'culture'; conversely, there could be no concept of culture without the idea of something outside culture – a pure, unsullied nature. Derrida proposes that our task is therefore to 'deconstruct' the oppositions produced by language in order to understand these interconnections:

> we must attempt to recapture the unity of gesture and speech, of body and language, of tool and thought before the originality of the one and the other is articulated and without allowing this profound unity to give rise to confusionism [sic].
>
> (Derrida 1974: 85)

INTRODUCING THE MATERIAL–DISCURSIVE ANALYSES IN THIS BOOK

A critical overview of a selection of discursive methods of research and analysis is provided in Chapter 2. This is intended primarily as an introduction to the nature and rationale of discursive methods for those with limited familiarity with qualitative research and discourse analysis – although experienced readers may also be interested in the discussion of issues such as ethics, coding, reflexivity and validation. The remaining chapters of the book illustrate a variety of theoretical perspectives and methodologies, applied to a wide range of health-related topics. From a discursive perspective, heterogeneity in approach is preferable to a universalist or 'essentialist' framework which maintains that one particular idea or method can be demonstrated to be superior or correct. As explained in Chapter 2, this kind of intellectual democracy does not imply an abdication of critical judgement, but quite the reverse – tolerance of multiple viewpoints creates an atmosphere which encourages fertile debate and awareness of the limitations of any single outlook.

Given the diversity of content, approaches and ideas represented in these chapters, my task as editor to group them into some apparently tidy conceptual structure has proved quite challenging. Nevertheless, there are two broad dimensions on which the chapters can be loosely ordered. The first is based on the theoretical stance adopted, and relates to the distinction between 'being' and 'having' a body referred to earlier. While I have argued that these two aspects of human life are intimately connected, for the purposes of analysis they are often isolated. Phenomenological approaches have been developed primarily for describing the subjective experience of 'being' a body, whereas discourse analysis has been predominantly concerned with the cultural and linguistic processes which construct the body as a social object. Since some contributors have focused more on one or other of these two aspects of embodied life, the chapters have been arranged so that the earlier ones emphasise the phenomenology of health and illness, the later ones are more oriented towards the social construction of the body, while the intermediate chapters combine both perspectives.

This categorisation happily coincides approximately with the second dimension on which the chapters are ranged, which is from the 'disordered' body to the 'normal' or healthy body. The dichotomy between health and disease is a highly ambiguous and hotly contested distinction; indeed, the problems surrounding the definitions of physical dysfunction constitute a recurring theme throughout the book. However, in conventional terms it is possible to view the earlier chapters as dealing mainly with medical 'complaints' such as heart disease, kidney failure, AIDS, deafness, dizziness and pain, whereas the later chapters are devoted to 'healthy' bodily activities such as sex, reproduction, eating and body decoration.

A phenomenological perspective is adopted in Chapter 3 by Radley and in Chapter 4 by Smith, Flowers and Osborn, who argue that social constructionist and discourse analytic approaches are not well suited to the purpose of studying non-verbal and subjective experience. Radley describes how states of health and illness are bodily enacted. Whereas medicine seeks to define health and illness as physiological conditions, in a social and phenomenological context one's state of health is defined and communicated by a certain way of relating to the world. Thus illness is designated by inactivity, while health must be demonstrated by a show of mastery, such as the ability to carry the shopping or to dig the garden. Physical sensations and transactions also play a central role in the descriptions of dialysis, pain and sexual relations presented by Smith, Flowers and Osborn. For example, the lack of control felt by a woman undergoing dialysis is epitomised by the experience of becoming part of an alien machine, in an equally alien hospital system. An intimate and moving account of the significance of unprotected sex for gay men explains how the spiritual symbolism of physical union is so profound as to transcend more rational – and also more materialistic – considerations of self-preservation, as lovers affirm their desire to share bodily contact, fluids, and even disease.

The next two chapters combine ecological psychology with social constructionism to analyse, respectively, deafness and disorientation. Both emphasise the role of the physical and social context in creating disability. In Chapter 5, Noble observes that hearing impairment is only experienced as a problem in so far as it interferes with the lifestyle and social activities of the deaf individual. Consequently, deaf people living in Martha's Vineyard earlier this century were not handicapped since virtually all members of the community could communicate by sign language. In Chapter 6, I examine how the potentially terrifying nature of disorientation in the modern world is created by the perceptual confusion provoked by artificial environments, such as shopping malls, motorways and 'virtual reality', combined with the modern Western imperative to maintain complete physical and emotional control.

Another theme I explore is the predicament of individuals who find that the dominant (medical and psychiatric–psychological) discourses do not offer them any satisfactory way of defining, communicating or dealing with their situation. Several of the succeeding chapters address related topics. Joffe provides an extensive analysis of the origins and consequences of scientific representations of AIDS. Drawing on interviews with black and white, gay and heterosexual men in Britain and South Africa, and the medical literature, she studies the way in which both scientific and lay beliefs reassuringly construct AIDS as a disease of the 'Other', whether this 'outgroup' is characterised as other nations or races, or as people who indulge in 'deviant' activities. These representations take up and feed into material practices, motivating the production of statistical data on the relative incidence of AIDS among groups defined by colour or by their activities, and culminating in the production of scientific papers about how AIDS might be linked to particular sexual practices or tribal rituals. The problem of deficient dominant discourses is also confronted by Ingham and Kirkland, who note that the inadequate and fragmentary nature of discourse about sexual relations can lead to confusion and misunderstandings, and ultimately to the material outcomes of unprotected sex. Their chapter highlights the taboo on young people's discourse about sex: many parents are too embarrassed to broach the subject; policy makers in the House of Lords ignore the views of young people, or dismiss them as 'the grubby half-truths of the playground'; young people themselves fear that discussion may disrupt the activity of sex. Scientific and lay discourses are again compared in the chapter by Woollett and Marshall, who undertake a feminist, social-constructionist analysis of discourse about pregnancy, juxtaposing the accounts of British Asian women with the medical and psychological literature. Whereas traditional medical discourse relegates the mother to a passive role as a 'container' for the child, and attempts to regularise women's varied physiological changes as simply 'normal' or 'abnormal', women's own descriptions of their bodily changes place these in a social context, for example, focusing on how nausea and tiredness interfere with care of the family.

The last two chapters examine the way in which discourse changes the body, which in turn inspires further discourse. Ogden reviews the psychological and sociological literature on eating behaviour and asks whether *descriptions* of eating have changed over the past century, whether *eating itself* has changed, or whether the two are linked; hence, just as discourse about sex may stimulate new forms of desire, discourse about eating and body shape may play a part in changing eating patterns. Applying her analysis to her own theory, she considers how her theorising about eating may itself reflect changing ideas about the nature of experience – ideas which contribute to the evolution of a new kind of person. In the final chapter, Soyland draws on discourse about body decoration (here, piercing and tattooing) to explore the relationship between social and bodily identity. His interviewees explain that their primary motive for self-decoration was not to appear extraordinary, but to express their authentic identity. This argument parallels the reasons reported by Kathy Davis (1995) for undergoing the more radical self-modification of cosmetic surgery; her interviewees sought surgery not to become outstandingly attractive but in order to achieve normality (by correcting perceived physical defects), and felt that they were best able to project their 'true' selves by means of this material alteration to their body.

A number of key themes repeatedly surface across several chapters. One is the problematic distinction between health and illness or disability mentioned above. Several of the chapters discuss the similarities and links between official–scientific and lay discourse, while many highlight the limitations and inadequacies of specific discourses. In keeping with the material–discursive theme of the book, numerous examples are given of the discursive power of the material world – how meaning is powerfully communicated through bodily activity or decoration, and in the form of buildings or machines. Finally, in the concluding section of each chapter, the material impact of discourse is considered and, in particular, the way in which the analyses presented here may substantially affect people's experiences of health and illness.

NOTES

1   The term 'discursive' is intended to embrace a wide range of theoretical perspectives, including social constructionism, post-structuralism and post-modernism, as well as methodologies such as hermeneutics and discourse analysis.
2   See French (1993) for an insightful discussion of the relationship between the social and material aspects of visual impairment.
3   This view of life, which is reminiscent of the Buddhist notion of 'becoming', is more explicitly developed by Maturana and Varela (1987) in their empirical analysis of the way in which living beings (even at the level of the single cell) create themselves developmentally by establishing both a system of internal organisation and a boundary between themselves and the environment.
4   By assigning a central importance to the intersection between organism and environment, Gibson's description of the material realm transcends the traditional image of a physically bounded body, in the same way that analysis of how the 'self' is constructed from discourse transcends the idea of the individualised mind (Henriques et al. 1984; Shotter and Gergen 1989).
5   This overview can only provide a very cursory and incomplete introduction to the many theoretical perspectives which I draw upon, and so the interested reader is recommended to follow up the ample references provided.

REFERENCES

Armstrong, D. (1987) 'Theoretical tensions in biopsychosocial medicine', *Social Science and Medicine* 25: 1213–1218.

Barrett, R. J. (1988) 'Clinical writing and the documentary construction of schizophrenia', *Culture, Medicine and Psychiatry* 12: 265–299.

Benton, T. (1991) 'Biology and social science: why the return of the repressed should be given a (cautious) welcome', *Sociology* 25: 1–29.

Berger, P. L. and Luckmann, T. (1966) *The Social Construction of Reality*, London: Penguin.

Bourdieu, P. and Wacquant, L. J. D. (1992) *An Invitation to Reflexive Sociology*, Cambridge: Polity Press.

Coulter, J. (1979) *The Social Construction of Mind*, London: Macmillan Press.

Csordas, T. J. (1994) 'Introduction: the body as representation and being-in-the-world', in T. J. Csordas (ed.) *Embodiment and Experience: The Existential Ground of Culture and Self*, Cambridge: Cambridge University Press.

Davis, K. (1995) *Reshaping the Female Body: The Dilemma of Cosmetic Surgery*, London: Routledge.

Deleuze, G. and Guattari, F. (1984) *Anti-Oedipus: Capitalism and Schizophrenia*, London: Athlone Press.

Derrida, J. (1974) *Of Grammatology*, Baltimore: Johns Hopkins University Press.

Engel, G. L. (1977) 'The need for a new medical model: a challenge for biomedicine', *Science* 196: 129–136.

—— (1982) 'The biopsychosocial model and medical education', *New England Journal of Medicine* 306: 802–805.

Featherstone, M. and Burrows, R. (1995) *Cyberspace/Cyberbodies/Cyberpunk: Cultures of Technological Embodiment*, London: Sage.

Fitzpatrick, R.M. (1991) 'Society and changing patterns of disease', in G. Scambler (ed.) *Sociology as Applied to Medicine*. London: Baillière Tindall.

Foucault, M. (1980) *Power/knowledge: Selected Interviews and Other Writings 1972–7*, London: Harvester Wheatsheaf.

—— (1988) 'Technologies of the self', in L. H. Martin, H. Gutman and P. H. Hutton (eds) *Technologies of the Self: A Seminar with Michel Foucault*, London: Tavistock.

—— (1989) *The Birth of the Clinic*, London: Routledge.

Fox, N. J. (1993) *Postmodernism, Sociology and Health*, Bristol: Open University Press.

Frank, A. W. (1993) 'The rhetoric of self-change: illness experience as narrative', *The Sociological Quarterly* 34: 39–52.

French, S. (1993) 'Disability, impairment or something in between?', in J. Swain, V. Finkelstein, S. French and M. Oliver (eds) *Disabling Barriers – Enabling Environments*, London: Sage.

Freund, P. E. S. (1990) 'The expressive body: a common ground for the sociology of emotions, health and illness', *Sociology of Health and Illness* 12: 452–477.

Gallagher, S. (1995) 'Bodily awareness and the self', in J. L. Bermúdez, A. Marcel and N. Eilan (eds) *The Body and the Self*, London: MIT Press.

Gergen, K. J. (1985) 'The social constructionist movement in modern psychology', *American Psychologist* 40: 266–275.

Gibson, J. J. (1966) *The Senses Considered as Perceptual Systems*, Prospect Heights: Waveland Press.

—— (1986) *The Ecological Approach to Visual Perception*, Hillsdale, NJ: Lawrence Erlbaum.

Gordon, D. R. (1988) 'Tenacious assumptions in modern medicine', in M. Lock and D. R. Gordon (eds) *Biomedicine Examined*, Dordrecht: Kluwer Academic.

Haraway, D. (1991) *Simians, Cyborgs and Women: The Reinvention of Nature*, London: Free Association Books.

Harper, D. J. (1992) 'Defining delusion and the serving of professional interests: the case of "paranoia"', *British Journal of Medical Psychology* 65: 357–369.

Harré, R. (1991) *Physical Being*, Oxford: Blackwell.

Harré, R. and Gillett, G. (1994) *The Discursive Mind*, London: Sage.

Henriques, J., Holloway, W., Urwin, C., Venn, C. and Walkerdine, V. (1984) *Changing the Subject: Psychology, Social Regulation and Subjectivity*, London: Methuen.

Herzlich, C. (1973) *Health and Illness*, London: Academic Press.

Hollway, W. (1989) *Subjectivity and Method in Psychology: Gender, Meaning and Science*, London: Sage.

Ibanez, T. (1994) 'Constructing a representation or representing a construction?', *Theory and Psychology* 4: 363–381.

Jackson, J. E. (1992) ' "After a while no one believes you": real and unreal pain', in M-J. DelVecchio Good, P. E. Brodwin, B. J. Good and A. Kleinman (eds) *Pain as Human Experience*, Berkeley, CA: University of California Press.

—— (1994) 'Chronic pain and the tension between the body as subject and object', in T. J. Csordas (ed.) *Embodiment and Experience: The Existential Ground of Culture and Self*, Cambridge: Cambridge University Press.

Johnson, M. (1987) *The Body in Mind: The Bodily Basis of Meaning, Imagination and Reason*, Chicago: University of Chicago Press.

Jost, J. J. (1995) 'Toward a Wittgensteinian social psychology of human development', *Theory and Psychology*, 5: 5–26.

Kirmayer, L. J. (1988) 'Mind and body as metaphors: hidden values in biomedicine', in M. Lock and D. R. Gordon (eds) *Biomedicine Examined*, Dordrecht: Kluwer Academic.

Lakoff, G. (1987) *Women, Fire and Dangerous Things*, Chicago: University of Chicago Press.

Lakoff, G. and Johnson, M. (1980) *Metaphors We Live By*, Chicago: University of Chicago Press.

Levin, D. M. (1985) *The Body's Recollection of Being*, London: Routledge & Kegan Paul.

Lewontin, R. C. (1993) *The Doctrine of DNA: Biology as Ideology*, London: Penguin.

Lings, A. (1994) *Foreign Bodies*, London: Routledge.

Lupton, D. (1993) 'Risk as moral danger: the social and political functions of risk discourse in public health', *International Journal of Health Services* 23: 425–435.

McNamee, S. and Gergen, K. J. (eds) (1992) *Therapy as Social Construction*, London: Sage.

Mahoney, M. J. (1993) 'Introduction to special section: theoretical developments in the cognitive psychotherapies', *Journal of Consulting and Clinical Psychology* 61: 187–193.

Manning, P. K. and Cullum-Swan, B. (1994) 'Narrative, content and semiotic analysis', in N. K. Denzin and Y. S. Lincoln (eds) *Handbook of Qualitative Research*, London: Sage.

Marks, D. F. (1996) 'Health psychology in context', *Journal of Health Psychology* 1: 7–21.

Maturana, H. R. and Varela, F. J. (1987) *The Tree of Knowledge: The Biological Roots of Human Understanding*, London: New Science Library.

Mauss, M. (1979) *Sociology and Psychology Essays*, London: Routledge & Kegan Paul.

Meltzoff, A. N. and Moore, M. K. (1995) 'Infants' understanding of people and things: from body imitation to folk psychology', in J. L. Bermúdez, A. Marcel and N. Eilan (eds) *The Body and the Self*, London: MIT Press.

Merleau-Ponty, M. (1962) *Phenomenology of Perception*, trans. C. Smith, London: Routledge & Kegan Paul.

Mishler, E. G. (1981) 'Social contexts of health care', in E. G. Mishler, L. R. Amarasingham, S. T. Hauser, S. D. Osherson, N. E. Waxter and R. Liem *Social Contexts of Health, Illness and Patient Care*, Cambridge: Cambridge University Press.

Ogden, J. (1994) 'Restraint theory and its implications for obesity treatment', *Clinical Psychology and Psychotherapy* 1: 191–201.

Phillips, M. J. (1990) 'Damaged goods: oral narratives of the experience of disability in American culture', *Social Science and Medicine* 30: 849–857.

Pierret, J. (1993) 'Constructing discourses about health and their social determinants', in A. Radley (ed.) *Worlds of Illness*, London: Routledge.

Pilgrim, D. (1992) 'Competing histories of madness', in R. P. Bentall (ed.) *Reconstructing Schizophrenia*, London: Routledge.

Pollock, K. (1993) 'Attitude of mind as a means of resisting illness', in A. Radley (ed.) *Worlds of Illness*, London: Routledge.

Potter, J. and Wetherell, M. (1987) *Discourse and Social Psychology*, London: Sage.

Radley, A. (1994) *Making Sense of Illness: The Social Psychology of Health and Disease*, London: Sage

—— (1995) 'The elusory body and social constructionist theory', *Body and Society* 1: 3–23.

Ricoeur, P. (1991) *From Text to Action: Essays in Hermeneutics* II, London: Athlone Press.

Riessman, C. K. (1990) 'Strategic uses of narrative in the presentation of self and illness: a research note', *Social Science and Medicine* 30: 1195–1200.

Sartre, J-P. (1948) *The Emotions: Outline of a Theory*, New York: Philosophical Library.

Schwartz, G. E. (1982) 'Testing the biopsychosocial model: the ultimate challenge facing behavioral medicine?', *Journal of Consulting and Clinical Psychology* 50: 1040–1053.

Shotter, J. (1990) 'Rom Harré: realism and the turn to social constructionism', in R. Bhaskar (ed.) *Rom Harré and His Critics*, Oxford: Blackwell.

—— (1993) *Conversational Realities*, London: Sage.

Shotter, J. and Gergen, K. J. (eds) (1989) *Texts of Identity*, London: Sage.

Silverman, D. (1987) *Communication and Medical Practice*, London: Sage.

Smith, J. A. (1996) 'Beyond the divide between cognition and discourse: using interpretative phenomenological analysis in health psychology', *Psychology and Health* 11: 261–271.

Soyland, A. J. (1994) 'Functions of the psychiatric case-summary', *Text* 14: 113–140.

Stainton-Rogers, W. (1991) *Explaining Health and Illness*, New York: Harvester Wheatsheaf.

—— (1996) 'Critical approaches to health psychology', *Journal of Health Psychology* 1: 65–77.

Stam, H. J. (1988) 'The practice of health psychology and behavioral medicine: whither theory?', in W. J. Baker, L. P. Mos, H. V. Rappard and H. J. Stam (eds) *Recent Trends in Theoretical Psychology*, New York: Springer-Verlag.

Taussig, M. T. (1980) 'Reification and the consciousness of the patient', *Social Science and Medicine* 14B: 3–13.

Toombs, S. K. (1992) *The Meaning of Illness*, Dordrecht: Kluwer Academic.

Turner, B. S. (1992) *Regulating Bodies: Essays in Medical Sociology*, London: Routledge.

Van den Berg, J. H. (1987) 'The human body and the significance of human movement', in J. J. Kockelmans (ed.) *Phenomenological Psychology: The Dutch School*, Dordrecht: Martinus Nijhoff.

Van der Merwe, W. L. and Voestermans, P. P. (1995) 'Wittgenstein's legacy and the challenge to psychology', *Theory and Psychology* 5: 27–48.

Ville, I., Ravaud, J-F., Diard, C. and Paicheter, H. (1994) 'Self-representations and physical impairment: a social constructionist approach', *Sociology of Health and Illness* 16: 301–321.

Waitzkin, H. (1991) *The Politics of Medical Encounters*, New Haven: Yale University Press.

White, D. and Wang, A. (1995) 'Universalism, humanism and postmodernism', *American Psychologist* 50: 392–393.

Wittgenstein, L. (1953) *Philosophical Investigations*, Oxford: Blackwell.

Yardley, L. (1994) *Vertigo and Dizziness*, London: Routledge.

—— (1996) 'Reconciling discursive and materialist perspectives on the psychology of health and illness: a re-construction of the biopsychosocial approach', *Theory and Psychology* 6: 485–508.

Chapter 2

Introducing discursive methods

Lucy Yardley

The principal aim of this chapter is to provide an introduction to the nature and rationale of discursive methods of inquiry and analysis for the benefit of those who have little familiarity with discursive research. However, discursive methods are constantly evolving, and this chapter also seeks to contribute to the continuing debate about how discursive analysts should carry out and justify their studies. The first half of the chapter consists of an overview of some of the more widely used methodologies, with appropriate references to health-related applications. The purpose of this overview is simply to acquaint the reader with the character and diversity of qualitative methodologies.[1] The second half then critically examines the difficult question of how the validity of the various modes of analysis can be established, and explores the problematic issues pertaining to ethics and relations of power that inevitably accompany any assertion of academic authority or expertise. Finally, the need and possibilities for *material*–discursive methodologies are briefly discussed.

Before proceeding to review discursive methods, it is first worth considering why (or indeed whether) a distinctive kind of discursive methodology is necessary. Why are the traditional psychological methods of experimental design, quantitative measurement and statistical analysis unsuitable for discursive research? The answer is that the rationale for any particular method of research is always based on a corresponding 'epistemology', or theory about how knowledge is obtained (Guba and Lincoln 1994). Realist theories of knowledge assume the existence of a stable reality which is independent of the observer, and propose that an accurate apprehension of this reality is best approached by means of precise, controlled, objective observation. Experimental design is therefore employed to isolate the variables of interest from complicating or confounding factors, while quantitative measurement and statistics are used in order to maximise the precision and objectivity of the analysis. In contrast, discursive theories of knowledge maintain that the 'reality' perceived by any individual (including both the scientists *and* the 'subjects' involved in a study) is produced by an interaction between their expectations and activities and the constraints and possibilities of the physical, socio-historical and linguistic context (see Chapter 1). It is therefore inappropriate to attempt to isolate the phenomenon studied from its context and futile to aspire to a neutral, objective perspective; instead, it is important to explicitly consider the way in which the context, the participants and the researcher have jointly contributed to the outcome of a discursive analysis. In addition, the emphasis on accurate measurement of isolated variables is replaced by the goal of elaborating a detailed, multi-layered interpretation of a particular situation.

Since the assumptions and goals of discursive research are quite different from those of realist investigation, different methods of pursuing these discursive objectives are needed. For example, discursive theory suggests that language and context have a profound influence on meaning. To investigate contextualised linguistic processes, it may be more appropriate therefore to undertake in-depth qualitative analysis of naturally occurring conversation than to quantify numerical responses to questionnaire items phrased by the researcher. Similarly, awareness of how the perception, understanding and expression of meaning is fundamentally related to the perspective of the perceiver–communicator has given rise to a variety of methodologies which acknowledge the perspectival nature of both reality and research. Phenomenological and life-story research can be used to explore and convey the meaning of people's lives; explicitly perspectival perspectives such as the 'feminist standpoint' (Riger 1992) may be adopted in order to communicate the situated knowledge of an under-represented minority group or alternative viewpoint; or participants may be involved in the research process not simply as 'subjects' providing raw data for transformation and interpretation by the expert scientist, but as active contributors to the design, conduct and implementation of the research, as commentators, analysts, and even authors.

Clearly, discursive theory does herald a new and distinctive approach to research which often entails innovative methods of investigation and analysis. It is for this reason that a chapter on methodology has been included in a book devoted to the topic of health and illness. Health psychology books which summarise quantitative, realist research do not usually find it necessary to explain or justify the methods whereby the reported findings were obtained, even if (as in the present book) the chapters provide an overview of the topics covered, and hence do not describe the details of the research process. But this is simply because specialist psychology books assume a thorough grounding in the basic rationale, methods and language of experimental psychology. This shared system of assumptions and knowledge permits the authors, for example, to criticise a clinical trial for failing to employ an adequate control group, or to note that a questionnaire was unreliable without having to explain why this could invalidate the research. At present it is not possible to assume that all health psychologists will share the knowledge of discursive methods and principles necessary to appreciate the basis and implications of the analyses of health and illness presented in the succeeding chapters. The following sections will therefore provide an introduction which, albeit necessarily brief, should elucidate some of the key characteristics of discursive methods and criteria.

DISCURSIVE METHODS

Quantitative and semi-quantitative methods

Having stated that the aims and axioms of discursive researchers call for a new approach to research, it may seem strange to then discuss the role of quantitative methods. However, from a discursive perspective there is no reason *per se* why phenomena should not be described using numbers as well as words. Indeed, just as qualitative methods are undoubtedly most suitable for some of the discursive purposes described above, quantification can be the most appropriate means to achieve specific aims – for example, to establish how many people in a community would like access to a particular health facility, or to determine whether changes in life circumstances are accompanied by changes in psychophysiological functioning. Moreover, scientific terminology, quantitative measures and statistical procedures can be viewed as a language or form of rhetoric which is very powerful in modern society (John 1992). In order to put across an argument to policy-makers, the general public, or to a community of medical scientists, it may therefore be necessary to adopt this language for the purpose of persuasive communication (Griffin and Phoenix 1994; Stenner and Eccleston 1994). This strategic, almost ironic (but *not* cynical), recourse to quantitative methods is by no means incompatible with discursive principles; indeed, a characteristic feature of postmodernist discursive approaches is the self-conscious utilisation of previous traditions and apparently disparate forms of knowledge and methodology, which are thereby transformed, reinterpreted and invigorated (Kvale 1992). Thus by using quantitative methods alongside qualitative analysis the rigour and credibility of both may be enhanced; for example, the latter could be employed as a sensitive and flexible framework for studying contextualised processes, while the former might be deployed to confirm statements about links between phenomena, or to test the generality of the qualitative findings (Steckler et al. 1992).

Some discursive researchers object to the use of quantitative methods in the social sciences on the grounds that by imitating the investigative techniques of the natural sciences they create a spurious and unhelpful impression of objectivity. From a discursive perspective, it is certainly important to avoid 'reifying' the results of quantitative research – treating figures as facts, and statistical analyses as precise representations of reality. But the tendency towards scientific reification can be counteracted by making the process of research itself a focus of study and an explicit part of the process of valida-tion (Banister et al. 1994). This strategy is known as 'reflexivity', and may range from disclosure of the researcher's personal ideological orientation and motives for undertaking the research, to a self-conscious reflection on how the context of the research may have affected the material obtained, how particular theoretical suppositions may have shaped the analysis, or the manner in which the conclusions presented have been constructed and justi-fied (e.g. Steier 1991; Wynne 1988). Although reflexivity is a concept which has been chiefly discussed as a way of enhancing the validity of qualitative research, it is equally relevant to quantitative research, and could be viewed as simply a discursive extension to existing conventions for methodological reporting and the interpretation of results. Realist researchers already acknowledge the need to discuss how samples were obtained or tests admin-istered, but discursive researchers may feel that it is equally important to explain why the participants in the study may have felt compelled to behave in a certain way, or to consider frankly how their own objectives motivated them to highlight particular aspects of the data.

Another reason why discursive researchers have tended to favour qualita-tive methods is that they are suitable for developing an understanding of subtle meanings and complex interactions, for analysing idiosyncrasies and inconsistencies, and for elucidating dynamic processes. These can be difficult to capture using quantitative methods, since the constraints of statistical testing limit the number of variables and inter-relationships which can be simultaneously considered, while the austere language of numbers tends to strip away the ambiguities, ironies and multiple intentions and connotations characteristic of human communication and behaviour. However, some researchers seek a compromise between the two methodologies (e.g. Berman et al. 1994; Pope and Mays 1995a,b). Qualitative methods may be used to gather observational, textual or biographical data. A procedure such as con-tent analysis is then employed to assign numerical codes to observations or text segments, according to strict classificatory rules which can be verified by assessing 'inter-rater reliability' (i.e. the reliability with which two or more raters can independently code the material in the same way). These codes are subsequently treated as summary indices of empirical observations, and can even in principle be statistically analysed if drawn from a large, random sample. For example, Borkan et al. (1991) interviewed elderly people with hip fractures following a fall and coded their accounts in terms of conceptu-al themes, such as whether the patient saw the fracture as a discrete mechan-ical problem or as a sign of general degeneration. Extensive inter-rater comparisons were used to ensure the reliability of the coding, and the rela-tionship of the coded attributes to outcome measures was assessed by analy-sis of variance.

This kind of 'soft-nosed positivist' or 'transcendental realist' research (Miles and Huberman 1984; Huberman and Miles 1994) is promoted as a way of combining the advantages of qualitative and quantitative methods. Whereas tightly controlled experimental and questionnaire designs require the researcher to define in advance of data collection which variables are relevant and which must be ignored or excluded, qualitative data collection allows the researcher to adopt a more 'inductive' approach – that is, to continue to build and elaborate hypotheses and explanations throughout the analytic process. It also permits the investigator to use naturally occurring, rich, linguistic data and interpretive coding. Temporal and causal relations between variables can be coded, facilitating description of processes of interaction and change. At the same time, the rigour of the coding process provides a guarantee that the interpretation of the data was consistent and explicit, while the semi-quantitative analyses can give an indication of the generality or uniqueness of particular findings.

Despite the multiple advantages of this kind of qualitative research (which include its acceptability and comprehensibility to realist and quantitative researchers), from a discursive viewpoint there may also be limitations and dangers associated with a semi-quantitative approach. In particular, the procedure of rigorous numerical coding tends to encourage a realist view of the data as a set of empirical facts which can be verified or disconfirmed by using multiple observers and observations. Rather than constructing an agreed description of reality in this way, many discursive analysts prefer to gain insight into differing personal perspectives, explore alternative 'readings' or interpretations of a phenomenon, or examine the wider socio-cultural systems of meaning on which all the participants in the research process draw. Some of the methods more suited to these purposes are considered below.

Phenomenological and hermeneutic analysis

Phenomenology and hermeneutics are not new methods of analysis, but have a long and venerable history (see Fewtrell and O'Connor 1994). Phenomenological analysis has been practised ever since the eighteenth-century German philosopher Kant recommended the systematic investigation of 'phenomena', which is the term he used for the contents and organisation of conscious experience. Hermeneutics is an even older tradition, having distant roots in the scholarly interpretation of religious texts. Central to both methods is a process of careful reflection and open-ended interpretation. Whereas phenomenology tends to focus more on the meanings of individuals and hermeneutics on the meanings of texts, because of the interrelatedness of people, society and language this distinction easily becomes blurred; indeed, as will become clear below, there are substantial conceptual commonalities and historical links not only between phenomenology and hermeneutics, but also between these and the various methods of discourse analysis discussed in the following section.

The oldest phenomenological method is referred to as 'transcendental' because it involves attempting to transcend or 'bracket' our preconceptions, and in particular to set aside the 'natural attitude' which corresponds to the realist illusion that what we perceive is objectively true. This is essentially achieved by means of reflection, coupled with introspective examination of one's own experiences and/or empathic identification with the experiences of others. Once our assumptions about what 'is' have been abandoned, it becomes possible to consider how things come to present or 'constitute' themselves in our consciousness in a particular way (Giorgi 1990), and how our intentions, activities and socio-historical situation create the meaning of phenomena. This is a continuously evolving process, since there can be no final, 'true' meaning so long as consciousness itself is constantly changing. The value of the analysis therefore is not so much in its ability to reveal the truth but in its contribution to the development of a new form of consciousness (Levin 1985).

The phenomenological method itself is also constantly evolving, and has been developed and applied in a number of different ways. A particularly significant development was introduced by Heidegger, a mid-twentieth-century German philosopher who argued that we cannot suspend our preconceptions, since these are the very categories and mechanisms of thought which make meaning possible (Ray 1994). Instead, the nature and effects of our preconceptions can be explored by studying the socio-historical evolution and formation of our 'being-in-the-world'. More recently, Ricoeur (1991: 34) has expanded this idea to encompass language, arguing that phenomenology 'must take the fundamental distortions of communication into account, in the same way as it considers the illusions of perception in the constitution of the thing'. Ricoeur portrays consciousness as an internal dialogue, and suggests that hermeneutic 'distanciation' (the need to consciously distance oneself from the object of study in order to interpret it) parallels the way in which consciousness interrupts the intentional flow of life in order to 'signify' it (i.e. represents it in an abstract form such as thought, imagery or language).

Recognition of the way in which socio-cultural processes are involved in the construction of shared meaning (or intersubjective consciousness) leads naturally to a more dialogical form of phenomenology, in which the introspective examination of subjective phenomena is supplemented or replaced by an exploration of how meaning is jointly created by social interaction. One implication of this interpretive or hermeneutic phenomenological approach is that descriptions of feelings and events given in an interview cannot be treated as a simple reflection of the subjective experience of the interviewee, but must be acknowledged as a joint product of both participants in the interview (Kvale 1983). Nevertheless, the phenomenological method is often employed in an attempt to achieve insight into the perspective of others and to uncritically present their understanding of a phenomenon, and thus has much in common with the 'experience of illness' approach (Conrad 1990), which aspires to a sensitive and penetrating description of the subjective experience of sufferers. This type of approach has proved particularly useful for highlighting the way in which non-medical factors influence the impact of disease and impairment; for example, the central role of anticipated stigmatisation (i.e. fear of being publicly exposed as 'abnormal' – see below) in motivating withdrawal from valued activities (e.g. Anderson and Bury 1988; Hétu et al. 1990; Yardley et al. 1992).

Interest in the processes of active co-construction of meaning has also given rise to methods of empirically researching social interaction such as 'ethnomethodology' and 'symbolic interactionism'. These approaches have been used to examine the social significance attached to everyday symbols, behaviour, and artefacts (Stern 1994), and the way in which talk and actions occurring in particular contexts are constrained by, but also produce, the implicit understanding of reality shared by co-participants in the interaction (Feldman 1995; Holstein and Gubrium 1994). For example, our (often unconscious) knowledge of the social 'rules' concerning what is possible, meaningful or allowable can be exposed by studying what happens when the rules are broken and the way in which justifications or attempts to explain incongruities are used to repair the damage to conceptions of reality (Tesch 1990). Goffman's (1963) analyses of 'stigma' – people's reactions to abnormalities of behaviour or appearance – provide a classic illustration of how deviations from expectations of normality profoundly disrupt social interaction.

The 'grounded theory' approach to qualitative analysis initiated by Glaser and Strauss (1967) has roots in the phenomenological tradition. This method, which has become increasingly popular in the field of health research, consists of gradually building up an explanation of a phenomenon by means of a repeated cycle of data collection, coding and analysis (Strauss and Corbin 1990). Open-ended interviews are used to generate relevant material, which is coded in great detail. After intensive and imaginative reflection on the relationship between these low-level, essentially descriptive codes, the researcher tentatively formulates some hypotheses concerning higher-level categories, dimensions and relationships. The researcher then carries out further interviews, deliberately seeking interviewees and asking questions which can clarify, confirm, contradict or elaborate these hypotheses. The cycle is continued until an account of the phenomenon which appears consistent and comprehensive has been constructed.

This approach to qualitative research has the virtue of ensuring that an intimate, meticulous knowledge of the topic is acquired, and is especially useful for elucidating subtle meanings and associations and complex interconnections. For example, Johnson's (1991) grounded theory analysis of recovery from heart attack reveals the importance of processes which might not be expected, such as the positive role of 'anticipatory worrying', which can be seen as a way of adjusting to the seriousness of the condition which is analogous to grieving. Corbin and Strauss's grounded analyses of chronic illness as an exhausting regime of work for both sufferer and carer also provide a new way of looking at illness which has significant implications for its management (Corbin and Strauss 1985; Strauss and Corbin 1988). However, it is important to acknowledge the extent to which the researcher contributes to the 'findings' of grounded theory research, which is sometimes presented as an inductive method – a means of arriving at an objective description of a pre-existent reality. Clearly, the investigator plays a crucial role in shaping the analysis, selecting the interviewees and questions, devising the interpretive coding, and constructing the explanatory framework (Lonkila 1995). Some researchers have suggested therefore that it may be valuable to explicitly recognise and enhance the constructive character of grounded theory analysis by integrating it with a more frankly discursive approach, which could help to uncover the socio-linguistic processes involved in the construction of meaning (Charmaz 1990; Henwood and Pidgeon 1995). A variety of discursive methodologies are considered in the following section.

Discourse analysis

Discourse analysis is concerned with elucidating the meanings and functions of discourse, and their links with social relations and the exercise of power. The notion of 'power' in this context does not refer to any crude concept of oppression or domination; power is portrayed by post-structuralists as a pervasive, constructive energy which is manifested not only in the organisation of social relations, but also in the desires and activities of individuals. 'Discourse' is a very inclusive term, which is sometimes taken to refer to actual speech or texts, or may be used to designate a coherent system of meanings (for example, a 'biomedical discourse'). Hence, discourse analysts are sometimes interested primarily in the microanalysis of how meaning and power is negotiated in conversations or documents, and at other times may focus on the macro level of discourses as symbolic systems which permeate and structure society and language. Many combine these approaches, showing how people draw on wider systems of meaning to construct and defend their own particular position or perspective (Potter et al. 1990).

Analyses of macro-level discourses are usually more theory-based than empirical, in the sense that their argument is seldom grounded in a systematic study of a particular set of observations, although it should be based on a profound and sophisticated knowledge of the topic and is generally illustrated by examples of the discourses identified and discussed. The analysis may draw on more than one theoretical perspective in order to generate an unconventional view of a situation or concept. For example, in his critique of the concept of 'care' in the context of illness and medicine, Fox (1993) draws on a combination of postmodernist and psychoanalytic theory to argue that professional care is inherently patronising and conservative because it is based on a repetition of parent–child relations in which both the health professional and the patient collude. In this kind of analysis, it is again less relevant to achieve a 'veridical' account (since truth is considered to be a situated, changeable concept) than to create an interesting, compelling or useful characterisation or story, although this does *not* mean that *any* story is seen as equally valid. (For further discussion of this issue, see the sections on validity below.)

Many discourse analysts draw attention to the way in which particular symbols or turns of phrase tend to structure our beliefs and practices. For example, in her eloquent dissertation on the social meanings attached to cancer, Sontag (1991) has illustrated how the metaphoric analogy of cancer with a hostile enemy tends to engender calls for chemical warfare on the invading force and a 'fighting spirit', rather than a more holistic, healing-based approach. Potter and Collie (1989) achieved a comparable aim by very different methods, employing an experimental design to empirically demonstrate how labelling new policies for housing the mentally handicapped as 'community care' promotes acceptance of the idea that handicapped people can be integrated into the community. As the preceding examples indicate, such analyses are not abstract intellectual exercises, but are concerned with the way in which dominant discourses impact on the lives of ordinary people. Indeed, the relationship between 'official' (e.g. scientific) and lay discourses is a central theme of social representations theory (Moscovici and Hewstone 1983).

The relationship between macro-level discourse and individual experience can be investigated by exploring the types of discourse which permeate and constrain everyday texts and talk, from advertisements and magazines to casual conversation (see Banister et al. 1994). Many different modes and levels of analysis are used to study conversations. The researcher may examine the way in which the speaker and listener draw on shared discourses or 'interpretive repertoires' to explain, legitimate or persuade (Potter and Wetherell 1987). Conversation may be approached as a linguistically explicit example of the socially distributed nature of meaning; thus certain speech acts only 'make sense' when completed by an appropriate response from the hearer (Leudar and Antaki 1988). A common theme is the function of certain linguistic strategies as a means of negotiating power relations.

The well-researched subject of talk between doctors and patients provides an illustration of these diverse approaches to conversation. By carefully quantifying the initiation of topics and the use of questions in a large sample of doctor–patient interactions, some researchers have shown how doctors attempt to control the agenda in consultations, discouraging talk about psycho-social issues by posing closed biomedical questions and failing to respond to patients' references to emotional or lifestyle matters (Campion et al. 1992; Mishler 1984; Tuckett et al. 1985). Close attention to the use of language has illuminated the way in which health professionals try to enlist the patient's support (Balint 1957); thus dentists invoke the impression of collaboration by using phrases such as 'Let's just . . . ' or 'Shall we . . . ?', the patient's reality is denied by statements such as 'It can't really hurt that much', while self-assessments ('That's a nice job') are used to reinforce a positive view of treatment (Anderson 1986). At the same time, patients may actually resist any effort by the doctor to venture outside the domain of bio-medicine (Silverman 1987), using the tactics of silence, evasion, concealment and refutation against attempts to monitor, control or normalise their behaviour (S. Freeman 1987; Bloor and McIntosh 1990).

Sometimes the 'conversations' used as material for discourse analysis are obtained by organising 'focus group' discussions (Kitzinger 1995), or by conducting interviews. It is important to attend to the way in which the investigator influences this material: by defining the topic and framing the questions; by implicitly demarcating the roles of the participants (e.g. as 'analyst/therapist' or 'interviewee'); by selectively tape-recording and tran-scribing only a portion of the conversation (experienced interviewers will be familiar with the way in which the conversation often changes radically *after* the tape-recorder has been turned off!); and by reacting to statements with indications of interest, sympathy, confusion or surprise (Hollway 1989; Leudar and Antaki 1996; Mishler 1986a,b).

Interviews are often used as a means of eliciting narratives, accounts or stories. These constitute an elemental form which allows people to imagina-tively organise and communicate their experiences by drawing on cultural conventions to elaborate themes, scripts and roles (Sarbin 1986). Narratives can hence be analysed as examples of the way in which people linguistically and cognitively structure their world, create meaningful identities, and make sense of their lives (M. Freeman 1993; Mishler 1986a,b). For instance, nar-rative accounts of the experience of illness typically explain how it relates to selfhood, weaving a biography which links the illness to life events and fami-ly history (Blaxter 1993), and describing the way in which illness has been reconciled with the sufferer's personality and lifestyle, either by resistance or accommodation (Frank 1993). Narratives exploit the dramatic form, and can thus be used to draw the listener–audience into the story-teller's experi-ence; the sufferer can set the scene, highlight key points by selectively report-ing events and dialogue, and enact the emotional content through gesture and non-verbal communication, including pregnant pauses, sighs or even moans (Brodwin 1992; Riessman 1990).

A variety of methods of analysing discourse have been suggested. Potter and Wetherell (1987) recommend repeated re-reading of the text in order to identify consistencies and inconsistencies, and to determine the functions of particular linguistic strategies by noting their effects. These procedures can be regarded as a form of 'deconstruction', a technique which is central to discourse analysis. Deconstruction is the process of revealing the ideological constraints on what can and cannot be said (Feldman 1995), and the dichotomies (known as 'logocentric oppositions') which connect the dominant discourses to those which are hidden or stifled (Parker 1988). These can be exposed by searching for the silences, omissions, hesitations and discrepancies which imply an alternative meaning to that expressed (Chase 1995; Steele 1986; Waitzkin and Britt 1993).

In this form of analysis a delicate balance must be maintained in order to avoid giving the mistaken impression that the content of an interaction is either simply a repetition of pre-existent discourses or a superficial exercise in self-presentation (Parker and Burman 1993). Although macro-level discourses do potentiate and circumscribe the content of a conversation, individuals create perspectives and positions which are flexible and idiosyncratic (indeed, often changeable and contradictory) by selecting arguments and images from a variety of the available discourses. Moreover, in doing so they are not engaging in some Machiavellian attempt to wield power and exert influence, but are participating in the continuous process of explanation and negotiation which is necessary in order to sustain our society and culture – the shared understanding of reality on which we base our beliefs and actions. The purpose of deconstruction is hence intended to be not only informative but also liberatory; by uncovering and challenging existing patterns of discourse, which underpin a certain set of social and power relations, possibilities for new ways of perceiving, talking and acting may be created (Parker 1990). The way in which discourse analysis can contribute to the construction of meaning and knowledge, and thus impact on power relations and social practices, is considered further in the following sections on the ethics and validity of discursive research.

ESTABLISHING THE VALIDITY OF DISCURSIVE RESEARCH

The epistemological and ideological dispute between realist (mainly quantitative) researchers and non-realist (mainly qualitative) researchers has become closely identified in recent years with the debate about the validity of qualitative research, which remains a hotly contested area of controversy. Qualitative researchers are accused of failing to satisfactorily demonstrate the reliability and objective validity of their data and findings. The discursive response is that in quantitative research 'reliability' is too often achieved by treating important inconsistencies and idiosyncrasies as 'error', and that objective validity is a mistaken ideal, since *all* views of reality are associated with a particular perspective. Discursive researchers believe that the material used in both qualitative *and* quantitative analysis is inevitably deeply influenced by the researcher. Rather than collecting neutral data, the investigator frames the question, picks the participants, and then interacts with them to produce the observations or texts used for analysis. Further processes of selection and interpretation shape the conclusions and presentation of the analysis: for example, the inclusion or omission of certain data; the examination of particular comparisons or associations; and the explanation of unexpected, ambiguous or inconsistent findings. Consequently, it is hypocritical to attempt to withdraw from the picture and treat the material or the findings of the research as an objective record of 'reality'.

This argument cannot readily be resolved because of the fundamental philosophical differences between realist and discursive research. Nevertheless, the extent of the rift between the two outlooks has often been exaggerated, since in practice both realist and discursive, quantitative and qualitative researchers necessarily seek to establish to the satisfaction of their peers that their findings are pertinent, sound and meaningful. In the following sections I will outline some of the diverse ways in which discursive researchers have attempted to enrich and emancipate the process of knowledge construction, and will consider a variety of responses to the problem of how the value of research can be demonstrated without appealing to a rhetoric of scientific objectivity.

Representativeness and generality

It will be clear from the first half of this chapter that qualitative researchers vary considerably in their attitudes to the issue of the 'representativeness' of their material. Some broadly concur with the principle that their sample should be sufficiently typical of a particular population that any conclusions drawn from the sample could be generalised to the population as a whole. However, qualitative research is generally much more intensive than quantitative research, and uses 'information-rich' contextualised data from a small number of individuals, rather than limited data from a large sample (Miller and Crabtree 1994). In order to ensure that this small sample includes the diverse perspectives of a range of individuals or sub-cultures, qualitative researchers may therefore employ sampling methods which explicitly target people whose views are believed to be especially pertinent, or different from those of other participants in the research project. One example is the grounded theory approach, whereby hypotheses formulated on the basis of data obtained from an initial sample of interviewees are tested by seeking further material from particular individuals or groups thought likely to provide information which could extend or refine the developing understanding of the phenomenon studied (Charmaz 1990; Strauss and Corbin 1990).

The case-study approach aspires towards an even more intensive rather than extensive mode of analysis – a detailed and profound insight into a particular, perhaps unique, account or experience rather than a set of broad generalisations about commonalities between different people. The rationale of this approach is to fully exploit one of the principal merits of qualitative methods, the analysis of meaning in depth and in context. The hermeneutic (i.e. interpretive) principle which underlies most qualitative analysis is that parts can only be properly understood in relation to the whole (and vice versa); for example, although a film is composed of successively presented scenes, it is only when the entire film has been viewed that the significance of some of the scenes can be fully appreciated in retrospect.[2] Indeed, some forms of qualitative research, such as narrative analysis, *require* a holistic overview. It is necessary to consider a narrative as a complete unit in order to interpret the 'point' or 'moral' of the story, to identify important gaps or inconsistencies in the 'plot', to comprehend the reasons why certain motives or circumstances are highlighted and others omitted, and to appreciate the origins and wider implications of the views and events which are related (Riessman 1993; Sarbin 1986). Consequently, even though for the purposes of comparison a narrative analyst may actually study several accounts from different people, the number that can be examined in the meticulous manner required for a thorough hermeneutic analysis is necessarily limited, and the interpretation derived from such an analysis is often best illustrated by presenting and discussing just one or two typical or particularly illuminating narratives (e.g. Mishler 1984).

Discursive analysts who have collected accounts from several people often eschew the ideal of representativeness because they are specifically interested in the *variability* in discourse. They may therefore simply select for presentation and analysis text segments which they consider especially interesting or revealing. Nevertheless, some notion of typicality itself still informs the selection of 'interesting' material, which is interesting because it uniquely exemplifies *or* contradicts what is seen as typical. For example, one way in which discourse analysts can identify the function of the inconsistencies and idiosyncrasies in individuals' accounts is by establishing the characteristics of the *stereotypic* public discourses (i.e. interpretive repertoires) on which they draw (Harré and Gillett 1994; Potter et al. 1990).

The validity of knowledge construction

Qualitative researchers also vary in their responses to the issue of the validity of their analysis and conclusions. Some adopt a broadly realist conception of validity, using well-defined coding schemes and inter-rater reliability checks to generate data which can be regarded as reasonably 'objective' and subjected to quantification and statistical analysis. Others regard the codes as an interpretation of the data rather than as indices of empirical facts, but nevertheless find that the development of an explicit coding procedure is a useful way of clarifying and refining emerging descriptions and hypotheses. A fully elaborated coding scheme can also provide a useful basis for comprehensively reporting how the analysis contributed to the process of knowledge construction. In addition, the extensive discussion with colleagues needed to achieve consistent coding across different raters can alert the investigators to ways in which their own assumptions and preoccupations may be affecting their perception of the material, and often proves a valuable source of fresh insights.

None the less, it is important to recognise that a rigid coding scheme with demonstrably good inter-rater reliability is neither a necessary nor a sufficient guarantee of quality in discursive research. Indeed, 'reliable' coding is not always the most appropriate and effective method of achieving rigorous concept development, reflexive self-awareness, sampling of diverse perspectives, and thorough reporting of the research process. In non-realist discourse analysis the coding system is not intended as a reliable set of measures of any empirical property of the data (Seidel and Kelle 1995); the coding of text segments simply represents a system of referencing which can facilitate the retrieval of a set of text segments which the analyst wishes for some reason to consider as a corpus (e.g. for comparison with a different set of text segments). In this type of research a high inter-rater reliability could be viewed merely as an indication that the analyst had undertaken the curious process of demonstrating that a colleague could be taught to use the same set of features and concepts to classify the material as they themselves had employed. Low-level procedural scrutiny of this kind is essentially irrelevant, unless the analyst wishes to make some assertion about the objectivity (or at least the shared inter-subjectivity) of the coding scheme. Moreover, codes which are sufficiently obvious that they can be reliably identified by multiple raters also tend to be somewhat crude, unimaginative, and insensitive to the ambiguities and nuances of meaning which can be discovered in the course of a thoughtful consideration of the material and its context. The constraints of reliable coding may therefore oblige the qualitative researcher to sacrifice some of the principal advantages of qualitative research.

Since the claims of discursive researchers cannot be verified by appeal to their objective truth, alternative forms of establishing their utility must be established. Some analysts appeal to the rigour and coherence of their analyses as proof of quality. But while comprehensiveness and consistency are undoubtedly desirable qualities in an analysis, the rhetorical effect of appeals to a 'systematic' method of analysis (e.g. Potter and Wetherell 1987; Strauss and Corbin 1990) can be to produce an illusion of almost scientific objectivity. This effect may be magnified when researchers claim to employ an inductive approach (i.e. to derive their theory and conclusions from the data) and recommend techniques for testing their own assertions that the conclusions 'fit' the material – for example, by deliberately seeking disconfirming instances (Miles and Huberman 1984). In grounded theory, for example, the thorough and well-specified set of procedures for generating a set of abstract categories, dimensions and relationships from interview data may give both analyst and reader the impression that this process can produce a description which is both comprehensive and accurate. However, any claim to allow the data to lead the inquiry or to 'speak for itself' is clearly disingenuous, since data is inevitably silent and lifeless except insofar as it is animated by the intentions and meanings of those (i.e. the researchers and the participants in the research) who jointly produce it (Charmaz 1990; Kvale 1983). The idea of referring to the coded material to 'test' the adequacy of theories developed from that coded material consequently contains a disturbing circularity. The coherence and explanatory power of any theory which endeavours to identify a pattern of relationships in the data is indeed an indication of its value, but to attempt to empirically 'test' the theory using coded observations is to mistake these codes for measures of reality, whereas they are more properly regarded as elements of the theory itself (Araujo 1995).

A similar objection can be directed at researchers who suggest that the 'triangulation' of methods and material (i.e. the use of a variety of methodological approaches and sources of data to investigate a single topic) can be employed as a way of converging on robust findings, which they claim should emerge repeatedly from the multiple analyses (Miles and Huberman 1984; Schwandt 1994; Silverman 1993). By utilising a variety of samples and analytic approaches, they aspire to counteract the subjectivity of *all* those involved in the research, whether respondents who misreport or observers who misrepresent the events or phenomena in question. But this approach to triangulation again implies a form of weak realism, since it is premised on the belief that it is possible to overcome the inevitable bias in the analysis in order to ascertain the 'truth'. In addition, some researchers would query not only the purpose but also the ethics of any attempt to verify or disconfirm the accounts of those involved in the research.

Researchers who have relinquished any conception of objective truth are compelled to formulate alternative means of justifying or validating their analyses. The practice of reflexivity, introduced in Chapter 1, can be used as a way of involving others in the process of knowledge construction and evaluation, and hence can help to defend the analysis from accusations of covert prejudice or excessive idiosyncrasy in interpretation. In principle, by reflexively disclosing how the conclusions were derived, including the goals and assumptions driving the research, investigators can render their findings so 'transparent' that readers will be able to make their own judgements about how these may have been affected by the research process (Banister et al. 1994; Stiles 1993). But if authors are incapable of providing an objective account of events – and especially their own activities and motives – then the ideal of candid reflexivity is impossible to attain. There is consequently a risk that reflexivity may degenerate into futile narcissism (Burman 1991), or will simply be used as a rhetorical device for deflecting suspicions of bias. Some similar advantages and problems are associated with the non-realist use of triangulation, which can be employed as a means of approaching a topic from multiple perspectives in order to derive a multi-faceted understanding rather than to converge on a unitary conclusion (see the following section). Consideration of a variety of types of information and a range of theoretical orientations and interpretations is a valuable method of enriching an analysis, but should not be mistaken for impartiality.

Expertise, power and persuasive validity

An intrinsic ethical ambivalence about the exercise of power needed to legitimate truth claims is responsible for many of the difficulties encountered by qualitative researchers in their efforts to develop satisfactory criteria for validation. Having relinquished the claim to scientific objectivity traditionally used by quantitative researchers as a means of justifying their assertions, qualitative researchers are faced with two stark alternatives: to reinstate their authority as experts by agreeing new conventions for evaluating and affirming the merit of an analysis or conclusion, or to openly admit that there is no gold standard by which the worth of any account can be assessed. Confronted with these equally unpalatable options, most researchers attempt a delicate and sometimes uneasy compromise by asserting only a limited local authority based on a combination of thorough and conscientious exploration and reporting, intellectual excellence, consensus of opinion and productive utility (e.g. Guba and Lincoln 1994). For example, an interpretation might be justified on the grounds that it was comprehensive and coherent, consistent with the data and theoretically sophisticated, and meaningful to both participants and peers.

Because these tentative and thoughtful forms of validation have the immense value of stimulating awareness of methodological issues other than sample size and statistical significance, they continually expose the intellectual and ethical dilemmas inherent in research. For example, one popular non-realist criterion for validating research is the goal of plausibility, persuasiveness, communicability or credibility (Leininger 1994; Mishler 1986b; Riessman 1993). This ideal refers partly to the consistency and rhetorical power of the research report, as judged by a community of academic peers – although the appropriate reference community may itself be very difficult to define, given the widely differing views on research quality held by, for example, phenomenologists, discourse analysts, and traditional quantitative researchers. In addition, most researchers feel that their interpretation should be meaningful, acceptable, and useful to the participants on whose accounts it was based, and may therefore include feedback from participants in the analytic process and report. This strategy is entirely suitable for some purposes, especially for phenomenological or advocacy approaches in which the investigator works with the participants to understand and describe their view of the world. However, many functionalist analyses of discourse seek to 'deconstruct' the rhetorical strategies of their participants in a manner which they might well not appreciate or concur with – or, indeed, fully understand. Instead of taking the participants' accounts at face value, this type of analysis examines how people tell their story, drawing on socially accepted forms of justification to present themselves in a particular way (e.g. Riessman 1990; Stenner 1993). Even if the participants are allowed to comment on these interpretations (Moir 1993), it would be disingenuous to suggest that this can redress the power imbalance inherent in the relationship between the person whose speech is analysed and the 'expert' who writes the final publication (Marks 1993).

Analysts who embrace the postmodern deconstruction and multiplicity of meaning have particular difficulty in subscribing to any standard definition of value or validity. Post-structuralist and postmodern authors are fundamentally opposed, on both intellectual and ideological grounds, to the idea that there can or should be a single 'correct' view or value system (Lyotard 1984). They have exposed how a dominant perspective or interpretation always simultaneously hides or suppresses, and yet implies, a different perspective (Hollinger 1994). For example, Sampson (1989) has shown how the dominant Western concept of the autonomous individual serves to conceal the pervasive power of state and corporate systems, while Oliver (1990) notes that the dominant portrayal of disability as an individual tragedy deflects attention from the way in which disability is created by exclusion from a socio-economic world geared towards the 'normal' person. Thus, for postmodern authors no universal absolute truths exist, and claims to validity can only be made in relation to a particular audience or goal (Altheide and Johnston 1994), and must be tempered with a reflexive critique of the assumptions upon which they rest and the conventions and practices by which they are justified (Gergen 1992). Indeed, radical postmodern conceptions of validity seek to undermine the stolid and authoritarian conception of expertise by embracing objectives such as creativity, tension, irony, empowerment and enlightenment, and encouraging the production of heterogeneous, changing, and open-ended interpretations (Lather 1993; Michael 1994).

By questioning the authority of *all* interpretations, the postmodern attitude undeniably makes it difficult to privilege a single perspective or champion a particular cause, such as feminism or patients' rights (Burman 1990). However, a tolerance of pluralism (multiple coexisting outlooks) does not, as some critics have argued, imply a nihilistic relativism – in other words, an intellectual and moral chaos which does not allow any value judgements to be made. Rather, it represents a recognition that the standards by which ideas are appraised must be co-operatively agreed and constantly revised and renewed. This position is neatly summarised by Feldman, who prefaces her book on qualitative methods with the statement that 'While I do not think all interpretations are equally reasonable or legitimate, I also understand that these concepts – reason and legitimacy – are culturally bounded' (1995: 2).

CONCLUDING COMMENTS: POSSIBILITIES FOR
MATERIAL–DISCURSIVE METHODS

The preceding discussion may appear to lead readers towards the disturbing conclusion that discursive research cannot be properly validated as there is no method of validation which is undisputed and universally accepted. However, this does not imply that discursive methods are intrinsically flawed or are inferior in this respect to quantitative methods, since the discursive critique of procedures for validating knowledge production is equally relevant to quantitative research. The uncertainty which surrounds the issue of validation can instead be seen as a positive feature of discursive research, one which encourages diversity and inventiveness as well as continual circumspection, reflection, self-awareness and critical debate.

The chapters in this book illustrate the heterogeneity of discursive approaches. As is customary in the context of a book (as opposed to a journal) the authors have been asked to provide an overview of their thesis rather than reporting the details of their procedures (for which interested readers are referred to their published articles, as appropriate). However, the variety of material on which they draw and the contrasting manner in which they treat this material provides a sample of the wide range of discursive modes of analysis. Some of the authors (Smith et al., Yardley) focus selectively on a few case-studies, while others (Joffe, Ingham and Kirkland, Woollett and Marshall, Soyland) sample discourse from a broad range of sources and interviewees. All the contributors implicitly or explicitly address theoretical matters to some extent, but also illustrate these by reference to empirical material. However, theoretical considerations are central to the chapters by Radley, Noble and Ogden, whereas the presentation of empirical research occupies a more prominent place in the chapters by Soyland, Woollett and Marshall, and Ingham and Kirkland. Some of the analyses are based principally on the talk of ordinary individuals (Smith et al., Soyland), while others relate this to the macro-level discourses of scientists, doctors, the media and policy-makers (Ogden, Joffe, Woollett and Marshall, Ingham and Kirkland, Yardley).

Since this book is consciously devoted to developing *material*–discursive approaches to health and illness, all the chapters contain some reflection on embodied being and/or other material factors and processes. And while these chapters are themselves by their very nature texts or discourses, they are also necessarily material objects – indeed, commodities. This dual existence represents a characteristic of material–discursive methodology which deserves further exploration. Three material aspects of discursive research are therefore briefly considered: the material influences on discursive products; the way in which the material can be incorporated into discursive analysis; and the material ramifications of academic discourses.

If discourses are not disembodied abstract disquisitions, but social products with material origins and implications, it seems pertinent to assess not only their discursive context but also the material circumstances in which they were produced. This means that in order to complement reflexive discussion of the discursive influences on knowledge production – for example, the conceptualisation, position and rhetoric adopted by the researcher – it may also be useful to appraise material influences on the research.[3] These include the factors of cost, time and access which might have led the researcher to approach particular potential interviewees (such as those at a convenient distance, or who were identified as suitable by a doctor or therapist), or which may have prevented certain people from taking part in the research (including illness or disability, family obligations or occupational pressures). The choice of method and analysis is also inevitably affected by availability of resources, such as people with time to transcribe and code text, or computer packages to assist with qualitative data analysis. A further consideration could be the way in which the source of funding and time constraints on production serve to regulate and circumscribe what can be studied, and the mode and presentation of the analysis. For example, the choice of research topic tends to be shaped by departmental strategies, public priorities, funding initiatives, and the possibilities for commercial exploitation or sponsorship, while most funding bodies expect analyses to be published in academic journals rather than (or as well as) being disseminated through the popular press, artistic and literary media, or the Internet.

The question of how the material can be incorporated into discursive analysis is confronted at the theoretical level by the preceding chapter, and is empirically addressed by the following chapters. Although many of the analyses in this book are based primarily on discourse, this can itself be viewed as a kind of 'virtual' embodiment. Bruner (1991) and Hermans (1995) have stressed the embodied nature of narrative, which is premised on a dialogue between speaker and audience, and which uses actors and locales as a way of simultaneously particularising experience and recreating social reality. It is thus possible to investigate the material by examining how it is reconstituted in talk – whether in scientific discourse about the experimentally determined 'facts' of AIDS (Joffe) or of eating behaviour (Ogden), or in students' talk about body decoration (Soyland) and women's talk about pregnancy (Woollett and Marshall). In addition, some contributors have chosen to supplement the analysis of discourse by descriptive ecological and phenomenological analysis of modes of non-verbal communication or of physical interaction with the environment (Radley, Noble, Yardley). The integration of discursive analysis with research into physical behaviour opens up a vista of exciting possibilities which have yet to be fully exploited in the field of health psychology; for example, the combination of discourse analysis with participant observation and ethnography, with measures of non-verbal communication or recordings of behaviour and with descriptions of physiological functioning.[4]

Lastly, but for health psychologists perhaps most importantly, it is necessary to consider the material consequences of discursive research. Discourse analysis has sometimes been portrayed as a kind of intellectual indulgence which lacks the practical significance of, say, a survey or a clinical trial. But whereas some realist researchers may indeed aspire simply to develop a neutral theory or provide an objective description, the very rationale for discursive research is to produce an effect – for example, to challenge existing practices, publicise suppressed discourses, or create an alternative way of looking at things. The material implications of a profound and persuasive discursive analysis can thus be just as far-reaching as the outcome of a trial of some innovative therapy; recent historical examples include the impact of feminist commentaries on sexist practices, and the way in which critiques of institutionalisation and the medicalisation of madness contributed to the demise of asylums. In order to illustrate the utility and pragmatism of discursive approaches to health and illness, each of the contributors to this volume has been asked to highlight briefly in their conclusions the practical import of their analysis. And while these include a variety of specific recommendations for changes in social policy, health education and health care practices, it is worth noting that the principal manner in which discourses exert their influence is through communication – in other words, their ability to subtly modify the future speech and actions of you, the reader!

NOTES

1 It is clearly beyond the scope of a single chapter to provide a detailed description of the wide variety of qualitative methods; for accessible introductory books on this topic see Smith et al. (1995) or Banister et al. (1994), while Denzin and Lincoln (1994) provide a more exhaustive review.
2 This principle is often referred to as the 'hermeneutic circle', which can be seen as relevant not only to the understanding of texts and narratives, but also human lives (M. Freeman 1993).
3 Analysis of the material and economic aspects of social practices has unfortunately come to be associated in some people's minds with a crude, reductionist form of ideological censure; what is needed is a mode of analysis which can simultaneously embrace the discursive dimension and is sensitive to the complexities and practicalities of professional endeavour.
4 For examples of how the meaning of individual experience can be related in a non-reductionist way to physiological function, see Csordas's (1994) fascinating exploration of the religious insights of a man with a temporal-parietal lobe brain tumour, or Sacks's (1985) stories of neurological deficit.

REFERENCES

Altheide, D. and Johnston, J. M. (1994) 'Criteria for assessing interpretive validity in qualitative research', in N. K. Denzin and Y. S. Lincoln (eds) *Handbook of Qualitative Research*, London: Sage.

Anderson, R. and Bury, M. (1988) *Living with Chronic Illness*, London: Unwin Hyman.

Anderson, W. T. (1986) 'The apostolic function of the dentist', in S. Fisher and A. D. Todd (eds) *Discourse and Institutional Authority*, New Jersey: Ablex Publishing Group.

Araujo, L. (1995) 'Designing and refining hierarchical coding frames', in U. Kelle (ed.) *Computer-aided Qualitative Data Analysis: Theory, Methods and Practice*, London: Sage.

Balint, M. (1957) *The Doctor, his Patient and the Illness*, Tunbridge Wells: Pitman Medical.

Banister, P., Burman, E., Parker, I., Taylor, M. and Tindall, C. (1994) *Qualitative Methods in Psychology: A Research Guide*, Buckingham: Open University Press.

Berman, P., Kendall, C. and Bhattacharya, K. (1994) 'The household production of health: integrating social science perspectives on micro-based health determinants', *Social Science and Medicine* 38: 205–215.

Blaxter, M. (1993) 'Why do the victims blame themselves?', in A. Radley (ed.) *Worlds of Illness*, London: Routledge.

Bloor, M. and McIntosh, J. (1990) 'Surveillance and concealment: a comparison of techniques of client resistance in therapeutic communities and health visiting', in S. Cunningham-Burley and N. P. McKeganey (eds) *Readings in Medical Sociology*, London: Tavistock/Routledge.

Borkan, J. M., Quirk, M. and Sullivan, M. (1991) 'Finding meaning after the fall: injury narratives from elderly hip fracture patients', *Social Science and Medicine* 33: 947–957.

Brodwin, P. E. (1992) 'Symptoms and social performances: the case of Diane Reden', in M-J. DelVecchio Good, P. E. Brodwin, B. J. Good and A. Kleinman (eds) *Pain as Human Experience*, Berkeley, CA: University of California Press.

Bruner, J. (1991) 'The narrative construction of reality', *Critical Inquiry* 18: 1–21.

Burman, E. (1990) 'Differing with deconstruction: a feminist critique', in I. Parker and J. Shotter (eds) *Deconstructing Social Psychology*, London: Routledge.

—— (1991) 'What discourse is not', *Philosophical Psychology* 3: 325–342.

Campion, P. D., Butler, N. M. and Cox, A. D. (1992) 'Principal agendas of doctors and patients in general practice consultations', *Family Practice* 9: 181–190.

Charmaz, K. (1990) ' "Discovering" chronic illness: using grounded theory', *Social Science and Medicine* 30: 1161–1172.

Chase, S. E. (1995) *Interpreting Experience: The Narrative Study of Lives*, London: Sage.

Conrad, P. (1990) 'Qualitative research on chonic illness: a commentary on method and conceptual development', *Social Science and Medicine* 30: 1257–1263.

Corbin, J. and Strauss, A. (1985) 'Managing chronic illness at home: three lines of work', *Qualitative Sociology* 8: 224–227.

Csordas, T. J. (1994) 'Words from the Holy People: a case study in cultural phenomenology', in T. J. Csordas (ed.) *Embodiment and Experience: The Existential Ground of Culture and Self*, Cambridge: Cambridge University Press.

Denzin, N. K. and Lincoln, Y. S. (eds) (1994) *Handbook of Qualitative Research*, London: Sage.

Feldman, M. S. (1995) *Strategies for Interpreting Qualitative Data*, London: Sage.

Fewtrell, D. and O'Connor, K. (1994) *Clinical Phenomenology and Cognitive Psychology*, London: Routledge.

Fox, N. J. (1993) *Postmodernism, Sociology and Health*, Buckingham: Open University Press.

Frank, A. W. (1993) 'The rhetoric of self-change: illness experience as narrative', *The Sociological Quarterly* 34: 39–52.

Freeman, M. (1993) *Rewriting the Self: History, Memory, Narrative*, London: Routledge.

Freeman, S. H. (1987) 'Health promotion talk in family practice encounters', *Social Science and Medicine* 25: 961–966.

Gergen, K. J. (1992) 'Toward a postmodern psychology', in S. Kvale (ed.) *Psychology and Postmodernism*, London: Sage.

Giorgi, A. (1990) 'Phenomenology, psychological science and common sense', in G. R. Semin and K. J. Gergen (eds) *Everyday Understanding*, London: Sage.

Glaser, B. G. and Strauss, A. L. (1967) *The Discovery of Grounded Theory*, Chicago: Aldine.

Goffman, E. (1963) *Stigma: Notes on the Management of a Spoiled Identity*, New Jersey: Prentice-Hall.

Griffin, C. and Phoenix, A. (1994) 'The relationship between qualitative and quantitative research: lessons from feminist psychology', *Journal of Community and Applied Psychology* 4: 287–298.

Guba, E. G. and Lincoln, Y. S. (1994) 'Competing paradigms in qualitative research', in N. K. Denzin and Y. S. Lincoln (eds) *Handbook of Qualitative Research*, London: Sage.

Harré, R. and Gillett, G. (1994) *The Discursive Mind*, London: Sage.

Henwood, K. and Pidgeon, N. (1995) 'Grounded theory and psychological research', *The Psychologist* 8: 115–118.

Hermans, H. J. M. (1995) 'The limitations of logic in defining the self', *Theory and Psychology* 5: 375–382.

Hétu, R., Riverin, L., Getty, L., Lalande, N. M. and St-Cyr, C. (1990) 'The reluctance to acknowledge hearing difficulties among hearing-impaired workers', *British Journal of Audiology* 24: 265–276.

Hollinger, R. (1994) *Postmodernism and the Social Sciences*, London: Sage.

Hollway, W. (1989) *Subjectivity and Method in Psychology: Gender, Meaning and Science*, London: Sage.

Holstein, J. A. and Gubrium, J. F. (1994) 'Phenomenology, ethnomethodology and interpretive practice', in N. K. Denzin and Y. S. Lincoln (eds) *Handbook of Qualitative Research*, London: Sage.

Huberman, A. M. and Miles, M. B. (1994) 'Data management and analysis methods', in N. K. Denzin and Y. S. Lincoln (eds) *Handbook of Qualitative Research*, London: Sage.

John, I. D. (1992) 'Statistics as rhetoric in psychology', *Australian Psychologist* 3: 144–149.

Johnson, J. L. (1991) 'Learning to live again: the process of adjustment following a heart attack', in J. M. Morse and J. L. Johnson (eds) *The Illness Experience*, London: Sage.

Kitzinger, J. (1995) 'Introducing focus groups', *British Medical Journal* 311: 299–302.

Kvale, S. (1983) 'The qualitative research interview: a phenomenological and a hermeneutical mode of understanding', *Journal of Phenomenological Psychology* 14: 171–196.

—— (ed.) (1992) *Psychology and Postmodernism*, London: Sage.

Lather, E. P. (1993) 'Fertile obsession: validity after poststructuralism', *Sociological Quarterly* 34: 673–693.

Leininger, M. (1994) 'Evaluation criteria and critique of qualitative research studies', in J. M. Morse (ed.) *Critical Issues in Qualitative Research Methods*, London: Sage.

Leudar, I. and Antaki, C. (1988) 'Completion and dynamics in explanation seeking', in C. Antaki (ed.) *Analysing Everyday Explanation*, London: Sage.

—— (1996) 'Discourse participation, reported speech and research practices in social psychology', *Theory and Psychology* 6: 5–29.

Levin, D. M. (1985) *The Body's Recollection of Being*, London: Routledge.

Lonkila, M. (1995) 'Grounded theory as an emerging paradigm for computer-assisted qualitative data analysis', in U. Kelle (ed.) *Computer-aided Qualitative Data Analysis: Theory, Methods and Practice*, London: Sage.

Lyotard, J-F. (1984) *The Postmodern Condition: A Report on Knowledge*, Manchester: Manchester University Press.

Marks, D. (1993) 'Case-conference analysis and action research', in E. Burman and I. Parker (eds) *Discourse Analytic Research: Repertoires and Readings of Texts in Action*, London: Routledge.

Michael, M. (1994) 'Discourse and uncertainty: postmodern variations', *Theory and Psychology* 4: 383–404.

Miles, M. B. and Huberman, A. M. (1984) *Qualitative Data Analysis*, Beverly Hills, CA: Sage.

Miller, W. L. and Crabtree, B. F. (1994) 'Clinical research', in N. K. Denzin and Y. S. Lincoln (eds) *Handbook of Qualitative Research*, London: Sage.

Mishler, E. G. (1984) *The Discourse of Medicine*, New Jersey: Ablex Publishing Group.

—— (1986a) *Research Interviewing*, Cambridge, MA: Harvard University Press.

—— (1986b) 'The analysis of interview-narratives', in T. R. Sarbin (ed.) *Narrative Psychology: The Storied Nature of Human Conduct*, New York: Praeger.

Moir, J. (1993) 'Occupational career choice: accounts and contradictions', in E. Burman and I. Parker (eds) *Discourse Analytic Research: Repertoires and Readings of Texts in Action*, London: Routledge.

Moscovici, S. and Hewstone, M. (1983) 'Social representations and social explanations: from the "naive" to the "amateur" scientist', in M. Hewstone (ed.) *Attribution Theory: Social and Functional Extensions*, Oxford: Blackwell.

Oliver, M. (1990) *The Politics of Disablement*, Basingstoke: Macmillan.

Parker, I. (1988) 'Deconstructing accounts', in C. Antaki (ed.) *Analysing Everyday Explanation*, London: Sage.

—— (1990) 'Discourse: definitions and contradictions', *Philosophical Psychology* 3: 189–204.

Parker, I. and Burman, E. (1993) 'Against discursive imperialism, empiricism and constructionism: thirty-two problems with discourse analysis', in E. Burman and I. Parker (eds) *Discourse Analytic Research: Repertoires and Readings of Texts in Action*, London: Routledge.

Pope, C. and Mays, N. (1995a) 'Reaching the parts other methods cannot reach: an introduction to qualitative methods in health and health services research', *British Medical Journal* 311: 42–45.

—— (1995b) 'Rigour and qualitative research', *British Medical Journal* 311: 109–111.

Potter, J. and Collie, F. (1989) ' "Community care" as persuasive rhetoric: a study of discourse', *Disability, Handicap and Society* 4: 57–64.

Potter, J. and Wetherell, M. (1987) *Discourse and Social Psychology*, London: Sage.

Potter, J., Wetherell, M., Gill, R. and Edwards, D. (1990) 'Discourse: noun, verb or social practice?', *Philosophical Psychology* 3: 205–217.

Ray, M. A. (1994) 'The richness of phenomenology: philosophic, theoretic and methodologic concerns', in J. M. Morse (ed.) *Critical Issues in Qualitative Research Methods*, London: Sage.

Ricoeur, P. (1991) *From Text to Action: Essays in Hermeneutics* II, London: Athlone Press.

Riessman, C. K. (1990) 'Strategic uses of narrative in the presentation of self and illness: a research note', *Social Science and Medicine* 30: 1195–1200.

—— (1993) *Narrative Analysis*, London: Sage.

Riger, S. (1992) 'Epistemological debates, feminist voices: science, social values, and the study of women', *American Psychologist* 47: 730–740.

Sacks, O. (1985). *The Man Who Mistook His Wife for a Hat*. London: Picador.

Sampson, E. E. (1989) 'The deconstruction of the self', in J. Shotter and K. J. Gergen (eds) *Texts of Identity*, London: Sage.

Sarbin, T. R. (ed.) (1986) *Narrative Psychology: The Storied Nature of Human Conduct*, New York: Praeger.

Schwandt, T. A. (1994) 'Constructionist, interpretive approaches to human inquiry', in N. K. Denzin and Y. S. Lincoln (eds) *Handbook of Qualitative Research*, London: Sage.

Seidel, J. and Kelle, U. (1995) 'Different functions of coding in the analysis of textual data', in U. Kelle (ed.) *Computer-aided Qualitative Data Analysis: Theory, Methods and Practice*, London: Sage.

Silverman, D. (1987) *Communication and Medical Practice: Social Relations in the Clinic*, London: Sage.

—— (1993) *Interpreting Qualitative Data*, London: Sage.

Smith, J. A., Harré, R. and van Langenhove, L. (1995) *Rethinking Methods in Psychology*, London: Sage.

Sontag, S. (1991) *Illness as Metaphor/AIDS and its Metaphors*, London: Penguin.

Steckler, A., McLeroy, K. R., Goodman, R. M., Bird, S. T. and McCormick, L. (1992) 'Toward integrating qualitative and quantitative methods: an introduction', *Health Education Quarterly* 19: 1–8.

Steele, R. S. (1986) 'Deconstructing histories: toward a systematic criticism of psychological narratives', in T. R. Sarbin (ed.) *Narrative Psychology: The Storied Nature of Human Conduct*, New York: Praeger.

Steier, F. (ed.) (1991) *Research and Reflexivity*, London: Sage.

Stenner, P. (1993) 'Discoursing jealousy', in E. Burman and I. Parker (eds) *Discourse Analytic Research: Repertoires and Readings of Texts in Action*, London: Routledge.

Stenner, P. and Eccleston, C. (1994) 'On the textuality of being: towards an invigorated social constructionism', *Theory and Psychology* 4: 85–103.

Stern, P. N. (1994) 'Eroding grounded theory', in J. M. Morse (ed.) *Critical Issues in Qualitative Research Methods*, London: Sage.

Stiles, W. B. (1993) 'Quality control in qualitative research', *Clinical Psychology Review* 13: 593–618.

Strauss, A. and Corbin, J. M. (1988) *Shaping a New Health Care System*, San Francisco: Jossey-Bass.

—— (1990) *Basics of Qualitative Research*, London: Sage.

Tesch, R. (1990) *Qualitative Research: Analysis Types and Software Tools*, New York: Falmer Press.

Tuckett, D., Boulton, M., Olson, C. and Williams, A. (1985) *Meetings Between Experts*, London: Tavistock.

Waitzkin, H. (1991) *The Politics of Medical Encounters*, New Haven: Yale University Press.

Waitzkin, H. and Britt, T. (1993) 'Processing narratives of self-destructive behavior in routine medical encounters: health promotion, disease prevention, and the discourse of health care', *Social Science and Medicine* 36: 1121–1136.

Wynne, A. (1988) 'Accounting for accounts of the diagnosis of multiple sclerosis', in S. Woolgar (ed.) *Knowledge and Reflexivity: New Frontiers in the Sociology of Knowledge*, London: Sage.

Yardley, L., Todd, A. M., Lacoudraye-Harter, M. M. and Ingham, R. (1992) 'Psychosocial consequences of vertigo', *Psychology and Health* 6: 85–96.

Chapter 3

What role does the body have in illness?

Alan Radley

INTRODUCTION

At first sight, the idea of asking the question that forms the title of this chapter seems faintly absurd. Surely, illness is, in an essential way, about disturbances to the body or to its normal way of functioning. It is likely that few would disagree with this statement. However, this discussion will analyse what this 'essential way' might be, and whether, indeed, there is one way or several. The idea that the body is the machinery that goes wrong when we are ill is but one way of looking at things, and by no means the most illuminating for students of psychology or social science. This chapter will explore what happens when people fall ill, when they seek medical help and when in situations where they must bear the symptoms of a chronic and perhaps serious condition. Using examples drawn from a variety of illness conditions, the discussion will show that although the body is perceived as 'the machinery that goes wrong', it is also understood to be more than this.

Because of its role as a medium of communication the body is also a way of *appearing well*, and of *appearing ill*. And because individuals must negotiate, with others, the movement between the states of health and illness, it is centrally involved in the communication of their personal conditions and social status. As well as this, it is the medium through which individuals live their lives, so that when ill they have to manage *with* the body that is affected by disease or injury.

This chapter addresses these issues by using interview material gathered from a group of forty-two men diagnosed as having serious coronary disease (a narrowing of the coronary arteries giving rise to angina pain and the risk of heart attack). A series of interviews (five in all) were conducted with the men, all of whom received coronary bypass grafting as the treatment for their condition. They were selected sequentially by taking their names from the surgical list. We also spoke with their spouses/partners, seeing the couples both prior to the operation and during the year afterwards. During these meetings, which took place in the home, husband and wife were first seen alone and then together. This allowed each of them to speak as individuals and then jointly as a couple, working out their response together. The structure of the interviews was open-ended, because the purpose was to obtain descriptions of the impact that the men's illness had upon the home, and the couples' ways of coping with this. The approach adopted to analysing the data was to view it as providing insights into the experience of the individuals concerned (i.e. a phenomenological perspective). Also, the fact that material was collected from partners, as well as from patients, meant that illness was seen in terms of the personal relationships of those involved, as well as the wider social context (i.e. a social, relational perspective). Therefore, the chapter approaches the body as being fundamental to how people act, both as ailing individuals and as members of a healthy social world.

THE DISEASED BODY AND THE IDEA OF ILLNESS

It can reasonably be said that the most widespread set of beliefs about illness in the industrialised world are based upon the concepts of Western medicine. From this point of view, the body is something that becomes diseased or injured so that it requires the attentions of physicians or surgeons to make it function properly once more. Within the terms of the medical model, the body is a physiological system which can only be understood in terms of concepts that analyse its constituent parts and their relations. It is also the object of the doctor's attention, so that to be a patient is to comply with medical authority in the furtherance of one's treatment.

This rather high-sounding introduction refers to the fact that, for most people in Western societies, being ill is inseparable from having one's symptoms diagnosed, going to the doctor or to the hospital, and having to follow the prescribed treatment regime. As part of this, people regard their bodies in particular ways, often using medical terminology to help make decisions about what they should do when they feel unwell. The body-for-doctors is a body of organs and functions, which, although it might not be wholly understood, is nevertheless more amenable to controlled investigation than it was in the past. Modern medicine, with its array of drugs and surgical techniques, has powers to see inside the body, to determine the early onset of disease, to alleviate suffering, and to bring about quite startling corrections of abnormality in bodily functioning. The procedures by which medicine tests and verifies its clinical procedures are those of natural science, which takes as axiomatic the need to 'objectify' its subject matter. That is, the ability of modern medicine to define the reality of disease and to offer treatment helps to shape the popular conception of the body as being a 'physical thing'.

In recent years, the assumption that all disease is the result of physico-chemical processes has been amended in the suggestion that some disease might have psychological or social causes (Engel 1977). This allows for aspects of the environment to be identified and measured to determine their effect upon the likelihood of people contracting certain diseases. An obvious example of this is the work on stress and coping and their contribution to illness, particularly as these concepts have been developed within the field of health psychology (Lazarus and Cohen 1977; Lazarus and Folkman 1984). However, it is important to note that this approach retains the idea of the body as a physiological system, to which are attached 'stress' or other 'pathogenic factors' by means of cause and effect relationships, or the implicative links of correlational analysis.

In contrast, many medical sociologists (and, more recently, some social psychologists) have set aside the idea of the diseased body in favour of examining people's experience of their illnesses. Where physicians have examined and treated the diseased body, these social scientists now study the sick person (or patient), and the context of his or her illness experience (Conrad 1987; Radley 1993). This distinction between disease and illness has been paralleled by a direction of focus towards the ideas, feelings and relationships of the individuals under study. Instead of factors that might contribute to the cause of disease, these studies examine the consequences of having been diagnosed as sick, and the various social contexts that have a bearing upon the quality of life of those affected. The majority of these studies have used some form of interview, in which patients (often with chronic, long-lasting illnesses) tell their story in their own words. A good example of this approach is the work of Kleinman (1988), who listened to the accounts given by people with chronic conditions. He makes explicit that this is a study of narrative, in that the experience of the individuals concerned is accessible only through their stories. In part, this is a phenomenological approach, in that the concern is to grasp the life-world of the person as it is given, without recourse to predetermined ideas. There are many examples in the literature of such studies of chronic illness experience, that attempt to reveal the situation of the sick or those who must try to live their lives as normally as possible (Anderson and Bury 1988; Pinder 1990; Yardley 1994). As part of this experience, the appearance of symptoms, their effect upon the person's life, and the strategies individuals use to deal with them are all important features to be examined.

One feature of work that has focused upon narrative has been an interest in the form of the stories themselves. Where phenomenological study attempts to read out the individual's experience from the account, researchers focusing upon discourse argue that there is no abiding experience that lies behind the words; rather, the experience of illness is fashioned in the telling. The study of accounts and of discourse is now well established in social psychology (Antaki 1994; Edwards and Potter 1992; Potter and Wetherell 1987). It emphasises that accounts are intentional, are strategically structured and draw upon both the immediate and other contexts to make their points. Examples using a similar approach, though within medical sociology, have existed for some time. In her study of families with handicapped children, Voysey (1975) chose to analyse what the parents said as statements aimed at justifying the hard choices they had had to make. Equally important, their accounts painted a picture of the families as being even more 'normal' than most, because of the way they had coped with the difficulties arising from their children's disabilities.

The distinction drawn above between the phenomenological and the discourse analytic approaches to accounts of illness experience is important for the argument to be made in this chapter. This is because of its implications for the treatment of the body in the course of understanding illness. In the context of illness, the phenomenological method aims at providing a description of the person's experience of his or her body as key to understanding the individual's situation. For the discourse analytic or narrative approach, any description of the body is no more (and no less) real than any other part of the story told. The body is, like all other elements in the account, a construction whose form and feeling are rhetorical features shaped in the telling. What is told about illness, and how it is told, cannot be dissociated from the context in which the account is given. As part of this, what is said about the body is part of the work of setting the boundaries and aims of the conversation (Radley and Billig 1996).

This can be illustrated by the case of someone going to the doctor with symptoms that they believe to be those of influenza. Telling the doctor about a bad headache, sore throat and feelings of fever are not merely descriptive of the patient's condition, but are designed to elicit treatment of a particular kind. Certain assumptions are conveyed about what the doctor can and 'ought to' do; these construct the person as someone with a legitimate claim to medical treatment – that is, as a patient.

The idea that signs of bodily discomfort do not exist in a ready-made state is consistent with the broad view of *social constructionism*. In the case of a specific episode (for example, seeing the doctor, telling a friend that you feel unwell), this means that the body is given meaning only in the account. Whatever feelings, disabilities or potentialities the person has are unknowable outside his or her way of talking about them. The idea of a 'real' body, an entity waiting to be referred to, that somehow exists beyond discourse, becomes an untenable proposition. This is the strong form of constructionism that has been contrasted with the weak variety, where the body is an inchoate (but very real) mass, which cognitions divide up and make sensible (Schacter and Singer 1962).

While there is no space here to discuss it in detail, social constructionism, in its historical form, argues that the body as a physical entity (a container with organs) is precisely a construction of modern medicine (Lupton 1994). It was only through the concepts and clinical techniques of modern medicine that such a body came to be discerned at all. Evidence from times prior to the emergence of modern medicine supports the argument that the diseased body was not seen in a universal fashion. To take a current example, in cultures where diarrhoea is prevalent among children, it is not seen as a symptom of illness, but remains a background mark of one's social and physical condition (Zola 1966).

Where does this brief analysis take us, as far as the body is concerned? It shows that what was formerly taken for granted (because the body was defined within biomedicine) has been placed in question; in addition, questions can now be raised about how *embodied individuals* treat each other. From the biomedical perspective, the body is an entity whose pathology can be objectively studied. It is something to which psychological and social phenomena can be related, where these, too, are treated as factors or variables. At the other extreme, the social constructionist position underlines that to speak of 'the body' is to endorse just this way of looking at things. From the position of a social constructionist psychology, the ailing body is discursively produced. It is the subject of narratives, outside of which it cannot be properly understood. Embodiment in illness is contextual and situated. What this embodied state 'is' depends upon whose body is being considered, by whom, in what context and for what purposes.

Ultimately, however, it also depends upon how it is spoken about, and therefore how it is seen. It is at this point that the constructionist position appears to deny the body any role other than that of being a field crisscrossed by the various discourses of patients, doctors, and healthy people. If this is the argument, then is this, indeed, the case? What about issues like pain and suffering? What about the demonstrable effectiveness of many interventions of modern medicine? Does the claim that the ailing body is a social construction mean that it is not 'real' in these senses of the word? The problem with tackling these questions head on is that we are drawn into a debate premised upon the opposition of the terms 'real' versus 'constructed'. As will be seen in the discussion to follow, better for us to examine what happens when people fall ill and when they attempt to recover good health.

FALLING ILL: THE SIGNIFICANCE OF INACTIVITY

The extent to which modern medicine has been able to inspect, internally examine and test the body runs parallel with its ability to predict the nature of the disease that afflicts it. The catheter that can enter the heart, the scanner that can picture the brain, and the procedures that can establish a thousand and one things on the basis of a blood sample, make it possible to follow diagnosis with effective treatment at an earlier and earlier stage of pathology. This means that, for the majority in the developed world, the historical situation of individuals literally falling ill before they receive any attention, is now past. Peculiarly, it seems, it is in situations where people suffer from ordinary ailments, like 'flu', that they sometimes 'fall ill' in the sense of taking to their beds.

It is necessary to make this point because the availability of medical techniques means that the experience of becoming ill does not often start with global or disabling symptoms. The following account was given by a man who was diagnosed as having coronary artery disease:

> I was involved with amateur dramatics and we were doing a production. You get tense, even amateurs, before the production and I started getting the chest pain and at the same time I was worried about redundancy at work and I put it down to just pressures, sort of nervous tension. I was also doing some work for a friend, rewiring his house for him, and the pain was getting more frequent and that was about 12 months ago. Then it cleared for a little while and then slowly it came back but not as strong as it had been. I was frightened to work odd times and I thought, 'This chest pain is over-exertion'.
>
> (Radley 1988: 63)

All too often it is small changes or sensations, such as those given in the above account, that lead people to go to the doctor. The explanation shows, in this case, that the first sign of disease appears in the course of everyday activity, and is accounted for by the man in terms of interruptions to the flow of ordinary life. The sign of discomfort stands out against the background of action. This is consistent with the more general condition of physical life, in which our bodies remain in the background of consciousness. Unless we are attending to our body, it is not there as an object, but as a condition of what phenomenologists call our 'being-in-the-world'.

The example of the man with chest pain can stand for many instances where specific aches, pains or changes to the body arise in a specific way. In these circumstances, the person recognises the dysfunction as something requiring attention, if not from a doctor then from someone else (or even oneself). In the account, the man's conclusion that it might be his own over-exertion suggests some monitoring of his future activity. With regard to his body, the incidents of chest pain raise questions within an otherwise healthy way of life. That is, the appearance of a bodily disturbance may be insufficient by itself to make the person either feel ill, to class themselves as having some disease, or even to require medical help. Clearly, one important aspect of this relates to uncertainty (lack of knowledge) about the nature of the sign. However, there is another aspect which is equally important, and concerns the body directly.

Early signs of dysfunction that can be contained can sometimes be suppressed or ignored. Examples of this include the headache that comes on while working on an essay that must be completed for the next day; the stomachache that is suffered during a visit to the parents of a friend. The containment of such signs depends upon the definition of the situation for the person concerned and for the others. If the essay is absolutely crucial, then the student might try to ignore it by working harder on the project. If, in the case of the second example, the parents must be impressed by their visitor, then it is vital that he or she keeps smiling and does not refuse too much of the food that is offered.

The point to be made here is that such containment is both an affirmation of normality and a display of good health that is made with the body. In the case of the essay writer, this affirmation might involve a redoubling of effort, a directing of intention that minimises the headache as perhaps a 'consequence' of hard work. This pain then signifies within the scheme of work, which means that the writing project is not just a cognitive (i.e. mental) exercise. To write an essay involves a physical commitment to a particular posture over a period of time, and to disattending away from sensations extraneous to the act of writing. Once the essay is written, the student might then become aware of the headache – or perhaps one should say, 'allow the headache to be felt'.

In the case of the individual with stomachache, the containment of the pain is both an affirmation and a display. Goffman (1971) has drawn attention to the need for individuals to manage their impressions (in this case, their bodily comportment) if others are to see them as worthy or attractive persons. In ordinary life, the containment of bodily eruptions (e.g. itches, belches and nasal mucus) is important if one is to retain a certain status as a socially creditable individual. In the case of symptoms, the status in question concerns one's health. While, ordinarily, people are not held to be at fault when they fall ill, the change in social status (from 'healthy' to 'sick') has repercussions upon other aspects of life. For this reason, the containment of the stomachache (smiling, trying to look as if one is enjoying the food) is necessary if the display congruent with being an 'agreeable and entertaining visitor' is to be maintained. While revealing the stomachache might not have serious consequences for the person's moral status (he or she will not be held to account for the illness), its revelation might well create uncertainty and embarrassment in the encounter.

These examples reveal that illness – as the appearance of symptoms – does not occur in isolation from the remainder of life. The 'ordinary' activities in which we engage are ongoing contexts in which the determination of how to handle these unwelcome experiences must take place. These ordinary activities are both functional and socio-evaluative. It matters that we are able to do certain things, that we do not let people down, that we go on in spite of our discomforts. The body's role in illness is, therefore, not a part played in a separately occurring state called 'sickness'. Rather, the 'deployment of the body' in its everyday activities involves an ongoing accommodation to the smaller or larger perturbations of physical life. It has been shown that people go to the doctor, not when symptoms are at their worst, but when this accommodation to them breaks down (Zola 1973).

What this means is that health and illness are not just cognitive categories that people apply to each other and to themselves. Being healthy is a condition that we sustain through our bodily appearance and conduct. The ability to carry out work and to conduct personal and social relationships is often sufficient for people to feel that they are not 'ill'. While the term 'sickness' designates a particular social status (those in society who are not healthy), the word 'illness' concerns the experience and identity of the person who is diagnosed as having a disease. So, it is possible for someone, like a man who has been diagnosed as having heart disease, to say that really he is not ill because:

> I'm not worried at all about it. I'm physically 100 per cent fit. I don't feel anything at all.

This was said in spite of his accepting the diagnosis made by the doctors he had consulted. There is no contradiction here, so long as one does not confuse sickness, as social status, with illness as the experience of the person who is afflicted with disease.

We can see from this that the body's role in illness is inseparable from its role in the world of health. It is often disruptions to our everyday activities, or our failure to contain or otherwise accommodate to symptoms, that lead us to attend to the problem, or to seek medical advice regarding it. With regard to the body, these everyday activities are manifold in that we have a body fit for work, a body that is pleasing to look upon, a body that moves with ease, a body whose natural functions operate smoothly. In each case, the non-conscious deployment of the body is, each day, an affirmation of its 'normality'. Therefore, it is not true to say that the body appears only with the arrival of symptoms. In this case, when the possibility of disease or dysfunction is present, the body-for-doctors appears as the background to the clinical interpretation of the given signs. For example, if a person thinks that a lump might be a sign of a serious disease and makes an appointment to see the doctor, his or her (whole) body is then projected in its biomedical aspect as an organic system under threat. That is, the diagnosis of disease (by self or doctor) requires the patient's participation within the discourse of medicine. This, in turn, necessitates the adoption of medicine's perspective, as part of which the body is made into a 'thing'. However, the appearance of the body in this aspect is not, as we have seen, the beginning or the end of the body's involvement in the determination and the affirmation of health or sickness.

Different diseases follow different courses, and the points at which people seek medical aid and receive treatment will in turn affect the course of their illness experience. In some cases, it is only later on that they will feel unwell; in other cases, treatment might relieve symptoms without the person having felt unwell at all.

The situation of falling ill, however, is within most people's everyday experience. Perhaps the most common example of this is the case of influenza, or similar debilitating conditions caused by a viral infection. In this case, there might be no distinct symptom that, by itself, warrants concern on the part of the individual, nor merits the attention of a physician. Instead, there is a general feeling of malaise, accompanied by headache, sore throat and a sense of incipient fever. How individuals respond to these symptoms will depend upon features of their everyday activities and commitments. What is likely is that, in so far as the symptoms are progressive, then those concerned will attempt to accommodate to them as far as possible. But at some point, it is likely that the person will acknowledge that he or she is 'not well' and take some action, such as going home, taking aspirin and perhaps going to bed.

This is a different situation to that of the person taking a distinct symptom to the doctor. In that situation, medical diagnosis precedes the person's occupancy of the sick role. In this latter situation, the individual herself (or himself) takes up that role by dint of an inability to fulfil everyday duties and obligations. In many cases, it is likely that the individual does not know, for sure, what is wrong in medical terms. And yet the experience of 'being ill' is so overwhelming that there can be no doubt that something is amiss.

The key issue here is the body's role in the determination of when one is 'so ill' as to 'be sick'. For the point has been made that the body (in its ordinary activities) is every day involved in the accommodation to small discomforts and minor dysfunctions. (Recourse to the reader's own experience is helpful here.) The crucial change happens when this accommodation is abandoned, when the feelings that one has been trying to suppress are sensed as overwhelmingly present. Even then, it is possible for the person to try to go on regardless, as they might if the situation were important or desperate enough to require it. For that reason, the move from health to illness in this example cannot be a literal state of being overwhelmed by symptoms. Instead, what is crucial is a giving up of one's projects and activities, an avowal that says, wordlessly, 'I am ill'. (Of course, there are conditions where the person is literally felled by disease – for example, heart attack, severe food poisoning and stroke.)

A useful analysis of this recourse to inactivity has been given by Herzlich (1973). She argued that giving up one's activities and defining oneself as ill are interchangeable in many people's experience. This is, in part, because inactivity marks the threshold of illness, the point which distinguishes between true illness and ailments with little more than a nuisance value. However, there is more to it than this. Giving up is not an abstract occurrence, but a redeployment of bodily potential. It has a positive function in that it serves to give some coherence to discomforts that were previously inchoate. As annoying headaches or vague feelings, they were matters to be minimised, if not suppressed. That is, the act of withdrawal from duties, of going home and getting into bed, is important in re-experiencing signs of bodily disturbance as symptoms of disease. Where beforehand one 'had a headache' or 'did not feel too good', one now says, 'I'm not well. I think I've got flu'.

As a result of this, symptoms are experienced in a different way, but not merely as objects of attention. What is important is that the withdrawal of one's effort from activity is simultaneously a willingness to experience the world through one's dysfunctional feelings. For the person concerned (let us assume a woman), this is a functional matter, because she now acknowledges that she is 'too hot' or 'too cold', that she cannot think straight because 'her head is throbbing'. And it is also a matter of appearance and identity, in so far as she presents herself to others as ill. She may take on a weary expression, hold her head in her hands or move in a slightly unsteady fashion. This use of the body is expressive of her condition, it displays for others her claim to be sick. And as this dramatic display of 'being ill' affirms for others her imminent occupancy of the sick role, it also confirms her own feelings of illness. The room is too hot, the light hurts her eyes, her books are heavy to carry. In effect, her world is out of sorts.

What this shows is that the body has a key role in falling ill. It is a way of being, an orientation that apprehends things in the light of its own inactivity. This inactivity is not just a negative withdrawal, an emptiness, but an attitude that, sensing the world through the pain and discomfort, organises those feelings into the illness condition. As a result, 'inwardly' we acknowledge that we are ill; 'outwardly' we demonstrate that we are crossing the threshold from being healthy to being sick. At no point in this do we have to know precisely what is wrong with us, or have made a diagnosis, or even mean to see a doctor. The ill body is not to be confused with the body of the patient, which is passive in anticipation of the doctor's examination and scrutiny. Of course, it happens sometimes that these two 'bodies' co-exist, as when the patient wishes to communicate his or her suffering to the doctor. What happens during the consultation, regarding the body, is extremely important, but space does not allow us to discuss that question in this chapter.

BEING ILL AND MAKING A RECOVERY

It is difficult, if not misleading, to try to examine the role of the body in illness 'in general'. One of the reasons for this is that different diseases, having different symptomatology, present the person with distinct problems to overcome. Difficulties in breathing, chest pain on exertion, inability to move specific muscle groups, various degrees of paralysis, and the whole spectrum of pain and fatigue mean that quite different demands will be made upon people suffering from different diseases. Even though, as psychologists and social scientists, we might want to formulate the problems of illness within a single theory, to do this without recognising these variations in bodily constraints would be to do less than justice to the data, to what is given.

Let us examine a few examples to make this point clear, and to begin to see what role the body has in recovery and in living with a long-lasting illness. As was pointed out in the context of falling ill, chronically sick individuals are not wholly defined by their condition. Being, for example, diabetic, or having rheumatoid arthritis or even cancer, does not mean lying in bed, but continuing with life in as normal a way as possible. Just what this involves will be reflected in some of the illustrative cases that will be described below. Before doing this, it is important to re-assert that 'the body' about which we speak is not (just) the biophysical entity with which medicine is concerned; nor is it (just) a social or cultural construction. For arthritis sufferers, joints are not only swollen and painful, but they also restrict movement. Wiener recounts this experience of a woman who contracted the disease at the age of twenty-two:

> It was harrowing. When I got up in the morning my feet were so painful I couldn't stand on them. I would slide out of bed and, with my elbow and rump, get into the bathroom. I learned to turn the faucets with my elbows.

> (Wiener 1975: 99)

Wiener makes the point that it is the variability of symptom occurrence, both in extent and degree, that makes the life of the arthritis sufferer so difficult.

For patients with multiple sclerosis similar problems occur, although it is sometimes a general feeling rather than specific discomfort that is at issue:

> Although I am an active MS patient it is difficult to overestimate the effect it has on one's whole life. The unpredictable level of energy is a constant stumbling block, my plans have to be very flexible and one's friends and relations very understanding. Additional illnesses, such as back trouble and a long-standing digestive problem, assume an awful significance and can seem like the last straw on top of the ever present MS difficulties.

> (Monks 1989: 81)

In these cases, bodily impairment is given apparently in feelings, but is actually fully disclosed in the attempt to carry out everyday actions. It is in this sense that, in ordinary life, the body has been said to be tacit or even absent in experience. For those with chronic illnesses, this condition is still true, except that the possible range of disclosures is widened with the variety of impairments that are encountered.

It would appear from this that the body in illness is a constraint, a limitation. That is, the signs of disease that appear either on its surface or in its impaired functioning provide what Wiener (1975) described as the 'physiological imperative'. However, there is more than a functional aspect to symptoms in the way that they hinder or prevent activity. The actions of the chronically ill are (potentially) visible to others, so that what, under a narrowed view, might be seen as a physical impairment only, becomes, in the light of social perception, evidence of handicap. Take this example of a woman suffering from Parkinson's disease, for whom questions of threatened identity are raised by the potential visibility of hindered action:

> That's the worst thing, the lack of grace. I used to have a friend who said to me that I was deft. I've lost that deftness and I don't like it. I come out of the bank with money, a purse, a handbag and umbrella, and I don't know how to put them away. I've got to think which hand to move first. I resent being ungraceful and clumsy.
>
> (Pinder 1990: 85)

For this individual (as for those suffering from symptoms of disorientation (Yardley 1994)), impaired movements, or those adapted as necessary, provide an unintended and unwanted display for others to see. This stigmatisation of some chronic conditions provides one source of motivation for patients to alter or to hide their actions or affected parts of the body.

Against this must be set what other people expect of the ill person. Part of being treated as a normal person is being able to act independently, to carry out everyday actions not only without needing assistance, but also without *appearing* to need assistance. In the case of men who had received surgical treatment for heart disease, several said that it was important to them to cope without the help of their wives (Radley 1988). Following his operation only four months earlier, one man told of how he and his wife would struggle over who should carry the shopping home from the supermarket.

There are two ways of explaining what is happening here. At one level, the sick who are recovering (and the chronically ill) are expected to undertake some duties in order to demonstrate either their will to get well, or their passage back into the world of health. We might call this the demands of society or culture. And yet these actions are also part of the ill person's ongoing and self-motivated engagements in the world, in which he or she wishes to play as full a part as possible. In this latter aspect, we see once more that the body is not restricted to illness, but continues to be a vital medium through which we achieve our everyday ends. In effect, it is often through the little things that we can or cannot do that we demonstrate – silently, and without comment – that we are fit to face the day, and fit to play our part in the world of the healthy.

Examples of this are mundane and plenty: we show we can move at will, attend to our personal needs, negotiate the home and working environment, and engage effectively and appropriately in relationships with others. We do not fall over, spill our drinks, fail to make the bathroom in time, or be unable to sustain a lengthy conversation. And during all of these things, we demonstrably appear to be in control of our bodies, and are able to contain any expressions of discomfort and show no evidence of illness that could bring us into question. In effect, to someone else's question, 'How are you today?', one can say 'Fine – OK' – and look it.

What this means is that 'the body' can be said to play a number of roles for the person who is chronically ill. It is the seat of disease, the source of impairment. In that sense it is unwanted. It places these people at risk, in its tendency to 'let them down', by appearing symptomatic or by preventing them carrying out everyday duties that they wish to undertake. It is yet the source of involvements and pleasures that are part of their ongoing engagements in the world. And it is the means by which the chronically ill can demonstrate their state of health to others, both functionally (in terms of achieving goals) and dramatically in terms of displaying their healthy powers and appearance to others. This underlines the point that 'physical and social constraints are not simple oppositions, because the individual's relationship to society is realised within bodily conduct, while disturbances of the body are defined and limited by social interpretations' (Radley 1989: 233).

Because these various aspects of the body are concurrent, and because they are in some sense contradictory, one of the special features of chronic illness is the way that individuals attempt to resolve these in the course of either making a recovery, or of living as 'normal' a life as possible. That resolution is achieved through action, and crucially involves the body as both its medium and focus.

ADJUSTMENT TO ILLNESS: RE-MAKING THE BODY-WORLD

The previous sections have drawn out two different aspects of the body's role in illness. One concerned inactivity as a giving-up, or withdrawal from duties, at the same time as it constitutes one's symptoms as signs of 'illness'. The other showed that the body is both the locus of disease, it is what 'lets us down', and as well as this, it is also the means by which we continue to establish ourselves as otherwise healthy people, the source of everyday pleasures that do not vanish (even if diminished) just because we are ill. There is a kind of contradiction here, in the sense that the body (and, indeed, the 'self') can appear to be both of these things at one time.

For the chronically ill, in particular, the problem is how to continue living with their ailment in the world of the healthy. The point has already been made that having a symptom or even a diagnosis of disease does not mean that people will define themselves as sick. One of the tasks faced by the chronically ill is how to re-establish themselves alongside the healthy once they have received treatment, or in the times between acute or disabling recurrences of symptoms.

The achievement of this task is a complicated one, varying with the disease in question. It also varies with the social situation of the sufferer, who is faced with having to come to terms with his or her situation in the context of ongoing relationships and social roles. Sometimes the condition is such that the person can take up duties and, to all intents and purposes, rejoin the world of the healthy. Often, however, it is not that easy, even for simple conditions. Having an operation to bypass a blocked coronary artery, or having a mastectomy, can leave a woman with the different, but equally difficult, tasks of being normal and healthy once again. The question is how to reverse that inactivity, and what attitude to take towards one's body which has proved unreliable and yet, to be healthy, is that on which one must rely.

Among the cohort of men who were interviewed following coronary bypass surgery were those who revealed one particular way of making this transition (Radley 1988). These particular patients had had a relatively good surgical outcome, in that they no longer suffered chest pain on exertion, for which symptom they had been referred. What was interesting was the way in which they took up activities as a way of defining themselves as being, once more, healthy individuals. Even in the hospital, one spoke of the benefits of activity this way:

> I like to think I help myself, by being determined I was going to get back to work in less than three months. And doing the exercises. . . . And the walking, they said do at least two miles a day. Well, I made it more or less four miles, and I think that may have helped a bit.
>
> (Radley 1988: 127)

Another mentioned that after discharge he spent time in the garden shed doing jobs of which his wife would not have approved. One example given was how he spent one afternoon chopping sticks while she was at work. What was interesting about this latter disclosure is that it was said in front of the wife, in the course of the interview. That is, it was not just the activity itself that was important, but its use as a demonstration to others (in this case, the wife) that the man was now recovered after his operation. It can also be analysed from the point of view of an account, where the manner of telling is the focus of interest (Radley and Billig 1996).

The chopping had, therefore, both functional and display characteristics, in that it was a field in which the man could explore and prove his physical capabilities, while also being the grounds upon which he could later claim from his wife that she should not worry about him – that she should treat him as 'healthy'. Indeed, the phrase 'back to normal' was frequently used by these patients, meaning not just an absence of symptoms, but the ability to carry out the ordinary acts of daily life without their being either remarkable or remarked upon.

This picture of a transition from illness back to health is, however, oversimplified. For most of the men in this sample, having had a heart attack, or having had major heart surgery, meant that their health was always a matter of concern for their families. For that reason, they were placed in a position of having to act as healthily as possible against the background of having been seriously ill. This kind of adjustment is what has been called the need to resolve the dual demands of symptoms and society (Radley 1989). One further example shows what this can involve.

The case concerned a man whose wife was worried about his health. In spite of this, he insisted on digging his garden, even though he knew it upset her. The act of digging did not merely assert that he was healthy, but actually said more than this. In the light of his condition, it conveyed something that words could not easily do. It displayed, in a single act, that he dug in spite of being ill. The digging cast his heart disease in a new light, reaffirmed his claim to be not just healthy, but in a sense healthier than normal. Not only did the garden get dug, but the man could evoke a sense of having overcome difficult odds. This evocation was more than a portrayal of having a certain identity, of being a member of the 'healthy' rather than the 'sick'. The act not only reconstructed his illness, but cast him in a new light. That is, it showed him as someone who had a certain kind of bravura, a certain enviable stance towards the world. This interpretation of events is, of course, not the only one that could be made of this episode. It was one that neither the man himself nor his wife spelled out in the course of the interviews. To perceive events in this way is a choice made by the researcher trying to understand features of adjustment to illness that involve communications between people that are non-verbal, but significant none the less.

With that caveat in mind, it can be argued that the body's role in this example is central. First, it is not the establishment of a particular identity that is at issue here. There is no substitute in everyday life for showing good health, and that must be done both functionally and in terms of appearance. Second, in action the body communicates the form of its resolution of those aspects that we said were contradictory. If a person has been ill, just how does he or she manage to carry out this or that activity? The answer to this question is not just to tell it, but to do and show it.

Third, the material aspect of the body is vital to what is done in the course of recovering good health. To display capacities one must engage with the world that gives them meaning. If I want to show I have recovered my strength I need weighty objects to carry; if I want to show I have recovered my stamina I need hills to climb. The argument is put this way to show that the evocation of 'healthy being' involves the body in taking up the world in order to transform it. This is parallel to the situation described earlier on, when it was said that inactivity – allowing events to be sensed through one's symptoms – constitutes the sick person and his or her world together.

For the sick person, therefore, to recover good health is the recovery of the world in its 'ordinary' aspect – to know it again in the way it was before. This does not have to happen deliberately. One patient who had undergone heart surgery said that he only knew he was better on the day that his dog escaped and he ran after it. He ran! And he was all right! This is the kind of mundane engagement through which the body's capacities, crucial for the membership of the everyday social world, are re-established. But it is important to say that these acts are not just isolated incidents, nor are they merely physical behaviours. Carried out with the body, in the presence of others (if not for their benefit), they are also expressive of a potential through which people lay claim to being 'healthy'. That display of ability, that evocation of coping, depends upon the exercise of the body in both its material and social aspects. As with the example of the men who chopped wood or dug their garden, recovering patients fashion a display of health with the body. This is more than mere appearance. Along with other people who help them, they re-make their social world as one that is both functionally and expressively a healthy one.

CONCLUDING COMMENTS

This chapter has attempted to draw out issues that show the body's role in health and illness using material gathered from interviews with patients and their partners. However, no direct observation of the things discussed are available from the interview data alone. Furthermore, no formal analysis of what people said (treated as discourse) has been attempted. From this perspective, such speculations about the body are not legitimate (and, some would say, should not be attempted). The arguments made are supported not by any findings taken separately, but by the reflection of different data against one another. This approach is broadly a phenomenological one, in its descriptive approach to the material collected. Among the advantages of using this approach are that (a) it allows a comprehension of how patients and carers experience their situation and elucidate it through reflection, (b) it shows how 'inner' (the body) and 'outer' (society) phenomena are given meaning by individuals in the course of attempts to re-orient themselves in the light of illness, and (c) it encourages a reformulation of theory in the attempt to define what is of general significance in this field, beyond the various descriptions of illness experience (Toombs 1992). The main practical implication of taking this line is that it reveals the limitation of interventions that rest upon the division of body, self and society into separate spheres. The successful alleviation of suffering, and the maintenance of health, require that practitioners understand how these things are woven together in the lives of the people concerned.

In summary, this chapter has emphasised that becoming ill and recovering good health involve more than physical change, and more than the re-labelling of signs of dysfunction. Physical changes do happen, and the apprehension of one's condition can be fundamentally affected by knowledge communicated verbally or in writing. However, the experience of illness also concerns one's body as a continuing medium for engaging the world. How one's body is deployed, in the sense of its organised activity in the light of symptoms of disease and their treatment, is crucial to the fashioning of a sense of illness, or of good health.

REFERENCES

Anderson, R. and Bury, M. (eds) (1988) *Living with Chronic Illness: The Experience of Patients and their Families*, London: Unwin Hyman.

Antaki, C. (1994) *Explaining and Arguing: The Social Organisation of Accounts*, London: Sage.

Conrad, P. (1987) 'The experience of illness: recent and new directions', in J. A. Roth and P. Conrad (eds) *Research in the Sociology of Health Care, vol. 6: The Experience of Chronic Illness*, Greenwich, CT: JAI Press.

Edwards, D. and Potter, J. (1992) *Discursive Psychology*, London: Sage.

Engel, G. L. (1977) 'The need for a new medical model: a challenge for biomedicine', *Science* 196: 129–136.

Goffman, E. (1971) *The Presentation of Self in Everyday Life*, Harmondsworth: Penguin.

Herzlich, C. (1973) *Health and Illness: A Social Psychological Analysis*,   trans. Douglas Graham, London: Academic Press.

Kleinman, A. M. (1988) *The Illness Narratives: Suffering, Healing and the Human Condition*, New York: Basic Books.

Lazarus, R. S. and Cohen, J. B. (1977) 'Environmental stress', in I. Altman and R. S. Lazarus (eds) *Stress and Coping: An Anthology*, second edition, New York: Columbia University Press.

Lazarus, R. S. and Folkman, S. (1984) 'Coping and adaptation', in W. G. Gentry (ed.) *Handbook of Behavioural Medicine*, London: Guilford.

Lupton, D. (1994) *Medicine as Culture: Illness, Disease and the Body in Western Societies*, London: Sage.

Monks, J. (1989) 'Experiencing symptoms in chronic illness: fatigue in multiple sclerosis', *International Disability Studies* 11: 78–83.

Pinder, R. (1990) *The Management of Chronic Illness: Patient and Doctor Perspectives on Parkinson's Disease*, Basingstoke: Macmillan.

Potter, J. and Wetherell, M. (1987) *Discourse and Social Psychology: Beyond Attitudes and Behaviour*, London: Sage.

Radley, A. (1988) *Prospects of Heart Surgery: Psychological Adjustment to Coronary Bypass Grafting*, New York: Springer-Verlag.

—— (1989) 'Style, discourse and constraint in adjustment to chronic illness', *Sociology of Health and Illness* 11: 230–252.

—— (1993) (ed.) *Worlds of Illness: Biographical and Cultural Perspectives on Health and Disease*, London: Routledge.

Radley, A. and Billig, M. (1996) 'Accounts of health and illness: dilemmas and representations', *Sociology of Health and Illness* 18: 220–240.

Schacter, S. and Singer, J. E. (1962) 'Cognitive, social and physiological determinants of emotional state', *Psychological Review* 69: 379–399.

Toombs, S. K. (1992) *The Meaning of Illness: A Phenomenological Account of the Different Perspectives of Physician and Patient*, Dordrecht: Kluwer Academic.

Voysey, M. (1975) *A Constant Burden: The Reconstitution of Family Life*, London: Routledge & Kegan Paul.

Wiener, C. L. (1975) 'The burden of rheumatoid arthritis: tolerating the uncertainty', *Social Science and Medicine* 9: 97–104.

Yardley, L. (1994) *Vertigo and Dizziness*, London: Routledge.

Zola, I. K. (1966) 'Culture and symptoms – an analysis of patients' presenting complaints', *American Sociological Review* 31: 615–630.

—— (1973) 'Pathways to the doctor – from person to patient', *Social Science and Medicine* 7: 677–689.

Chapter 4

Interpretative phenomenological analysis and the psychology of health and illness[1]

Jonathan A. Smith, Paul Flowers and Mike Osborn

INTRODUCTION

This chapter is concerned with the ways in which individuals construe, make sense of, and talk about issues concerning health and illness. We consider the health domain is a particularly useful one in which to carry out such research because we take as our starting point both the existence of bodily states and also the degree to which individuals consider these states to be important. This is especially true when the body malfunctions and illness occurs. In these circumstances, people often consider their sense of identity is threatened and may expend considerable mental energy reflecting on what is occurring to them: Why is this happening to me? Did I bring it on myself? Will it be the same tomorrow and in the future?

An approach which we consider is consonant with the picture presented above is introduced. Interpretative phenomenological analysis is a method which attempts to tap into a natural propensity for self-reflection on the part of participants. Obviously the degree to which individuals are used to expressing such reflections, orally or in writing, can vary and some people need more encouraging and facilitating than others. But a central premise of the method is allowing participants to tell their own story, in their own words, about the topic under investigation.

However, research is not a simple, singular process and the original account from the participant in the form of an interview transcript or diary entry, for example, then needs to be analysed closely by the investigator. Interpretative phenomenological analysis is about attempting to discover meanings, not eliciting facts, but trying to find out what a person's health condition means to them requires considerable interpretative work on the part of the researcher. The resultant analytic account can therefore be said to be the joint product of the reflection by both participant and researcher.

This chapter provides a brief theoretical contextualisation for interpretative phenomenological analysis and then argues for the particular relevance it has for health psychology. It is worth pointing out that this approach aims to have a dialogue with, and to help enlarge, the discipline of health psychology – not to attack or stand outside it. As will become apparent, we believe interpretative phenomenological analysis can make a valuable contribution in enriching the way mainstream psychology conceives of the individual's experience of health and illness.

Three illustrations of interpretative phenomenological analysis applied to the psychology of health and illness are given: two instances are taken from the field of chronic illness, the third from the area of preventive health behaviour.

The first example is from a study examining how patients respond to renal dialysis, which is an extremely arduous treatment regime for serious kidney failure. The project involves analysis of long semi-structured interviews with a relatively small number of patients. Because the study is based on a case-study design, looking at each patient in their own terms, an example from a single case is provided here. A particular theme, 'the importance of control', emerges from this case analysis and is in turn related to existing work on this construct.

The second example is from a project exploring the experience of chronic lower back pain. Participants in the study are volunteers from a specialist pain clinic and they again took part in semi-structured interviews exploring the way they thought and felt about their medical condition. This example draws from two of the participants in the study in order to illustrate how themes which emerged during analysis are instantiated at the individual level. Two important themes – 'the uncertainty of pain' and 'the equivocal nature of social comparisons' – are described.

In order to illustrate the diversity of interpretative phenomenological analysis, the third example is taken from a very different health field. Here gay men talk about their conceptions of sex and sexual behaviour. While the topic is very different, the theoretical assumptions and the method used in this study closely resemble those of the previous two. This section illustrates the development of one theme emerging from the interview transcripts – how sex acts need to be contextually defined. In particular, this example is concerned with how the interpersonal context can make a great difference to conceptions of apparently identical sexual behaviours. This has important implications for sexual health promotion.

INTERPRETATIVE PHENOMENOLOGICAL ANALYSIS AND HEALTH PSYCHOLOGY

The aim of interpretative phenomenological analysis (IPA) is to explore the participant's view of the world and to adopt, as far as is possible, an 'insider's perspective' (Conrad 1987) of the topic under investigation. Thus, the approach is phenomenological in that it is concerned with an individual's personal perception or account of an object or event as opposed to an attempt to produce an objective statement of the object or event itself. At the same time, IPA also recognises that the research exercise is a dynamic process. While one attempts to get close to the participant's personal world, one cannot do this directly or completely. Access is both dependant on, and complicated by, the researcher's own conceptions which are required in order to make sense of that other personal world through a process of inter-pretative activity. Hence the term interpretative phenomenological analysis is used to signal these dual facets of the approach (Smith 1994a, 1995a, 1996).

While interpretative phenomenological analysis and related qualitative approaches have only recently begun to establish a higher profile in psychol-ogy, they connect to a long intellectual history in the social sciences more generally. One important theoretical touchstone for this form of qualitative methodology – phenomenology – has already been discussed above. It has a long pedigree in the social sciences and originated with Husserl's attempts to construct a philosophical science of perception at the turn of the century. A second important theoretical influence on this type of qualitative methodol-ogy is symbolic interactionism. Symbolic interactionism emerged in the USA in the 1930s, influenced both by phenomenology and more immediate-ly by the pragmatism of, for example, Dewey, and represented an explicit rejection of the positivist paradigm beginning to take hold in the social sci-ences. Symbolic interactionism argues that the meanings individuals ascribe to events should be of central concern to the social scientist, and also that those meanings are only obtained through a process of interpretation. It also considers that meanings occur (and are made sense of) in, and as a result of, social interactions. (For more on the general theoretical underpin-ning to qualitative research, see Bryman 1988; for more on phenomenology, see Giorgi 1995; for more on symbolic interactionism, see Denzin 1995.)

It is important to distinguish IPA from discourse analysis (Potter and Wetherell 1987; Edwards and Potter 1992) which has developed a strong position in social psychology, particularly in the UK. While IPA shares with discourse analysis (DA) a commitment to the importance of language and qualitative analysis, where IPA researchers would typically differ from dis-course analysts is in their perception of the status of cognition. DA is gener-ally sceptical of the possibility of mapping verbal reports on to underlying cognitions and is concerned with attempting to elucidate the interactive tasks being performed by verbal statements. Thus, DA regards verbal reports as behaviours in their own right which should be the focus of func-tional analyses. IPA by contrast is concerned with cognitions, that is, with understanding what the particular respondent thinks or believes about the topic under discussion. Thus, while recognising that a person's thoughts are not transparently available from, for example, interview transcripts, IPA engages in the analytic process with the hope of being able to say something about that thinking.

Why should this approach be of particular interest to a health psychologist? We would suggest that IPA and health psychology could form a useful alliance. It can be argued that health psychology is premised on the existence of real and discrete bodies. Thus, while there is obviously room for an intellectual debate about boundaries within, and the appropriate unit of analysis for, health psychology (for example a systems or community approach or an individual focus), there will always remain a place within the discipline for concern with the individually diseased body (see Shilling 1993 for related discussion). Thus, for example, while societal accounts may provide valid explanations for the distribution and transmission of illness, the individual body still provides an exemplary unit for determining the existence of, and possible boundaries for, the illness.

Furthermore, health psychology, as currently practised, is also premised on the assumption that people think about their bodies, and that what they have to say about these bodies in some way relates to those thoughts. Thus, when asking a diabetic to complete a questionnaire about their illness, a health psychologist assumes a chain of connection between physical condition, cognition and verbal response. Many of the assumptions underlying this approach draw directly from the social cognition paradigm in social psychology (Smith 1996).

This chain is questioned by DA. While discourse analysts may be interested in, for example, cultural discourses of illness or in how illness is constructed in talk, the relationship between that talk and underlying cognitions is considered problematic. Presumably DA would have similar conceptual reservations with the second link in the chain – the relationship between cognition and physical state. Thus DA and social-cognitively oriented health psychology have radically different research agendas (Potter and Wetherell 1995).

For IPA, the body and its perception may provide an excellent crucible for research. While recognising the gap which can exist between an object and the individual's perception of it, a phenomenological researcher may indeed be interested in elucidating the nature of that gap. Therefore, the existence of real entities such as bodies and illnesses provides a useful background against which to consider personal accounts of physical processes. And a phenomenologist may choose, for example, to focus on the way two people may speak very differently about what is ostensibly, and medically categorised as, the equivalent illness precisely because of the light that may be shed on the subjective perceptual processes which are operating in the person's interpretation of their health status. Similarly, it has already been suggested that the IPA researcher will recognise the degree of interpretative work required to address the corresponding gap between personal account and underlying cognitions, but the point is that the IPA researcher is also generally still concerned with attempting to tackle that gap as well.

Thus space for a dialogue between IPA and the currently dominant social-cognitive approach to health psychology seems to open up. While IPA may perceive the nature of the links in a particular way, it shares with the social-cognitive paradigm a belief in, and concern with, the chain of connection between account, cognition and physical state. (See Abraham and Sheeran 1993 for related discussion of the parallel chain between account, cognition and behaviour.)

And what does the health psychologist gain from employing IPA? The answer from IPA might take a strong and a weak form. According to the strong version, it would be argued that quantitative psychology's requirement to separate and measure the relationship between objectively assessed variables may be appropriate for certain research questions. Other questions may more usefully be addressed by employing a qualitative methodology.

The weak version of IPA's response would advocate a collaborative endeavour between quantitative and qualitative researchers where each is able to contribute to any particular research project. Thus, while quantitative research can operate at a macro level, constructing broad models of, for example, cognition and behaviour relationships, qualitative research will work at the micro level, exploring the content of particular individuals' beliefs and responses and illuminating the processes operating within the models.

INTERPRETATIVE PHENOMENOLOGICAL APPROACHES TO CHRONIC ILLNESS

While the interpretative phenomenological approach has suffered neglect in mainstream psychology, it links to a long tradition in medical sociology. Thus, from Goffman (1968) and Glaser and Strauss (1967) onwards, contemporary sociology has found a place for research on health-related issues using a range of non-quantitative methodologies (including phenomenological interviewing, participant observation and ethnography) to address a wide range of issues – for example, lay perceptions of health and illness, doctor–patient communication, institutionalisation (see Silverman 1985 and Conrad 1987).

Let us take one area – the experience of chronic illness – and compare its treatment by health psychology and medical sociology. In general, psychological studies have concentrated on measuring outcomes associated with the illness, or assessing the relationship between individual differences such as locus of control and coping (for example: Christensen et al. 1991; Marks et al. 1986). While there has been some psychological research examining common-sense representations or patients' personal models of illness (for example: Hampson et al. 1990; Lau et al. 1989) most of this work has been quantitative. As yet, there appears to be little work done by psychologists in exploring, through the detailed qualitative analysis of verbal reports, how particular individuals attempt to make sense of, or find meaning in, their illness, and it seems somewhat ironic that in order to explore this phenomenology of illness one turns to sociological rather than psychological studies.

A number of researchers in medical sociology have attempted to get closer to the individual's own sense of what chronic illness means by conducting qualitative studies (for collections, see: Anderson and Bury 1988; Social Science and Medicine 1990). Typically these studies are less concerned with testing predetermined constructs than with examining individual themes elicited from the transcripts of intensive, semi-structured interviews with patients. So, for example, Williams (1984) illustrates how arthritis sufferers attempt to make sense of their illness by placing it within a coherent social–biographical context. Thus, one man considers his illness as resulting from, and illustrative of, the exploitation of workers by employers – a theme which gives his own biographical account an internal coherence. A second respondent conceptualises her arthritis in the context of the stressful relational roles of women, and particular losses she suffered around the onset of her illness – her daughter leaving home in distressing circumstances and her husband also becoming very ill.

Taylor (1983) is still unusual in being a well-known psychologist who has published qualitative work on patients' conceptions of chronic illness. Taylor discusses the strategies employed by cancer victims in coping with their illness. She suggests her interviews reveal three central themes: a search for meaning in the experience; an attempt to regain mastery of one's life; an attempt to enhance self-esteem. Taylor provides instances from the women's own accounts to support her case. For example, Taylor argues that, in terms of re-establishing mastery, a common strategy employed by the women was the perception of a discontinuity between the present and past – that is, a separation of the previous cause and course of the illness from a present more successful position and prognosis. Thus, one woman accuses a first husband of being a boorish rapist and considers the relationship to be implicated in her having become ill. In contrast, her current husband provides unstinting support and so helps to keep her well. The qualitative methodology illustrates both the particularity and the adaptability of these strategies. Taylor's use of the method therefore supports her argument that an individual will attempt to find a currently self-enhancing account or explanation which can then be discarded later if no longer appropriate.

At present, therefore, there appears a clear disciplinary split. Psychologists have tended to use quantitative, variable-centred methodologies to try to model components of coping with illness while a number of sociologists have employed qualitative, phenomenological approaches in an attempt to get closer to how individuals themselves perceive their illness and to capture the process of their particular attempts to deal with it. There would clearly be value in some convergence of the two disciplines because much of the territory explored by phenomenologically-oriented medical sociologists is as psychological as it is sociological. It is hoped that the relative infancy of health psychology will allow it to bypass traditional boundaries and facilitate the cross-fertilisation with these currents in medical sociology.

Thus there would seem to be a clear place for psychological studies dealing with chronic illness. Such studies would examine in detail the concerns of particular individuals faced with specific conditions through an intensive examination of respondents' texts, in the form of either written accounts or interview transcripts.

The next part of this chapter provides two extended illustrations of IPA applied to different areas of the psychology of chronic illness – the patient's perception of renal dialysis, and the experience of chronic back pain. These examples draw from the authors' own work: the first illustration is from a project by the first author, the second from that of the third author.

IPA IN PRACTICE: A CASE STUDY OF THE PATIENT'S EXPERIENCE OF DIALYSIS TREATMENT FOR KIDNEY FAILURE

Haemodialysis is a treatment regime for end-stage renal disease (ESRD). During dialysis, the patient is connected to a machine which takes over the function of the damaged kidneys, extracting, cleansing and replacing the blood. Treatment sessions are long and frequent, commonly lasting three hours three times a week, and can take place either in hospital or, if the patient has their own machine, at home. Psychological research on ESRD, and more particularly haemodialysis treatment, tends to paint a gloomy picture of its effects on psychological well-being with high levels of depression and anxiety being reported. Most of the existing studies on ESRD have, not surprisingly, adopted the quantitative paradigm. This study, by contrast, aims to explore in detail the perceptions of a dialysis patient by examining one woman's account of her experience. A semi-structured interview with the woman was subjected to interpretative phenomenological analysis.[2]

Carole is 44 years old and has been dialysing in hospital for six months. She is a musician and is married with two daughters. Carole has not been selected as a special case, nor at this stage is it being claimed that she is representative of haemodialysis patients in general. Rather, she represents a particular case of a patient's response to dialysis in order to help us gain a more detailed picture of this phenomenon (Smith et al. 1995). Only a part of the data from Carole is presented here. See Smith (1995b) for the complete case study.

A construct which emerges strongly from Carole's interview is her sense of lacking control over the treatment regime. The term *emerge* is used to highlight the fact that Carole was not responding to questions about control – she introduced the concept into the conversation.

When asked about her experience of dialysis, Carole expresses considerable concern over the effect the treatment is having on her. She describes the physical restriction of the regime and expresses frustration at the unrelenting routine:[3]

> You're just so sort of passive in the whole situation 'cos once the machine is in operation you have to keep still and you can't move much otherwise the damn thing alarms all the time.
>
> And I'm sort of really fed up with the repetition of it [ ] and the worst bit is like going home afterwards and feeling an absolute wreck [ ] thinking, O God you know I feel like this again, I've got to face it all over again in two days time.

Thus the severe restriction has to occur so frequently that as soon as Carole is over one session she is already preparing herself for the next one. She perceives herself as having no control over the situation:

> I just hate that being out of control [ ] being sort of tethered to one place and to this machine and becoming part of this machine. [ ] It's like being tethered to the situation (laughs) and not having the power to change it or to be perhaps a part of it. You just play your part which is quite a passive one and get on with it really.

So Carole sees herself as being both part of, and not part of, the system. Although she feels as though she is part of the hospital machine, she also feels detached from both the workings and the community of that machine, rather like an outsider who intrudes occasionally.

The intention is for Carole to transfer to home dialysis some time in the near future. Reflecting on the difference having her own machine will make, Carole says:

> I think when I get it home and it's mine and I get it on my own premises and it's a part of my life and put in its place, its little back room, then I think, Yeah, it's under my control, and I use it. I'm not dominated by it and dialysing at home would be: I'm still being myself, I've still got my identity, but I'm just giving myself some treatment that evening.

Rather than Carole having to enter the machine's territory – the hospital – the machine will be installed in Carole's home and will become hers. Consequently the machine (and dialysis) will be relegated to its subordinate status, as it is 'put in its place'. Carole clearly perceives the greater control this will bring her as being a crucial element in asserting her sense of identity. Thus, as the centrality of treatment fades, so Carole's sense of being a person separate from being a dialysis patient can come to the fore once more.

Carole goes on:

> You can go and see the machine when it's not working maybe, you know, sort of get to know it [laughs] have a bit of poke around and see what this

and that is. [ ] I do like equipment. I like to know how it works. [ ] As long as you're in sort of total control then it'll be a lot sort of better.

This suggests part of the reason Carole feels intimidated by hospital dialysis is her lack of knowledge of the equipment and its workings. At present, she is dependent on the staff who operate the machine and her lack of knowledge disempowers her. Once she is dialysing at home, her sense of personal control can also be enhanced by greater knowledge of, and responsibility for, the process.

So how does Carole's account link to the existing research on chronic illness? Control clearly is a construct of considerable importance in the health psychology literature, as well as informing the existing work on renal dialysis. Many current models of stress-control relationships emphasise the cognitive component. Thus Abramson et al. (1978) argue that the attributions an individual makes for a relevant stressor can lead to learned helplessness. Taylor et al. (1984) report Thompson's (1981) review of the literature as suggesting that, of the strategies available, 'cognitive control may be most uniformly successful in reducing stress' (Taylor et al. 1984: 491), cognitive control referring to the ability of the individual to think of the situation in different terms. Rotter's (1966) locus of control construct is a measure of an individual's *perceived* level of control. And the existing work on dialysis does point to a high degree of perceived external locus of control in haemodialysis patients (Poll and Kaplan De Nour 1980) – that is, a tendency to believe that they do not have control over their situation.

The emphasis on cognition facilitates a convergence between qualitative IPA studies like the one illustrated here and existing social cognition work. If the way an individual thinks about and labels a potentially stressful situation is an important factor in determining their response to the stressor, then the examination of detailed case studies of individuals' accounts of stressful situations should be able to enrich the cognitive model. In related vein, Thompson (1981) and Taylor (1983) argue for the importance of exploring the *meaning* of stressful events and situations to the person undergoing them.

This is exactly where studies like the one presented here are able to make a contribution. First, we have a detailed account of what dialysis means to a particular patient. Dialysis treatment has for Carole come to mean restriction, entrapment, passivity. These are not descriptions of the treatment itself, but rather of the meaning of the treatment for Carole at this stage in time. Other patients may have different perceptions and Carole may view her treatment differently at other times – for example, when she begins to dialyse at home. Second, Carole herself introduces the topic of control. This helps us to gain a sense of the strength of this construct for her, and we also learn more about what it is in the regime which can help induce perceived lack of control. Third, we also find out more about what regaining control would mean to Carole. Having the machine on her own territory, taking more responsibility for it and getting to know how it works will, she feels, all increase her sense of being in control. Again, the phenomenological slant is important. It is the perception of control which is significant rather than control *per se* and this is Carole's perception. Other patients' conceptions of what would increase control may be very different and a next stage might involve analysing the accounts of other patients to look for convergences and divergences in their perceptions. Finally, the flexible methodology employed has thrown up an important link between personal control and identity. Feeling in control is for Carole an important aspect of affirming her sense of identity. Thus, the definition, parameters and implications of control as a construct can be broadened.

It can be argued, therefore, that a social-cognitive model of stress and control relationships can be strengthened by looking in detail at how individuals talk about the stressful situations they face and how they deal with them, and by close consideration of the meanings they attach to them. Such work should enable us to gain a much richer picture of what control actually means, and its potency as a construct will thereby be enhanced.

A FURTHER CASE OF IPA AND CHRONIC ILLNESS: DEALING WITH CHRONIC BENIGN LOWER BACK PAIN

The previous section illustrated how one area of chronic illness – the experience of renal dialysis – could be beneficially explored using IPA. It is, of course, not the only area, and in this section we provide a further example of IPA applied to chronic illness – this time, the condition of chronic benign lower back pain (CLBP) which is a major health problem for individual sufferers, their social networks, and society as a whole. Sufferers can report high levels of distress, pain and disability with no respite, and it is one of the most common causes of time lost at work. CLBP places a high demand on the physical health services, which in many cases is inappropriate as 85 per cent of cases are not amenable to a discrete medical diagnosis or treatment, but are ascribed to natural processes of 'wear and tear' (Clabber Moffat et al. 1995).

In CLBP, distress, disability and biological pathology are only loosely correlated, and it is considered that the psycho-social factors play the lead role in mediating the individual sufferer's condition (Waddell 1987). Our understanding of each dimension of the chronic pain phenomenon is far from complete and cannot explain the range of individual variability (Aronoff 1992). As yet, most of the psychological research conducted on CLBP is within the quantitative, empirical tradition. As implied earlier in the discussion regarding disciplinary differences in relation to the understanding of chronic illness, qualitative work that attends explicitly to the meaning of chronic pain and explores the processes at play as the sufferer attempts to make sense of their experience is, at present, more often to be found within medical sociology (e.g. Baszanger 1992; Bury 1988).

This section draws from two case studies of CLBP which are, in turn, part of a wider study of how chronic pain sufferers experienced their condition (Osborn and Smith 1996). Linda is 50 years old and has been in persistent back pain for over ten years. She has been through a succession of failed treatments before being told that no more can be done for her. Deborah is 46 years old, has been in pain for at least eight years, and has a similar history of treatment. As in the dialysis project, semi-structured interviews were conducted with patients and they were asked to describe their pain and their experiences of living with it. The resultant transcripts were subjected to IPA, and two of the themes that emerged – the inability to make sense of pain and the equivocal nature of social comparisons – are illustrated here.

Neither participant was directed to talk about their situation in any particular way, but both referred quickly to the confusion they felt towards their pain. Linda described at length how she has failed consistently to understand why she remained in pain and recounted a sense of disbelief at its chronic presence:

> I just keep asking myself, you know, why the pain is there. I haven't got an answer 'cos I don't know how I feel really. It's just that I think it shouldn't be there. Why should I have it? And after all this time I would have thought it would have eased up and gone away, but it hasn't. As far as I'm concerned, I haven't broken anything, I haven't done anything, so why have I got it?

Deborah, too, did not understand why her pain had become chronic:

> Well, I always thought you had pain to tell you when there was something wrong, so why have I got it?

Despite their lengthy pain careers and extensive contact with the health services, Linda and Deborah could not explain why they had pain. They were not experts in their condition. To them, it was not benign, but senseless and unpredictable and left them considering an uncertain, but seemingly bleak, future:

> But I don't know why you have to keep suffering it, and suffering it, and suffering it, for ever and ever.
>
> (Deborah)

> I just hope that I don't end up sort of not being able to get about. That's what frightens me. I think, well, you know, it's not gonna get any better and I just hope it doesn't get any worse. It's just so it gets you mad, you know, very frustrated because it's there and it won't go away.
>
> (Linda)

In her uncertainty, Linda in particular feared for a bleak, immobile future that she felt she could only 'hope' to avert. The threat and frustration she related to her pain situation prompted her to be self-critical:

> I'm sort of mad at myself and getting aerated with myself, not with any-body else, because it's there and I can't get it to go away. It's just frustrating. I think, well, if I'm like this at my age, what am I going to be like at seventy?

In the presence of this uncertainty, Deborah and Linda both used comparisons with others to evaluate their lives in pain. Linda described how she felt looking at her peers who were active and pain-free:

> I'm only fifty. They say life begins at forty, and I should be doing this and that and the other, but I can't. It's frustrating that people of my own age are a lot, you know, you see them, they're flying their kite and things like that and you feel as if you can't, well you can't.

Linda compared herself with others, but fell short of her expectations. Through the metaphor of 'flying their kite', Linda emphasised the denial of joy or physical celebration in her life that she felt had been imposed by her pain and highlighted her contemporary frustrations. The strength of the metaphor emphasised the restrictions she felt she endured.

Deborah tended to use downward comparisons, and she described how she tried in vain to mitigate the sense of loss she felt as a result of her pain:

> I try to tell myself I'm luckier than a lot of people, you know. I haven't got cancer. I've done heaps more things than other people have done. So I think well, you always think well, there's loads of people far worse off than you, you know, so you try to think of other people who are permanently in wheelchairs and it's supposed to make you feel better, but basically it's frightening.

Deborah looked at others in a worse position than herself, but received no reassurance. As she reflected on her situation in this way, she became anxious and found it 'frightening' to consider such a prospect. As Linda considered the future, her comparisons reflected a similarly threatening sense of pessimism:

> I've seen other people, I don't know exactly what she died of, she was getting these aches and pains and next thing I see her in a wheelchair and then her speech went. She started with aches and pains, but I think there must have been something more. I hope I never get like that. It starts off with one thing, I hope nothing else.

Despite her diagnosis of a benign chronic pain condition, Linda only selected those with malignant or terminal conditions as comparisons. She admitted that back pain was not the principal problem in their conditions, but remained anxious and concerned that she could not guarantee avoiding a similar sense of decline for herself:

> I hope I never get like that. I hope that I'm no worse than I am now, that I'm mobile. Because my mother, she died, she'd only just got her bus pass when she died. But it wasn't her back. She always suffered with her heart.

As Deborah and Linda described their life in pain, uncertainty and confusion emerged as, to them, it remained painful, inexplicable and uncontrollable. Their chronic pain resonated with a sense of loss, threat and frustration. Their use of social comparison reflected these concerns and tended only to emphasise the gloomy prospects they perceived for themselves.

Uncertainty is a recurrent theme in the literature on chronic illness, both in health psychology (Radley 1994) and medical sociology (Locker 1991), and was referred to continually by Linda and Deborah. One aspect is its relationship to control, a construct which has already been introduced in the previous section on the experience of dialysis, where the importance of the individual's perception of control was highlighted. In contrast to the experience of haemodialysis, where lack of control over treatment was the stressor, for Linda and Deborah it was the pain itself that was perceived to be uncontrollable.

Uncertainty in chronic pain has also been shown to correlate with helplessness and reported pain intensity (Williams and Thorn 1989; Idler 1993), particularly if it is believed to be due to chance, to endure with no relief, or to be mysterious in origin. According to attribution theory, it is an important human need to establish a cause in the face of such mystery (Brewin 1988), to both explain the world we inhabit and feel a sense of control over it. Particular attributional styles are thought to have affective consequences for the individual concerned. However, for Linda and Deborah, their frustration and hopelessness appeared not to be consequent upon a discrete attributional category, but a result of a more fundamental inability to attribute any cause at all. They complained that they simply 'should not' have such pain and in trying to understand their situation, where pain persisted in the absence of injury, they could find no acceptable answers and remained confused and anxious.

Linda and Deborah used social comparison repeatedly in their accounts of their predicament. Festinger's (1954) original theory of social comparison suggests that people need to have stable appraisals of themselves and will resort to comparison with others in the absence of any more objective measures. This is often the case in chronic illness and the use of comparison amongst patients has been well documented (Molleman et al. 1986).

There is a debate within current social psychological research as to the affective consequence of downward comparisons; those made with others in a worse situation, or with a 'worse-world'. In particular, do they always promote positive affect and well-being under stressful conditions (e.g. Taylor and Lobel 1989; DeVellis et al. 1990)? Or can they actually cause the reverse and produce negative affect (e.g. Buunck et al. 1990; Hemphill and Lehman 1991)? Studies have suggested that comparison and affect are not directly related, but mediated by other factors (Jensen and Kardy 1992; Vanderzee et al. 1995).

Linda and Deborah's downward comparisons suggest they do not always represent beneficent coping strategies. Linda, despite her diagnosis of benign pain, made comparisons only with those with malignant conditions in her account of her situation. Although she made many downward comparisons, they only emphasised her feelings of pessimism and threat. Deborah felt that she should feel better as a result of a comparison with those with cancer or in a wheelchair, but instead described how the process actually promoted fear. Faced with an uncertain future, neither Deborah nor Linda could look to a 'worse-world' with any confidence that they might not inhabit it themselves one day. Their comparisons appeared to give them a concrete representation of the bleak outlook they had of the future and this, if anything, reinforced rather than ameliorated their sense of threat and pessimism.

Although it played an important role in prompting the use of social comparison, the uncertainty and frustration that Linda and Deborah related to their pain appeared to deny them any benefit that the comparison with a 'worse-world' is reputed to offer. For them, social comparison served primarily an evaluative function and reflected and reinforced, rather than helped to change, their affective state. In the absence of any facility to determine an acceptable cause, or establish a sense of control, social comparison appeared only to confirm and exacerbate their worst fears.

IPA AND GAY MEN'S CONCEPTIONS OF SEX AND SEXUAL BEHAVIOUR

Thus far, this chapter has focused on what IPA can offer to the psychology of chronic illness. However, that does not prescribe the limits of IPA's potential contribution to health psychology. In this final section, we present an illustration of IPA research from a different domain – the psychology of sexual health. The study reported here is concerned with enhancing our understanding of gay men's attitudes towards sex, sexual behaviour and sexual decision-making.

A major task of health psychologists working in the field of sexual health is to try to help limit HIV infection and re-infection. Given the novelty of what was, at that time, an unidentified infectious agent, the early 1980s witnessed a plethora of epidemiological studies that sought to delineate transmission routes and affirm the validity of the emerging notions of safer sex. The identification of the HIV virus and the efficacy of condoms in preventing its spread led to the promotion and provision of condoms as the central means of reducing HIV infection amongst gay men. However, despite the profound health behaviour change reported amongst gay men in adopting safer sex, the level of unsafe sex, and subsequently the rates of HIV infection in that group, continue to rise (e.g. Hart et al. 1993). Consequently, a fuller understanding of gay men's sexual decision-making is needed.

The study reported here employed IPA to explore gay men's understandings of sexual decision-making and condom use. Interviews were conducted with gay men living in a small town in Yorkshire. The accounts which emerge can be contrasted with the more singular account employed across much of health psychology, epidemiology and indeed health promotion. The differences between these accounts are important because, arguably, much of the psychology and the promotion of sexual health have been premised upon the latter (a medical understanding of sex) when, in actual fact, a more appropriate and perhaps more effective response would be based around the former (gay men's understandings of sex). (For more details of the complete project, see Flowers et al. 1996a,b.)

As with chronic illness, sexual health research addresses a distinctly embodied experience. In this respect, any useful psychology of safer sex must concern itself with the interaction of individual bodies changing the pool of HIV infection. However, as this chapter shows, it is not enough to premise a psychological understanding of sexual health solely at that physical level.

Let us first look in a little more detail at the historical legacy of sexological research and its medicalisation of sexuality. Gagnon and Simon (1974) outlined the difficulties presented by such a limited understanding of sex – an understanding that focuses upon the somatic: the sex organs and reproduction. Over twenty years later, the psychology of sexual health is still limited by these same constraints. Matching the urgency of a rapidly spreading epidemic, epidemiological studies sought to delineate HIV transmission routes in terms of sexual acts and provided much needed information regarding the relative chance of HIV infection from unprotected anal or oral sex (e.g. Darrow et al. 1987; Kingsley et al. 1987). It is not surprising then that an emerging psychology of sexual health took, as its focus, this same level – that of the physical act – as a theoretical basis.

What is problematic about the resulting psychology of sexual health is its incomplete account of sexual decision-making and its employment of a unitary understanding of sexual behaviour. This somatic slant emphasises the apparent constancy offered by a focus upon particular sexual acts (especially anal intercourse) and neglects contextual differences in terms of the relational, spatial and temporal location of that activity. This is troubling because, when one looks at the accounts of gay men talking about the meaning of sex, one finds the apparent unity of a single conception of sex breaking down. For example, Richard describes two differing understandings of the same physical act (penetrative anal sex):

> If it's somebody casual, a fuck's a fuck isn't it? But when you're making love with somebody, there's like the emotional feeling. It's not just sort of the feeling that you get in your dick and once you've, you know, once you've come, I mean that's it, isn't it, but when you're making love with somebody, you can come and then still carry on from there, you know. It's just totally, totally different.

Richard explains the difference between what he describes as 'a fuck' and 'making love'. The identical nature of penetrative sex in both situations begins to point to the inadequacy of a psychology of sexual health premised upon a somatic understanding of sex.

Richard's distinction, between fucking and making love, draws attention to one particular context – that of the romantic relationship. Across the sexual behaviour literature, there are robust findings which show that penetrative sex is more likely to occur within close relationships than outside them (e.g. McLean et al. 1994). Richard's account points to why this could be so:

> When you're penetrating someone, you sort of become one piece, you're joined together aren't you? And that's why I think it's more intimate than any other sexual experience that you can have between two people, you know, a wank's a wank isn't it? You can have fun with a wank but when you actually penetrate somebody that's just like the ultimate.

Within a relationship, the meanings of penetration become particularly potent. Anal penetration is understood to represent a distinct union. This union is a chance for one partner to be inside another, unified both physically and psychologically. It is understood as being the most intimate and the ultimate of all sexual acts. Brent casts further light on this:

> *Brent*   So you get like, Jake's being screwed is sacred.
> *Interviewer*   Why's that?
> *Brent*   I don't know. He just holds it really sacred that you've got to find somebody right and that's why he made me wait, and I thought, 'This kid dun't want sex with me all t' time. 'Cos he dun't. He just wants to be with me, and that's nice. So you dun't feel like a cash machine, cos that's what I once said to Neil, I says, 'Thy makes me feel like a cash machine, press right button and you get what you want.' With Jake, you dun't, we just like being together and we enjoy together. That's it.

Again, Brent addresses the meaning of the sexual activity as opposed to the physical sensations. His understanding of the sexual activity is concerned mainly with the dynamics of his relationship. This stands in sharp contrast to the somatic focus of a unitary understanding of anal penetration. It also shows how the couple's relationship is privileged above and beyond the respective individuals' physical needs and pleasure.

Within this understanding – of penetration as intimate and enjoining – the exchange of semen can also be seen to have especial importance. As Philip explains:

> *Philip* He cumed inside me. A lovely feeling. You know, there's som'at there of somebody that you care about, you love, I used to like it.
>
> *Interviewer* So what is it about their cum that means so much?
>
> *Philip* (*Sighs*) It gives you a feeling, it gives you a buzz. You know – I've had his seed inside of me, things like that, just sit here thinking about it hours after. And then you go to the toilet and it goes plop, plop, plop! Yeah, me body sort of went 'Oh he's gone now'. He's there, he's just like there. I'm still like it now.

As Philip describes it, his lover's 'seed' is understood to represent his lover himself. This can be understood as the natural consequence of the apparent meaning of penetration – the logic of unity, sharing, giving, receiving and becoming one. As penetration is understood in romantic relationships to be the ultimate coming together of two disparate selves, so the exchange of semen represents the exchange of those selves. As Philip says, on losing his lover's semen – 'He's gone now'.

This takes us to an issue of critical importance in appreciating the meanings of sex. In reviewing the impact of major psycho-social factors upon sexual behaviour change amongst gay men, Flowers et al. (1996c) report a problematic finding – that 'relationship status' was associated with unsafe sex more often and more consistently than any other variable. That is, the closer the relationship, the greater the chance of unsafe sex. The gay men's accounts in this study help to cast light on this finding. For if semen exchange has particular symbolic importance in signifying intimacy, then this level of intimacy can, of course, be compromised by the use of condoms.

Daniel explicitly discusses this problematic relation between condom use and intimacy:

> Well when I was going out with Harry, like I weren't fucking, blah de blah, just the general things, um, but with Harry it were more like being there for each other, and like wanting to sort of like be inside each other. Like I wanted him inside of me, and part of me inside of him, and which in a relationship can also be a big thing with sort of the safe sex thing. Of actually wanting to be so close to the other person, that you actually, you know, you know it carried all these risks and still you're having to put a barrier between you and someone you love. And even if it's only a few inches of barrier, if you like, it's still something artificial that's there,

which is otherwise a very sort of spiritual, animal type, primeval type of experience.

Daniel highlights the 'naturalness' of unprotected penetration and hints at its symbolic and historical legitimacy as the culmination of sex and the expression of a couple's togetherness. The condom acts as a barrier to this fulfilment. Thus, unprotected sex can in fact come to represent an expression of love and commitment:

> That were the day that I told him I loved him and he says, 'Oh you can't love another man'. I says, 'I love you enough to fuck you without a condom on. Yeah, yeah,' I says, 'I want to fuck you without a condom on or you fuck me, I want you to come inside me or I'll fuck you and come inside you.'
>
> (Philip)

In the next passage, Daniel takes such thoughts to one logical conclusion, representing the ultimate privileging of the relationship above the self:

> I've not been in the situation, but if we really loved somebody and that's what you wanted to do, even if you knew they were HIV, I think that would even come into the equation, if you know, if you were wanting, you know, wanting to die with somebody, or even if you loved somebody that much I suppose, wanting somebody's virus inside 'em. You know they've got it, then you want it as well, sort of thing.

Thus HIV itself can take on a role in constructing the meanings of sexual behaviour. Becoming infected knowingly can be seen as the ultimate expression of prioritising the relationship of the selves beyond the bodies and the couple above the individuals. This might also be described as the ultimate expression of love.

By employing IPA, a rich portrayal of gay men's conceptions of sex and sexual decision-making emerges. The extracts above point to a wealth of motivations and cognitions which appear to relate directly to the use and non-use of condoms. However, they are not premised upon a somatic understanding of sexual health. Decisions relating to penetration and condom use appear to be based around the meaning of sexual acts, and these meanings are to do with the status accorded to particular acts within a particular context and especially point to the relational signification of sex.

The study has particular relevance for the understanding of unprotected sex. As the work reported here would suggest, much of the unprotected sex that occurs in relationships does not occur because of a lack of relevant safer sex knowledge or inaccurate perceptions of risk, as would be suggested by the extant literature. Neither does a costs-and-benefits analysis premised upon loss of sensation and the gains of disease prevention seem relevant. Instead, it appears that men are making deliberate and informed decisions not to use condoms, in full knowledge of the risks they may be taking, because of the particular meanings such unprotected sex confers. This illustrates the value of attending to participants' accounts when attempting to make sense of a phenomenon and, therefore, the valuable role IPA can make in enriching the understandings offered by health psychology. Further research of this type could then inform future health promotion campaigns in terms of changing how safer-sex messages are constructed and delivered – for example, offering alternative conceptions of how commitment and intimacy can be expressed sexually.

Of course, we would not want to generalise from this study to the whole gay community. This study was conducted in a small town in Yorkshire. It is likely that one would find very different conceptions in bigger metropolitan centres (for more details, see Flowers et al. 1996b). Further studies could be conducted explicitly concerned with major cultural differences in how gay men conceive of sex.

CONCLUDING COMMENTS

This chapter has introduced interpretative phenomenological analysis, argued for the particular role it can play in the psychology of health and illness and provided three examples of IPA working in practice.

We would, finally, like to reflect on some issues that arise when using IPA. First, it is important to recognise that doing this type of research is personally demanding in a number of ways: talking with patients about serious health conditions can, of course, be distressing; good interviewing requires particular skills which take time to develop; qualitative analysis is slow and painstaking and one does not know until late in the project exactly what is going to be produced. Doing IPA requires being comfortable with the particular personal demands which follow from the approach.

An interesting connection to the issue of personal involvement concerns the relationship which is established between researcher and participant. It is often argued that this type of research method is more democratic and participant centred than many others. While we would ourselves concur with this general claim, it is important to remember that IPA research still takes place within particular parameters. Thus, while the interview takes the form of a conversation, it is usually a pretty one-sided conversation. Good practice in phenomenological interviewing is generally considered to involve minimal intervention on the part of the interviewer, in order to allow the respondent to tell their own story (Smith 1995a). However, doing this type of work can sometimes leave one with something of a feeling of intruding. One has learnt a great deal about the other person; they have disclosed often intimate details about themselves, but this has not been reciprocated by the researcher. This is perhaps an inevitable consequence of conducting research as conventionally defined, however non-conventional one's particular methodology might be. However, an awareness of these issues is important and one should at all times be attentive to showing respect to one's respondents and helping to maintain their dignity. We consider it good practice to encourage the participant to ask whatever questions they may have at the end of the interview and, if necessary, be prepared to talk about oneself more openly at this point, once the main body of the interview has been completed.

There are, of course, also various strategies which can be adopted with the aim of including the participant more closely in the research project. Preliminary analyses can be taken back to the participant and their responses to these can be included within the final write up. Smith (1994b) describes a form of dialogical analysis where the participant shares in the analytic endeavour. More radically still, co-operative inquiry researchers try to enlist participants as co-researchers who have an equal stake at every stage of the research project – from inception to dissemination (Reason and Heron 1995).

One possible limitation of IPA is that the intensive involvement required means that the numbers of participants in such studies are almost always quite small, and this obviously raises questions about generalisability. However, the main aim of IPA is indeed to capture how particular individuals perceive and respond to their experiences and, therefore, the value of each case is highlighted. In this way, IPA has a different epistemological commitment to that of mainstream psychology where issues of reliability, sample size and so forth have particular status. And even single cases can make a contribution to the wider field, for example, in terms of problematising existing concepts or helping to develop ways of looking at new areas of study. With a set of cases, one can go even further and begin to develop case law or, through a process of analytic induction, begin to generate grounded theory (Smith 1994a; Smith et al. 1995).

What contribution can IPA research make above and beyond the particular findings generated by individual studies? First, as has been intimated at a number of points in this chapter, we see IPA as able to contribute to the wider discipline of health psychology, by helping to illuminate both the individual conditions and issues researched (e.g. kidney failure and renal dialysis, back pain, sexual behaviour and safer sex) and also the general concepts and constructs employed (e.g. control, social comparison, relational commitment). Thus, as more studies are conducted using IPA, then they can contribute to a cumulative data set of cases of related topics.

Second, the detailed findings from IPA studies can be used to suggest and guide changes in practice in the health setting. So, Carole's account of dialysis could be used to consider modifications to the treatment regime she would find beneficial. Of course, the whole point of this work is to indicate the importance of taking account of individual requirements when contemplating such changes, but even a single case can lead to useful reflection on current practice and its possible shortcomings.

Findings from IPA studies may also provide suggestions for psychological therapeutic interventions. In the second example in this chapter, we saw how social comparisons tended to work in negative ways for some chronic back pain patients. Such findings could serve as useful cues for interventions aimed at trying to help the patient to better understand the chronic nature of their condition and construct more self-enhancing comparisons.

Finally, our example from discussions with gay men about sex and sexual behaviour suggests how findings from IPA studies might help inform preventative health interventions. A detailed examination of participants' own accounts provided important insights into how gay men themselves conceived sex. This clearly impacted on their perception of safe sex and condom use and demonstrates the value of exploring participants' understandings in order to facilitate the construction of more valid and efficacious health promotion strategies.

NOTES

1 The first part of this chapter – up to and including the example of the experience of renal dialysis – is an abridged version of a paper which first appeared as: Smith, J. A. (1996) 'Beyond the divide between cognition and discourse: using interpretative phenomenological analysis in health psychology', *Psychology and Health* 11: 261–271. (Permission obtained from the publishers.)
2 The names of all participants and people referred to by them in this chapter have been altered in order to protect confidentiality.
3 Square brackets [ ] indicate where material has been omitted.

REFERENCES

Abraham, C. and Sheeran, P. (1993) 'In search of a psychology of safer sex promotion: beyond beliefs and texts', *Health Education Research* 8: 245–254.
Abramson, L., Seligman, M. and Teasdale, J. (1978) 'Learned helplessness in humans: critique and reformulation', *Journal of Abnormal Psychology* 87: 49–74.
Anderson, R. and Bury, M. (eds) (1988) *Living with Chronic Illness*, London: Unwin Hyman.
Aronoff, G. (1992) *Evaluation and Treatment of Chronic Pain*, Baltimore: Williams & Wilkins.
Baszanger, I. (1992) 'Deciphering chronic pain', *Sociology of Health and Illness* 14: 181–215.
Brewin, C. (1988) *Cognitive Foundations of Clinical Psychology*, London: Erlbaum.
Bryman, A. (1988) *Quantity and Quality in Social Research*, London: Unwin Hyman.
Bury, M. (1988) 'Meanings at risk with arthritis', in R. Anderson and M. Bury (eds) *Living with Chronic Illness*, London: Unwin Hyman.
Buunck, B. P., Collins, R. L., Taylor, S. E., Van Yperen, N. and Dakof, G. A. (1990) 'The affective consequences of social comparison: either direction has its ups and downs', *Journal of Personality and Social Psychology* 59: 1238–1249.
Christensen, A., Turner, C., Smith, T., Holman, J. and Gregory, M. (1991) 'Health locus of control and depression in end-stage renal disease', *Journal of Clinical and Consulting Psychology* 59: 419–424.

Clabber Moffat, J., Richardson, G., Sheldon, T. and Maynard, A. (1995) *The Cost of Back Pain*, York: Centre for Health Economics.

Conrad, P. (1987) 'The experience of illness: recent and new directions', *Research in the Sociology of Health Care* 6: 1–31.

Darrow, W., Echenberg, D. F., Jaffe, H. W., O'Malley, P. M., Byers, R. H., Getchell, J. P. and Curran, J. W. (1987) 'Risk factors for human immunodeficiency virus infections in homosexual men', *American Journal of Public Health* 77: 479–483.

Denzin, N. (1995) 'Symbolic Interactionism', in J. A. Smith, R. Harré and L. Van Langenhove (eds) *Rethinking Psychology*, London: Sage.

DeVellis, R. F., Holt, K., Renner, B. R., Blalock, S. J., Blanchard, L. W., Cook, H. L., Klotz, M. L., Mikow, V. and Harring, K. (1990) 'The relationship of social comparison to rheumatoid arthritis symptoms and affect', *Basic and Applied Social Psychology* 11: 1–18.

Edwards, D. and Potter, J. (1992) *Discursive Psychology*, London: Sage.

Festinger, L. A. (1954) 'A theory of social comparison processes', *Human Relations* 7: 117–140.

Flowers, P., Smith, J. A., Sheeran, P. and Beail, N. (1996a) 'Health and romance: understanding unprotected sex in relationships between men', *British Journal of Health Psychology* (in press).

—— (1996b) 'Identities and gay men's sexual decision making', in P. Aggleton, P. Davies and G. Hart (eds) *AIDS: Activism and Alliances*, London: Taylor & Francis (in press).

Flowers, P., Sheeran, P., Beail, N. and Smith J. A. (1996c) 'The role of psychosocial factors in HIV risk-reduction among gay and bisexual men: a quantitative review', *Psychology and Health* (in press).

Gagnon, J. H. and Simon, W. (1974) *Sexual Conduct: The Social Sources of Human Sexuality*, London: Hutchinson.

Giorgi, A. (1995) 'Phenomenological psychology', in J. A. Smith, R. Harré and L. Van Langenhove (eds) *Rethinking Psychology*, London: Sage.

Glaser, B. and Strauss, A. (1967) *Awareness of Dying*, Chicago: Aldine.

Goffman, E. (1968) *Asylums*, Harmondsworth: Penguin.

Hampson, S., Glasgow, R. and Toobert, D. (1990) 'Personal models of diabetes and their relations to self-care activities', *Health Psychology* 9: 632–646.

Hart, G. J., Dawson, J., Fitzpatrick, R. M., Boulton, M., McLean, J., Brookes, M. and Parry, J. V. (1993) 'Risk behaviour, anti-HIV and anti-hepatitis B core prevalence in clinic and non-clinic samples of gay men in England, 1991–1992', *AIDS* 7: 863–869.

Hemphill, K. J. and Lehman, D. R. (1991) 'Social comparisons and their affective consequences: the importance of comparison dimension and individual difference variables', *Journal of Social and Clinical Psychology* 10: 372–394.

Idler, E. L. (1993) 'Perceptions of pain and perceptions of health', *Motivation and Emotion* 17: 205–224.

Jensen, M. P. and Kardy, P. (1992) 'Comparative self-evaluation and depressive affect among chronic pain patients: an examination of selective evaluation theory', *Cognitive Therapy and Research* 16: 297–308.

Kingsley, L. A., Kaslow, R., Rinaldo, C. R., Detre, K., Odaka, N., VanRaden, M., Detels, R., Polk, B. F., Chmiel, J., Kelsey, S. H., Ostrow, D. and Visscher, B. (1987) 'Risk factors for seroconversion to human immunodeficiency virus among male homosexuals', *The Lancet* i: 345–348.

Lau, R., Bernard, T. and Hartman, K. (1989) 'Further explorations of common-sense representations of common illnesses', *Health Psychology* 8: 195–219.

Locker, D. (1991) 'Living with chronic illness', in G. Scambler (ed.) *Sociology as Applied to Medicine*, London: Baillière Tindall.

McLean, J., Boulton, M., Brookes, M., Lakhani, D., Fitzpatrick, R., Dawson, J., McKechnie, R. and Hart, G. (1994) 'Regular partners and risky behaviour: why do gay men have unprotected intercourse?', *AIDS Care* 6: 331–341.

Marks, G., Richardson, J., Graham, J. and Levine, A. (1986) 'Role of health locus of control beliefs and expectations of treatment efficacy in adjustment to cancer', *Journal of Personality and Social Psychology* 51: 443–450.

Molleman, E., Pruyn, J. and Van Knippenberg, A. (1986) 'Social comparison processes among cancer patients', *British Journal of Social Psychology* 25: 1–13.

Osborn, M. and Smith, J. A. (1996) 'Personal experiences of chronic pain: an interpretative phenomenological perspective' (submitted for publication).

Poll, I. and Kaplan De Nour, A. (1980) 'Locus of control and adjustment to chronic hemodialysis', *Psychological Medicine* 10: 153–157.

Potter, J. and Wetherell, M. (1987) *Discourse and Social Psychology: Beyond Attitudes and Behaviour*, London: Sage.

—— (1995) 'Discourse analysis', in J. A. Smith, R. Harré and L. Van Langenhove (eds) *Rethinking Methods in Psychology*, London: Sage.

Radley, A. (1994) *Making Sense of Illness: A Social Psychology of Health and Illness*, London: Sage.

Reason, P. and Heron, J. (1995) 'Co-operative inquiry', in J. A. Smith, R. Harré and L. Van Langenhove (eds) *Rethinking Methods in Psychology*, London: Sage.

Rotter, J. (1966) 'Generalized expectancies for the internal versus external control of reinforcement', *Psychological Monographs* 90: 1–28.

Shilling, C. (1993) *The Body and Social Theory*, London: Sage.

Silverman, D. (1985) *Qualitative Methodology and Sociology*, Aldershot: Gower.

Smith, J. A. (1994a) 'Reconstructing selves: an analysis of discrepancies between women's contemporaneous and retrospective accounts of the transition to motherhood', *British Journal of Psychology* 85: 371–392.

—— (1994b) 'Towards reflexive practice: engaging participants as co-researchers or co-analysts in psychological inquiry', *Journal of Community and Applied Social Psychology* 4: 253–260.

—— (1995a) 'Semi structured interviewing and qualitative analysis', in J. A. Smith, R. Harré and L. Van Langenhove (eds) *Rethinking Methods in Psychology*, London: Sage.

—— (1995b) 'Dialysis and depersonalization: a phenomenological case-study of the psychological impact of haemodialysis treament for kidney failure' (submitted for publication).

—— (1996) 'Beyond the divide between cognition and discourse: using interpretative phenomenological analysis in health psychology', *Psychology and Health* 11: 261–271.

Smith, J. A., Harré, R. and Van Langenhove, L. (1995) 'Idiography and the case study', in J. A. Smith, R. Harré and L. Van Langenhove (eds) *Rethinking Methods in Psychology*, London: Sage.

Social Science and Medicine (1990) *Qualitative Research on Chronic Illness* vol. 30, no. 11 (special issue).

Taylor, S. (1983) 'Adjustment to threatening events: a theory of cognitive adaptation', *American Psychologist* 38: 1161–1173.

Taylor, S. E. and Lobel, M. (1989) 'Social comparison activity under threat: downward evaluation and upward contacts', *Psychological Review* 4: 569–575.

Taylor, S., Lichtman, R. and Wood, J. (1984) 'Attributions, beliefs about control, and adjustment to breast cancer', *Journal of Personality and Social Psychology* 46: 489–502.

Thompson, S. (1981) 'Will it hurt less if I can control it? A complex answer to a simple question', *Psychological Bulletin* 90: 89–101.

Vanderzee, K. I., Buunk, B. P. and Sanderman, R. (1995) 'Social comparison as a mediator between health problems and subjective health evaluations', *British Journal of Social Psychology* 34: 53–65.

Waddell, G. (1987) 'A new clinical model for the treatment of low back pain', *Spine* 12: 632–644.

Williams, D. A. and Thorn, B. E. (1989) 'An empirical assessment of pain beliefs', *Pain* 36: 351–358.

Williams, G. (1984) 'The genesis of chronic illness: narrative reconstruction', *Sociology of Health and Illness* 6: 175.

Chapter 5

Social and material ecologies for hearing impairment

William Noble

INTRODUCTION

In this chapter, work from various quarters is considered in order to pick out features of the meaning of the concept 'hearing impairment'. At first, it is straightforward to see what that term means. It may commonly be understood, for instance, to describe the consequence for perceptual experience of a material disorder (injury/disease) affecting the auditory pathway. That way of characterising hearing impairment is from the perspective of the doctor's surgery or the audiological clinic, and is quite intelligible in the world of psychology and related professional domains. What I aim to do is a colouring-in exercise to bring about a more broad-range understanding of the concept of hearing impairment, and how it functions in the hands of different people. In the course of this exercise, my intention is to introduce readers to the variety of perspectives that may be taken in relation to the issues and experiences associated with impairment of hearing. A particular concern is to get across features of hearing impairment from the perspective of the person who sustains it and that of their close family.

I will be speaking from the kind of 'off-centre' position found in some types of analytic writing about deviance (e.g. Goffman 1963). My theoretical commitment combines an ecological approach to perception with a 'social constructionist' view of mental life. The ecological approach to perception (Gibson 1979) takes it that animals (thus, humans) detect spatio-temporal structures of energy which directly specify features of and events in their surroundings. Such an approach contrasts with one in which 'reality' is put together by a central information processing system (a 'personal construction' of the mind or brain). A major feature of the ecological approach is that animals, and the environments they inhabit, cannot be considered independently of each other; rather, they are mutually dependent elements in an overall system. The forms and behaviours of animate organisms, and the niches in which they subsist, are intimately linked. The social constructionist view of mind (Coulter 1979; Mead 1934) takes the category of 'the mental' to describe, for any individual person, conduct deriving from that person's unique history of interpersonal interaction in a linguistic community. The stress on language is due to the equation of 'mentality' and 'language-using' (Noble and Davidson 1996). Such an equation has particular significance for discussion of mentality and hearing impairment, because language and communication are central issues in the experience of that kind of impairment.

A foundational claim connected with this theoretical combination is that human life is constituted by material and discursive ecologies in interaction with each other (Noble 1993). By this, I mean that there are inescapable material contexts within which ordinary lives are conducted, and that people make things of their circumstances through the discursive practices they engage in. For example, people in urban habitats may spend time 'in the countryside', say, as a form of leisure, or for the pursuit of a hobby like butterfly netting, or as part of acting on behalf of a community interest group (conservationists), or to escape difficult personal circumstances (on the run, getting away from the family). The material ecology of the 'countryside' is broadly invariant across the range of such interests and engagements, but what is made of what is there will vary significantly through the different lenses of those various interests. Those interests will, in turn, be shaped up in discursive interaction with relevant others. Ultimately, features of any material ecology may well be altered in different ways, in consequence of the different discourses and practices engaged in with respect to it.

As part of the theoretical orientation just outlined, I side with a view (Coulter 1982) that the matter of analytic interest is the activity of individuals in social engagement with themselves and each other, rather than that social 'structures' or 'systems' have interesting things to tell us about people's conduct. Social engagement is strongly typified by the varieties of conversational interaction people undertake (Sacks 1992). At the same time it must be recognised that the moves available to people are constrained by their own capacities in relation to the social and material ecologies they inhabit (Yardley 1996).

One material-cum-discursive ecology for hearing impairment to be considered in this chapter is that of whatever arrangements exist for the provision of 'hearing health care'. Such arrangements vary over time and space; my remarks will attempt to get a fix on key elements typical of such a service in industrialised societies.

What is the place of this chapter in this collection? A good question – if for no other reason than that the dimension of health–illness may not even come into consideration in the context of hearing impairment – my reference to 'hearing health care' notwithstanding. I offer a critique of the concept of 'hearing health' in the fourth section below. The absence of linkage between any question of health in the context of lack of hearing can be seen in relation to a particular social ecology, namely, the world of capital-'D' 'Deafness'. In that world there is a radical departure from anything connoted by the common understanding of 'hearing impairment' signalled in the opening paragraph. Capital-'D' 'Deafness' indicates a culture, not a condition, as I explain in the next section.

Before I get to that, certain related points must be made in advance. A reader may want to take the general concept of 'hearing impairment' to cover all instances of departure from normal hearing. The term 'deafness' (small-'d') is used similarly, in common parlance, to cover all such instances. For the purposes of the following analysis, though, I need to establish a distinction that has critical consequences for understanding what is afoot in this corner of reality. Thus, I use the term 'deafness' to denote complete, or nearly complete, absence of hearing, and that of 'hearing impairment' to cover 'less than normal hearing' – from relatively slight hearing loss up to some limit that includes residual hearing on which the person none the less relies. Someone who is 'hard-of-hearing' comes under the description of having 'hearing impairment'; someone quite unable to hear, and/or so extremely impaired as not to rely on their hearing, is small-'d' deaf. Notwithstanding this definitional distinction, I will return to consider, in the third section, small-'d' deaf as popularly covering all instances of non-normal hearing.

Other matters to clarify are as follows. I will occasionally use the word 'speak' to refer, in a metaphoric sense, to any form of *verbal* utterance, be it vocal or manual. Thus, we can consider speaking in one or other of the several sign languages of the world – articulation by means of the fingers, hands and arms (often assisted by the face); just as we can consider speaking in one or other of the several vocal languages of the world – articulation by means of the larynx, tongue, oral cavity, teeth and lips. As a generic term I will use the capital-'S' 'Sign' to indicate manual language having 'design features' (Hockett and Altmann 1968) equivalent to a vocal language like English. Finally, I note that Sign is typically not a manual code for a mainstream vocal language like English. Natural sign languages are separate and distinct languages in their own right. Someone who speaks Australian Sign Language and Australian English possesses two languages.

CAPITAL-'D' DEAFNESS AND SMALL-'D' DEAFNESS

The world of (capital-'D') Deaf people may be characterised as a world whose inhabitants normally deploy a manual–visual rather than vocal–auditory language and who take for granted communication by that and related means, just as hearing people take for granted their vocal–auditory communication mode. People who constitute the world of capital-'D' Deafness are usually – but need not be – small-'d' deaf, as I defined that above.

The absence of hearing in the world of Deafness is usually a matter of secondary interest to those who form this sort of community. If attended to at all, not-hearing might be taken as a mark of difference, the more significant mark being the language that characterises Deaf life (Padden and Humphries 1988). Absence of hearing is not seen in Deaf worlds as any sign of inferiority, and certainly not as pathology (Dolnick 1993). Padden and Humphries (1988) explain that for children raised as members of Deaf families, the word 'deaf' denotes simply 'us'. The use of capital 'D' in this realm of social life is thus to indicate cultural membership rather than deviation from a biological norm.

These remarks are a simplification in the sense that there is no homogeneous 'Deaf community' to be found at any national or regional level. The point to stress, rather, is that the social and material contexts for capital-'D' Deafness are likely to be better captured by the descriptive techniques of social anthropology (e.g. Lane 1984; Rutherford 1988; Stokoe et al. 1976), than by a 'clinical gaze' (Foucault 1973) aimed at 'symptoms' displayed by the physically embodied individual. In a later section, I return to discussion of the appropriateness of clinical approaches to 'hearing impairment', as earlier defined.

I propose a conceptual fiction at this point, called 'people in the mainstream of the community'. This stands for that (non-existent) set of people sometimes referred to as 'the man in the street', 'the average person'. For my purposes, 'mainstreamers' take unaided hearing for granted as a design feature of standard-plan humans. Though no individual can be 'the average person', it is probably safe to say that the majority of people make this assumption about unaided hearing implicitly. For mainstream people, the word 'deaf' has a range of meanings, but – by contrast with its cultural connotation at the hands of Deaf members – for them, most saliently, the term literally denotes 'unable to hear'. The potential for profound differences of meaning attached to the term 'deaf' features time and again, as when one considers what 'deaf' means in the question (spoken in an aggravated tone), 'Are you *deaf*?!'

The world of Deaf people has gained somewhat in mainstream consciousness. There is an increasing appearance of Sign in public activities, such as educational, entertainment and political gatherings. Also, there are TV shows like 'Reasonable doubt', featuring Marlee Matlin, who acted alongside William Hurt in the movie *Children of a lesser god* (these examples may be opaque to readers unexposed to North American media). Such manifestations serve to make Deafness as 'cultural difference' more intelligible to the majority. Even so, forms of human life reliant on Sign continue to represent a challenge to the contemporary mainstream of existence. In my own experience, (hearing) students struggle with the idea that you can 'think' in such a language. This is because they take language and thought to be, at base, dependent on vocal utterance – hence, that normal human life entails vocal speech.

That assumption, as a prevailing feature of the mainstream social ecology, has its associated material devices in the form of personally worn hearing aids and cochlear implants. In combination, these promote a discourse (e.g. McCormick 1991) which maintains deafness as a deficiency to be corrected, rather than a potentially different form of life. Here it must be stressed that, although hereditary deafness exists, historically, by far the greater proportion of deaf children have been born into hearing families. The occurrence of deafness is thus often isolated within a family group whose members may be completely strange to, and highly unnerved about, its nature. If there is a culture of Deafness it is not readily accessible to the members of such a social grouping. The 'correction of deficiency' perspective is a natural one to adopt in these circumstances.

Nevertheless, commentators who are wise to elements of this scene, such as Armstrong (1985) and Ross (1992), report strong indications that many people born deaf or hearing impaired, and initially drawn into the 'correction' perspective on deafness, later re-orient to a Sign-based approach, presumably due to the less than satisfactory correction achieved. There are several reasons to expect that corrective efforts – in the sense of attempts to improve auditory contact with the world – visited upon those born deaf or severely hearing impaired, will vary from moderately successful to completely ineffective (Conrad 1979).

For many, removal from a 'corrective' perspective will undoubtedly be accompanied by a discursive shift to embrace Deafness as culture. Such a shift, akin to religious conversion, is what Berger and Luckmann (1966), in discussion of the construction of social worlds, termed 'alternation'. Deaf communities are typically constituted of members socialised from birth into that way of being, as well as those 'alternating' from the mainstream (Foster 1989).

It is not my aim to engage in the debate between the 'correction of deficiency' and 'culture' perspectives on deafness. The purpose is to draw attention to the fact of those different views, that they are strongly defended and contested, hence to show this as an instance of interplay between material and social ecologies related to absence of hearing. In a deficiency approach, attention is centred on special educational facilities for aural–oral training, on the advantages flowing from participation in the vocal communicative mode, and on decision-taking with respect to appropriate prosthetic fitting, including the surgical alterations entailed in the fitting of implants and the like. In a culture approach, the focus is on the community of Sign users as a natural social habitat, on the equivalence of Sign to any other natural language, and on political activism to raise the status of those who rely on this form of language.

The opposition between 'deficiency' and 'culture' perspectives is itself contingent on particular background conditions. It arises due to the expectation that 'normal' existence entails articulate vocal speech and an unaided ability to hear. Ordinarily that expectation is unchallenged, but conditions do occur in which a sufficiently large proportion of a regional population has been deaf from birth.

Martha's Vineyard is an island lying off the coast of Massachusetts, on the eastern side of the continental USA. Historical conditions have been such that, until early in this century, and over many generations, there was a large contingent of people with hereditary deafness living there. As a consequence, Sign was not only a common language among them, but also between them and the island's hearing inhabitants (Groce 1985). As a further consequence, normal hearing capacity was of no great relevance as regards membership of the category of 'mainstream person'. Because a majority language did not require hearing for its production and comprehension, one criterion usually assumed for standard-plan humanness was not in force. A 'normal' human being is one who can speak more or less fluently. On Martha's Vineyard, that condition was able to be fulfilled by the fact of Sign.

Social conditions like these are not likely to be reproduced in the contemporary world, and the presence of a device like the cochlear implant serves to confound discourse about aiming for equivalent conditions – for example, having Sign as a language taught in mainstream schools (Selover 1988). The cochlear implant is a device that transforms environmental acoustic energy into patterns of activity in a single or multi-channel electrode set which directly stimulates the auditory nerve. The device provides an analogue of features of the audible world, and is of varying effectiveness (e.g. Carney et al. 1993). It has, none the less, been popularly referred to as a 'bionic' ear, and as having miraculous (curative) properties. Such rhetoric has several effects, among them the maintenance of a deficiency perspective on deafness, hence maintenance of its stigmatising status.

HEARING IMPAIRMENT (POPULARLY, SMALL-'D' DEAFNESS)

Connotations of 'deaf'

In this, the main section of the chapter, I want to discuss hearing impairment as I defined that term at the start – namely, that which does *not* constitute complete or nearly complete absence of hearing. Yet I also wish to reintroduce the term (small-'d') 'deaf' in consideration of that sort of case. This is not perverseness; rather, I am concerned to illuminate the semantic force in popular use of the term 'deaf', given that it tends to be applied to any case of impaired hearing.

The word 'deaf' carries more than the intension of 'inability to hear'. Historically, it has been accompanied by the term 'dumb', and Sign is sometimes referred to as 'deaf-and-dumb' language. Someone born deaf (in the sense defined at the start) is unlikely to learn to vocalise, hence will be dumb, in the sense of mute.

The term 'dumb' more prominently carries the meaning 'stupid'. That is not an entirely misplaced meaning. Someone born deaf who does not speak vocally will have difficulty accessing the senses of things referred to in the mainstream vocal language of the community they happen to be born into. Even if they learn whichever sign language is spoken locally, this is still a different language, not a visual code for a mainstream vocal language. (There are such codes, for example, as Signed English, but they are typically limited to the classroom in their use.) Thus, the common stock of knowledge that usually allows an ordinary member of a community to act competently (to not be dumb) may often be beyond the reach of someone born deaf. This is why, it must be stressed, the more universal use of Sign on Martha's Vineyard is so critical: it counters the exclusion, and the resulting social 'dumbness', that arise from non-access to a mainstream language. I note at this point that a vital function of an invented code like Signed English is to assist speakers of Sign to grasp the syntactic conventions of that vocal language, the better to learn to *read* its written form.

As I said at the start, language and human mentality are equated in the theoretical position from which I offer analysis of this (or any) feature of the human scene. In the case of Sign, and its functionality within the community at large, 'mindedness' may be seen as fostered in proportion to the degree of language-based social commerce. If a circumstance arises, as on Martha's Vineyard, that enables deaf and hearing members to routinely communicate using the same language, 'like-mindedness' (which, here, I do not want to mean agreeableness) emerges among them.

The upshot of all this is that deafness can (though it need not) have critical implications for matters of intelligence, competence, and the like. Deafness is thus not just deficiency in sensory sensitivity – the link between deafness and dumbness adds significantly to the stigmatising nature of this status. It is thus that the meaning of 'deaf' in the question 'Are you *deaf*?!' connotes social ineptitude or stupidity.

There is a spread of meaning from the potential 'dumbness' of those who are deaf ('deaf' as defined at the start of this chapter) to those whose hearing has become impaired, yet who are otherwise members of mainstream communities. In the case of someone who is born or becomes deaf, this is an inescapable status; its stigmatising potential will vary with the social and material circumstances the person inhabits. Someone who becomes deaf in adult life and is successfully fitted with an implant may be able to retain their place in the mainstream. This is because, having been socialised into mainstream membership, including the mainstream language, the prosthesis might function adequately enough to enable continued comprehension and production of that language.

Nevertheless, there will be problems in maintaining adequate auditory contact with the world. These problems are common to all forms of personally-worn hearing aids, and they concern comprehension of critical signals like speech in contexts of competing noise (Plomp 1994). Reports concur (e.g. Walden et al. 1984; Cox and Gilmore 1990) that optimum benefit of hearing aids, including cochlear implants (Hirsch 1993), is in quiet conditions and one-to-one communication–listening, and when the person talking can be clearly seen. Despite the limitation of benefit when those conditions are not met (which is, of course, not infrequent), the predicament for a person postlingually deaf or hearing impaired will be less drastic than were they unable to achieve any help from implanted or personally-worn amplification technology.

Hearing impairment as a status

In the case of someone whose hearing becomes impaired, yet not to the point of being inescapably identified with the status of deafness, a different set of dynamics is observed. For all the reasons I am trying to reveal in this chapter, such a person may well be motivated to avoid identifying with the status of non-normal hearing, since to attract the commonplace description of being 'deaf' is to be saddled with a number of undesired characteristics concerning competence, intelligence, and so on. Despite the efforts via public media to raise the status of Deaf membership, those same media remain the places where small-'d'-deaf and impaired-hearing behaviours (never distinguished, in any case) are a source of jokes and mockery.

Who, born into a world in which hearing is taken for granted, would willingly 'alternate' to the world of hearing impairment/deafness? Evidence has accumulated informally and, in recent times, more systematically, that, if it can be done, avoidance of this status is, indeed, strongly pursued. For example, in a survey of inhabitants of retirement homes (Franks and Beckmann 1985), it was noted that only one-fifth of those who had clearly measurable loss of hearing used a hearing aid. This survey, conducted in the north-western region of the USA, revealed that one of the two main factors motivating avoidance of the use of hearing aids was their effect of drawing attention to a personal disability; the other factor was cost.

Even when cost is not a factor, as in the United Kingdom where hearing aids are available as part of welfare provisions financed by the State, the take-up rate in comparable groups – those with an evident hearing impairment – is similar (less than 25 per cent) to that observed in the American sample (Davis 1989). We are left with the likelihood that the other strong factor reported by the US sample, namely, identifiability as disabled, inhibits many people from making the move to reduce the disabling effect of impaired hearing.

Of course, a point will be reached at which hearing is sufficiently impaired that the person may be forced to acknowledge that something has to be done. A recent survey of hearing levels among new clients of

Australian Hearing Services (Lovegrove et al. 1992) shows the average measured impairment in that sample to be significantly greater than the level observed among people in the UK survey (Davis 1989) who reported that they had 'great difficulty' hearing in background-noise conditions. The Australian average was closer to the level observed in people in the UK survey who reported having 'moderate difficulty' hearing even in optimum conditions, a finding confirmed in a subsequent survey of hearing aid clients (Macrae and Dillon, personal communication). A similar value to the Australian data was observed among first-time seekers of a hearing aid in Denmark, another country with hearing aid provision financed by the State (Salomon et al. 1988). Thus, the degree of departure from adequate hearing has to be substantial, on average, before people will seek assistance. Even then, it appears that only about 20 to 25 per cent of those with such substantial impairment actually take that step.

Reports vary about the significance of the decision to seek a hearing aid. One fairly authoritative account (Goldstein and Stephens 1981) argues that the majority of persons attending at clinics have a positive attitude to what is called 'audiological rehabilitation' – a procedure that invariably includes the fitting of one or more personally-worn hearing aid(s). The report from Australia by Lovegrove et al. (1992) suggests that over 90 per cent of clients keep using the aid(s), although for daily durations that vary considerably among users. This result confirms in general terms an early account (Kasden and Robinson 1971) that a high proportion of people who take the step of getting a hearing aid, keep using it. About 85 per cent of the people in the Australian sample reported satisfaction with the rehabilitation service outcome, in terms of its having met certain specific goals.

Though most people fitted with a hearing aid keep using it, reports show that about half of them use the aid for only limited periods in the day. The item identified in the Lovegrove et al. (1992) report as showing most beneficial effect was listening to television and radio. It was also the item most clients sought to attain improvement with, in terms of goal-setting. This finding agrees with one from the study by Salomon et al. (1988) that among people aged over seventy, those who sought a hearing aid rated television as an important element of their lives. Those who did not seek an aid, rated television as less significant in their lives. (Some not seeking a hearing aid, had impaired hearing as severe as those who did.) Taken together, these findings provoke more than one interpretation. It may truly be the case that TV/radio listening is somehow the key to seeking a hearing aid, and that the fairly common use pattern of a few hours per day indicates the aid is used for that purpose only. At the same time, use of a hearing aid indoors to listen to radio or television (and coincidentally to hear a spouse in conversation) may be a sign of avoidance of use in contexts where the aid is visible to others besides the spouse, a proposal consistent with results from a recent Quebec study (Waridel 1993).

Such a use-pattern would also be consistent with the general observation of a low level of desire to use hearing aids among those whose hearing is far from adequate.

One factor to be noted from a parallel study by the Danish group (Vesterager et al. 1988), is that the partnership rate among those not seeking a hearing aid was lower than among those who did. Furthermore, of those not seeking an aid, yet who clearly had hearing problems, none reported problems in hearing a spouse (but did report problems hearing others). Likeliest is that non-seekers were living alone. It is typically observed that spouses are the catalysts for hearing aid seeking – I return to the consideration of family dynamics and hearing impairment presently. A common anecdote from family members is that relatives who are finally coerced into attending a hearing aid clinic, go through all the motions of testing and fitting, then put the device in a drawer. The foregoing data could be taken to contradict that story. Perhaps, or maybe the hearing aid goes in the drawer when there are visitors, or it is time to go out, and comes out of the drawer when it is time to watch TV.

I detail this matter because it focuses on a phenomenon that has not been well researched or understood (and demands closer attention) – namely, the management of a personal identity 'spoiled' by this particular form of stigmatising sign (Goffman 1963). In considering social as well as material ecologies for impaired hearing it is vital to witness the moves people make in such management. By so doing, wiser approaches may be taken in assisting them to address the problems they experience. Those problems are real, and can be very damaging for the personal and social lives of those who sustain impairment of their auditory system. Discussion has concentrated so far on the factors that may plausibly animate a motive to avoid being identified as 'deaf'. Whether the person is so identified or not, their experiences of frustration from conversational breakdown and the social, hence emotional, isolation that flow from avoidance of such difficulty, can have injurious effects on personal well-being, giving rise to depression (Herbst and Humphrey 1980; Thomas 1984), and contributing to psychotic states (Almeida et al. 1995).

Stigma's effects

Before proceeding, it is useful to note the distinctions made by the World Health Organisation (1980) among the terms 'disorder', 'impairment', 'disability', and 'handicap'. Disorder, in the WHO scheme, is a physical state of disease/injury in an organ; impairment (in this case, hearing impairment) is the consequence of disorder, and shows up in clinical tests of various kinds; disabilities are the actual difficulties experienced in hearing in everyday settings; finally, handicaps are the disadvantages and psycho-social consequences that result from impairments and disabilities – such things as being stigmatised, isolated, considered socially incompetent (Jones et al. 1987).

A body of research that helps provide a model of stigma management has examined the experience of hearing impairment as a family affair. From interviews with families in which the male partner has a hearing impairment due to noise at work, it emerges very clearly that the consequences of the disabling effects of impairment radiate as handicaps co-suffered by other family members (Hétu et al. 1987). The effort at management of a potentially spoiled identity shows up in terms of reluctance to acknowledge difficulties in hearing (Hallberg and Barrenäs 1993; Hétu et al. 1990). A consequence is that wives become interpreters for and protectors of their husbands; they become unable to act independently at social gatherings, so as not to have the husband's impaired communicative competence revealed. At the same time, life in the family itself becomes degraded (e.g. Blaikie and Guthrie 1984; Hétu et al. 1993); mishearings and non-hearings are often read as increasing failures in being able to relate to each other; tension and frustration attend what ought to be the normal conversational traffic of family life; intimacy is reduced due to the effort involved in communicating, and there are consequent feelings of anger, grief and isolation.

The stigmatising power of 'deafness' is so great that this is put up with, rather than perceived as a problem that is ruining people's lives. Concealment of a status that is shameful thus perpetuates the tortured nature of family life (Hétu 1996).

The social ecology that pressures 'deafness' to be concealed also perpetuates material ecologies that do nothing to make life easier for those whose hearing is impaired. The everyday built environment includes barriers to easy communication – 'wallpaper' music in stores; hard and reverberant surfaces that increase the level of interfering noise; poor lighting, and grilles and other barriers to seeing people in service areas (Noble and Hétu 1994). All this is unremarked because there is no perception of hearing impairment as an issue in everyday life.

An ironic but telling note can be uttered here. The theory, mentioned at the start, which has inspired the present, ecological approach to issues of hearing impairment, is that of James Gibson. Though best known for his work on visual and haptic perception, Gibson once wrote a general treatise (Gibson 1966) which necessarily included coverage of the audible world and hearing as a perceptual system. In that work Gibson also included a survey of 'causes of deficient perception'. This addressed such matters as the obscuring of signals, camouflage, haze and dust, illusions of different sorts, and adaptations and after-effects from overstimulation. In the course of the survey, Gibson delivered a little lecture (1966: 304), explaining that while the theorist of perception (himself) must strive to understand what was perceivable, and why it sometimes was or was not perceived, he must not take inquiry to the individual level and ask how he himself, as a particular person, perceives.

That point stated, Gibson then noted that:

> Perception is deficient in the lower animals as compared to the higher animals, and . . . is less efficient in the human child than in the human adult, but let us confine the question to the last case only – to the supposedly normal observer. We exclude from consideration all deficiencies due to disease or injury.

The irony is that Gibson was himself profoundly hearing impaired, a fact he wrote about, but only when in biographical mode (Gibson 1967). It surely helps to sustain the 'non-existence' of hearing (or any other sensory) impairment in the social ecology when an influential psychologist of perception adds to the stock of knowledge in a way that expressly proscribes reference to the impaired (his own) case.

'HEARING HEALTH' AND THE ECOLOGY OF THE CLINIC

I said at the start, that the dimension of health/illness may not come into the picture where hearing impairment is concerned, despite my reference to 'hearing health care', and that this could be witnessed with respect to capital-'D' deafness, discussed above. There is a second way in which the use of 'health' in connection with impaired hearing is inappropriate, and considering that second way brings us to what I think is the right orientation to clinical intervention.

'Hearing health' is actually a misnomer. An injury-cum-disease process might be the cause of 'poor hearing', but the word 'poor' in this context is not the same as its meaning when we describe someone as being in 'poor health'. Some forms of poor health may, among other things, cause poor hearing; equally, poor hearing may arise from causes that have no effects other than on the 'health' of organs usually permitting normal hearing. Poor hearing is not, itself, a case of ill-health. Any 'health' issue is not with regard to hearing impairment *as such*. Appropriate questions about health in the context of hearing impairment are to do with emotional health and well-being, and the threats to those that result from the ruptures to everyday life that hearing impairment generates. I hope I have been able to give a clear enough sense of those 'mental health' effects by reference to the evidence mentioned throughout the previous section.

The reference to 'hearing health' turns out to be more than a quibble about words. Use of the word 'health', in cases of hearing disorder, carries with it the risk of down-playing an individual's or a family's needs considered in terms of disabilities and handicaps, with a focus instead on needs considered in terms of impairment. To show this, let me reiterate words I used a moment ago: 'poor hearing may arise from causes that have no effects other than on the "health" of organs usually permitting normal hearing'. We may, properly, speak about the health or otherwise of cochlear hair cells or middle-ear connective tissue. If medical or surgical means can somehow remedy disorders of those organs, we can speak of a cure for their diseased state. Now, in the absence of possibilities for intervention at that level, it is tempting to take reduction of impairment by means of prosthesis as a substitute for restoration to a state of 'health'. Physical disorder in an organ, and its possible cure, can reasonably be described in terms of changed states of health. But impairment, and the restoration of function which the prosthesis may give rise to, are not states of ill or good health. Hearing, in this sense, is not a state; it is a capacity.

A disease in your leg is a state of ill-health in that limb which may inhibit the function of walking; cure of the disease by medical or surgical intervention may restore that function. The lessened mobility cannot be seen as illhealth, nor its restoration the return of health. Those alterations of function are the disabling and enabling of capacities. A prosthesis in the form of callipers may help to restore function, with the state of health in the limb unaffected. But we would not speak of 'walking health', and nor should we speak of 'hearing health'. An observer not wise to the intervention may mistakenly think that the limb is restored to health if the callipers are out of sight and the capacity to walk on even ground looks fairly normal. So with a hearing aid, especially one that is small enough not to call attention to itself, and a context, such as one-to-one conversation in quiet conditions, where the person can function quite fluently. An observer might be tempted to think that the hearing system has been restored to a healthy condition, when no such restoration has occurred. Rather, the degree of impairment has been reduced, while the health of the auditory system may remain unchanged.

A challenge to the coherence of the term 'hearing health' is not to say that *other* aspects of the person's health and well-being are unaffected as a result of interventions using hearing prosthesis. Just as, by the use of devices to aid walking, the person's state of general fitness could improve, as well as their sense of autonomy, so by the use of aids to hearing the person's feeling of social isolation, their level of stress or emotional disturbance, could well decline. This has, indeed, been reported (Abrams et al. 1992; Taylor 1993).

But it is not straightforward to adjust the rhetoric of 'audiological rehabilitation'. The discursive and material ecologies of the hearing clinic are replete with reference to health. In many countries 'audiological rehabilitation' is in the hands of doctors and nurses, so the health theme is explicit. In many others, specialist practitioners emulate medical practices, and the clinic is filled with devices and machinery for inspecting parts of ears and evaluating various esoteric features of auditory capacity – bolstering the 'clinical gaze'.

In some cases this orientation makes sense. Surgical or medical procedures may be appropriate to address certain problems; childhood middle ear infection, for example (Kenna 1994), or otosclerosis (Farrior 1994). What is more, in addition to the cochlear implant, surgical procedures may offer benefit in the fitting of certain types of acoustic prostheses (Mylanus et al. 1994). A clinical medical approach may thus, at times, be appropriately found at the boundary between treatment of disorder, and reduction of disabilities and handicaps.

More typically, though, into the ecology of the clinic come individuals, often accompanied by their spouse or another close family member, whose lives have reached the point where normal transactions and relations have broken down: something is needed to relieve the deterioration in both personal and interpersonal circumstances. This is not an issue to do with illness, at least not directly; rather, there is a breakdown in taken-for-granted ways of being in the everyday world. Furthermore, because no two people and their circumstances are alike, the nature of that deviation from expected ways of being will have unique, as well as common, features. Yet the ecology (and economy) of the clinic are not oriented to the particular issues the individual or individual family is facing: the clinic orientation is centred on the hearing prosthesis; it promotes an approach that seeks to ensure adherence to 'best practice' prescription guidelines based on physical and psychophysical measurements (Byrne and Dillon 1986). The orientation is to reduction of impairment. Issues about avoidance of the status of 'deaf', about fear of being stigmatised, and the increased likelihood of these handicaps through the advertisement of one's status by public use of a hearing aid, are not part of the game.

These remarks are not offered in a hostile tone. They are preliminary to a conclusion that when some notice *is* paid to the individual or individual family's needs, taking account of the goals that the parties feel able to set for themselves and address, a more satisfactory outcome ensues (Dillon et al. 1991a,b). Notable, though, is the comparative modesty of the problems people identify and the goals they seek to meet. This, it strikes me, reflects the fearfulness that surrounds hearing impairment as a status, making people highly circumscribed in what they will disclose or acknowledge, even though they have taken the major step of attending the clinic.

CONCLUDING COMMENTS

It must be acknowledged that the critique offered here is based on a mix of knowledge sources, including reportage and personal judgement, as well as interpretation of, and extrapolation from, more standard empirical inquiries. The position of the present writer is that of unapologetic analyst and cool commentator; someone else surveying the same landscape could well come up with a different story about hearing impairment in our time. The issues identified here would not, thereby, be dispelled, even if the tone were more inspirational.

I close with some practical points: the issue of impaired hearing is among us all; and it is enlarging, particularly as life-expectancy increases. Psychology has several contributions to offer: analysis – the sort made in this critique, for example; identification of psycho-social issues and features, for individuals and families; appropriate orientation to those features in any intervention or service provision; keeping a weather eye out, in more general practice, for hearing problems as underlying family relations problems, mood disorders, or psychotic symptoms. Any such contribution will beneficially include orientation to the specific needs articulated by the persons affected, and will refrain from the introduction of our own form of the 'clinical gaze'.

REFERENCES

Abrams, H. B., Hnath-Chisolm, T., Guerreiro, S. M. and Ritterman, S. I. (1992) 'The effects of intervention strategy on self-perception of hearing handicap', *Ear and Hearing* 13: 371–377.

Almeida, O. P., Howard, R. J., Levy, R. and David, A. S. (1995) 'Psychotic states arising in late life (late paraphrenia): the role of risk factors', *British Journal of Psychiatry* 166: 215–228.

Armstrong, D. F. (1985) 'Will it ever? A review of "When the Mind Hears" by Harlan Lane', *Sign Language Studies* 48: 223–248.

Berger, P. L. and Luckmann, T. (1966) *The Social Construction of Reality*, Harmondsworth: Penguin.

Blaikie, N. W. and Guthrie, R. V. (1984) *Noise and the Family: An Enquiry into Some Effects of Noise-induced Deafness*, Royal Melbourne Institute of Technology, Faculty of Humanities and Social Sciences.

Byrne, D. and Dillon, H. (1986) 'The National Acoustic Laboratories' new procedure for selecting the gain and frequency response of a hearing aid', *Ear and Hearing* 7: 257–265.

Carney, A. E., Osberger, M. J., Carney, E., Robbins, A. M., Renshaw, J. and Miyamotc, R. T. (1993) 'A comparison of speech discrimination with cochlear implants and tactile aids', *Journal of the Acoustical Society of America* 94: 2036–2049.

Conrad, R. (1979) *The Deaf Schoolchild: Language and Cognitive Function*, London: Harper & Row.

Coulter, J. (1979) *The Social Construction of Mind*, London: Macmillan.

—— (1982) 'Remarks on the conceptualization of social structure', *Philosophy of the Social Sciences* 12: 33–46.

Cox, R. M. and Gilmore, C. (1990) 'Development of the profile of hearing aid performance (PHAP)', *Journal of Speech and Hearing Research* 33: 343–355.

Davis, A. (1989) 'The prevalence of hearing impairment and reported hearing disability among adults in Great Britain', *International Journal of Epidemiology* 18: 911–917.

Dillon, H., Koritschoner, E., Battaglia, J., Lovegrove, R., Ginis, J., Mavrias, G., Carnie, L., Ray, P., Forsythe, L., Towers, E., Goulias, H. and Macaskill, F. (1991a) 'Rehabilitation effectiveness. I: assessing the needs of clients entering a national hearing rehabilitation program', *Australian Journal of Audiology* 13: 55–65.

—— (1991b) 'Rehabilitation effectiveness. II: assessing the outcomes for clients of a national hearing rehabilitation program', *Australian Journal of Audiology* 13: 68–82.

Dolnick, E. (1993) 'Deafness as culture', *The Atlantic Monthly*, September: 37–53.

Farrior, J. B. (1994) 'Small fenestra stapedectomy for management of progressive conductive deafness', *Southern Medical Journal* 87: 17–22.

Foster, S. (1989) 'Social alienation and peer identification: a study of the social construction of deafness', *Human Organization* 48: 226–235.

Foucault, M. (1973) *The Birth of the Clinic*, trans. A. M. Sheridan Smith, New York: Pantheon.

Franks, J. R. and Beckmann, N. J. (1985) 'Rejection of hearing aids: attitudes of a geriatric sample', *Ear and Hearing* 6: 161–166.

Gibson, J. J. (1966) *The Senses Considered as Perceptual Systems*, Boston: Houghton-Mifflin.

—— (1967) 'James J. Gibson', in E. G. Boring and G. Lindzey (eds) *A History of Psychology in Autobiography*, New York: Appleton.

—— (1979) *The Ecological Approach to Visual Perception*, Boston: Houghton-Mifflin.

Goffman, E. (1963) *Stigma*, Englewood Cliffs: Prentice-Hall.

Goldstein, D. P. and Stephens, S. D. G. (1981) 'Audiological rehabilitation: management model I', *Audiology* 20: 432–452.

Groce, N. E. (1985) *Everyone Here Spoke Sign Language*, Cambridge, MA: Harvard University Press.

Hallberg, L. R-M. and Barrenäs, M-L. (1993) 'Living with a male with noise-induced hearing loss: experiences from the perspective of spouses', *British Journal of Audiology* 27: 255–261.

Herbst, K. G. and Humphrey, C. (1980) 'Hearing impairment and mental state in the elderly living at home', *British Medical Journal* 281: 903–905.

Hétu, R. (1996) 'The stigma attached to hearing impairment', *Scandinavian Audiology* 25 (Suppl. 43): 12–24.

Hétu, R., Jones, L. and Getty, L. (1993) 'The impact of acquired hearing impairment on intimate relationships: implications for rehabilitation', *Audiology* 32: 363–381.

Hétu, R., Lalonde, M. and Getty, L. (1987) 'Psychosocial disadvantages associated with occupational hearing loss as experienced in the family', *Audiology* 26: 141–152.

Hétu, R., Riverin, L., Getty, L., Lalande, N. and St Cyr, C. (1990) 'The reluctance to acknowledge hearing problems among noise exposed workers', *British Journal of Audiology* 24: 265–276.

Hirsch, H. G. (1993) 'Intelligibility improvement of noisy speech for people with cochlear implants', *Speech Communication* 12: 261–266.

Hockett, C. F. and Altmann, S. A. (1968) 'A note on design features', in T. A. Sebeok (ed.) *Animal Communication*, Bloomington: Indiana University Press.

Jones, L., Kyle, J. and Wood, P. (1987) *Words Apart*, London: Tavistock.

Kasden, S. D. and Robinson, M. (1971) 'Otologic-audiologic hearing aid evaluation', *Archives of Otolaryngology* 93: 34–36.

Kenna, M. A. (1994) 'Treatment of chronic suppurative otitis media', *Otolaryngology Clinics of North America* 27: 457–472.

Lane, H. (1984) *When the Mind Hears*, New York: Random House.

Lovegrove, R., Battaglia, J., Dillon, H. and Oong, R. (1992) *Report on Outcomes Assessment Measures for New Clients*, Australian Hearing Services, Sydney.

McCormick, B. (1991) 'Paediatric cochlear implantation in the United Kingdom – a delayed journey on a well marked route', *British Journal of Audiology* 25: 145–149.

Mead, G. H. (1934) *Mind, Self, and Society*, Chicago: University of Chicago Press.

Mylanus, E. A., Cremers, C. W., Snik, A. F. and Van den Berge, N. (1994) 'Clinical results of percutaneous implants in the temporal bone', *Archives of Otolaryngology, Head and Neck Surgery* 120: 81–85.

Noble, W. (1993) 'Meaning and the "discursive ecology": further to the debate on ecological perceptual theory', *Journal for the Theory of Social Behaviour* 23: 375–398.

Noble, W. and Davidson, I. (1996) *Human Evolution, Language and Mind*, Cambridge: Cambridge University Press.

Noble, W. and Hétu, R. (1994) 'An ecological approach to disability and handicap in relation to impaired hearing', *Audiology* 33: 117–126.

Padden, C. and Humphries, T. (1988) *Deaf in America*, Cambridge, MA: Harvard University Press.

Plomp, R. (1994) 'Noise, amplification and compression: considerations of three main issues in hearing aid design', *Ear and Hearing* 15: 2–12.

Ross, M. (1992) 'Implications of audiologic success', *Journal of the American Academy of Audiology* 3: 1–4.

Rutherford, S. D. (1988) 'The culture of American Deaf people', *Sign Language Studies* 59: 129–147.

Sacks, H. (1992) *Lectures on Conversation*, Oxford: Blackwell.

Salomon, G., Vesterager, V. and Jagd, M. (1988) 'Age-related hearing difficulties: I. Hearing impairment, disability and handicap – a controlled study', *Audiology* 27: 164–178.

Selover, P. J. (1988) 'American Sign Language in the high school system', *Sign Language Studies* 59: 205–212.

Stokoe, W. C., Bernard, H. R. and Padden, C. (1976) 'An elite group in deaf society', *Sign Language Studies* 12: 189–210.

Taylor, K. (1993) 'Self-perceived and audiometric evaluations of hearing aid benefit in the elderly', *Ear and Hearing* 14: 390–394.

Thomas, A. J. (1984) *Acquired Hearing Loss: Psychological and Psychosocial Implications*, London: Academic Press.

Vesterager, V., Salomon, G. and Jagd, M. (1988) 'Age-related hearing difficulties: II. Psychological and sociological consequences of hearing problems – a controlled study', *Audiology* 27: 179–192.

Walden, B. E., Demorest, M. E. and Hepler, E. L. (1984) 'Self-report approach to assessing benefit derived from amplification', *Journal of Speech and Hearing Research* 27: 49–56.

Waridel, S. (1993) *Etude qualitative des désavantages psycho-sociaux vécus par des femmes atteintes d'une perte auditive acquise*, Maître d'Orthophonie et d'Audiologie, Université de Montréal.

World Health Organisation (1980) *International Classification of Impairments, Disabilities and Handicaps*, Geneva: WHO.

Yardley, L. (1996) 'Reconciling discursive and materialist perspectives on health and illness: a re-construction of the biopsychosocial approach', *Theory and Psychology* 6: 485–508.

Chapter 6

Disorientation in the (post) modern world

Lucy Yardley

This chapter seeks to develop an 'ecological–constructionist' analysis of the context of disorientation and dizziness. The social constructionist aspect of this analysis is represented by a focus on how discourse and practice have contributed to contemporary conceptualisations and experiences of disorientation. Since medical discourse and practice have a particularly profound influence over the way in which 'health problems' are construed, the first half of the chapter will be devoted principally to a consideration of how complaints of dizziness have been interpreted and managed by medical professionals over the past century. However, medical and scientific discourse is embedded in a wider system of shared meanings and values, and in the second half of the chapter I shall explore some of the metaphoric connotations of orientation and disorientation conveyed in literary and philosophical writings, and contemporary language and culture. Material aspects of disorientation will be addressed by an 'ecological' analysis of the way in which disorientation affects the functional relationship between the individual and their environment. Whereas reductionist physiological explanations for dizziness attempt to isolate the physical from the psychic causes, the ecological perspective reveals that the material and psycho-social aspects of this functional relationship are intimately linked.

Three central issues are considered in this chapter. The first is the problem of mind–body dualism, which is entrenched in the discourse, institutions and practices of medicine, but poses acute social and phenomenological problems for people experiencing disorientation. A second theme is the uncertainty and consequent loss of control which characterises disorientation; this topic is used to demonstrate the parallels and connections between the socio-cultural and physical realms. Third, the individualistic focus of traditional therapeutic approaches to disorientation is contrasted with the ecological–constructionist emphasis on the context of disorientation. In order to construct this alternative account of disorientation, I will draw on very diverse sources of material, ranging from experimental studies of perceptual–motor function to phenomenological explorations of the nature of being. This conscious eclecticism represents an attempt to bring together materialist and linguistic, physical and psycho-social, quantitative and qualitative research on the topic, and to show that all of these can usefully contribute to a multi-layered description of the phenomenon.

In addition, discursive themes and issues identified in the analysis will be illustrated using examples drawn from the discourse of three women who define themselves as suffering from an ambiguous and distressing mixture of physical and mental disequilibrium. For reasons of anonymity, the names of the women have been changed. 'Sally' was referred to me by a doctor for a programme of physical and psychological rehabilitation for disorientation, while 'Clare' was encountered by chance in the course of my work as a lec-turer in medical psychology. Both agreed to a tape-recorded interview which was later transcribed in full. Both had a long history of disorientation, start-ing with severe childhood travel sickness, and had recently received a diag-nosis of organic impairment of the balance system (i.e. vestibular dysfunction). Since vestibular dysfunction is a common and usually tran-sient complaint, this diagnosis does not necessarily fully explain their chron-ic dizziness, and both had also been treated for anxiety. The third woman, 'Elizabeth', wrote me a letter summarising her experiences of vestibular dis-order and anxiety. The excerpts presented are frankly selective, and no attempt is made to assert or assess their generality or typicality; indeed, the texts from which they are taken were chosen precisely because they appeared to address the themes in this chapter in an explicit and interesting manner. However, a variety of studies are referenced in this chapter which provide more conventional evidence that the situation and expressed attitudes of these individuals are not particularly exceptional, and more extensive docu-mentation is provided by my current study of ninety-six transcribed inter-views with a random sample of sufferers (Yardley et al. 1996).

A strictly 'symptom-based' approach is adopted in this analysis, which focuses on the specific phenomenon of disorientation, whether attributed to physical causes (e.g. vestibular dysfunction or travel sickness) or to psycho-logical causes (e.g. anxiety or panic disorder). Numerous investigations have indicated that most people diagnosed as agoraphobic report dizziness as a particularly prominent somatic symptom (e.g. Barlow et al. 1985; Noyes et al. 1987; Schneier et al. 1991), and that agoraphobic behaviour often appears to be triggered by physical illness and/or disorienting environments (e.g. Chambless et al. 1985; Eaton and Keyl 1990; Jacob et al. 1989; Shulman et al. 1994). The places characteristically feared and avoided by people with what has been termed 'situational' agoraphobia (e.g. shopping malls and carparks, lifts and escalators, underground trains and motorways) overlap to a remarkable degree with the environments which people with organic balance disorders find disorienting, and therefore disconcerting (Yardley 1994a). Consequently, there will be many references in this chapter to theories and observations related to the 'agoraphobic' avoidance of disorienting environments. However, these observations are not intended to imply that the complex syndrome or entity known by psychiatrists as 'panic disorder with agoraphobia' is synonymous with disorientation, or can be reduced to or explained by the symptom of disorientation.

DUALIST AND INDIVIDUALIST APPROACHES TO DISORIENTATION

For the past century, explanations for dizziness and disorientation have been characterised by an artificial dichotomy between mental and physical causation. Although early case histories of disorientation noted the frequent co-occurrence of dizziness (sometimes clearly due to organic disorders of the balance system) and situational panic or agoraphobia (Freud 1924: 82; Gordon 1986; Guye 1899), a holistic approach to the problem was incompatible with the growing institutional differentiation and competition between the disciplines of physical medicine and psychiatry (and later psychology). Around this time, physiologists were expanding their understanding of how the biomechanics and pathology of the vestibular system could contribute to perceptions and illusions of movement (e.g. Barany 1907), while Freud and his followers were developing an appreciation of how psychic disturbance could be manifested in somatic symptoms (e.g. Freud 1924). Since then, each discipline has continued to elaborate a distinct system of aetiological explanation and diagnosis, with the result that complaints of disorientation now elicit entirely different patterns of treatment, depending on whether they are attributed to a somatic or psychic cause.

The somatic model

If a physiological disorder is suspected, much effort is devoted to seeking evidence of physiological dysfunction and the patient may undergo a lengthy process of examination and testing for the purpose of differential diagnosis (e.g. Jacobson et al. 1993; Linstrom 1992; Sharpe and Barber 1993). This emphasis on diagnosis is reflected in medical textbooks and articles on 'vertigo' (the medical term for an illusion of movement) and its management, in which 80–90 per cent of the text is typically devoted to aetiology and diagnostic procedures (e.g. Linstrom 1992; McCormick et al. 1992; Sharpe and Barber 1993). However, owing to the multiplicity, subtlety and complexity of the causes of disorientation, a definite organic diagnosis is often elusive and treatment ineffective (McCormick et al. 1992; Sullivan et al. 1993). The consequence can be an indefinitely prolonged state of uncertainty and impotence, since in the meantime the patient has no means of managing their condition other than to comply with treatment. As the search for a physical pathology and cure becomes more protracted and frustrating, the likelihood increases that a diagnosis of 'psychogenic' dizziness will be assigned by default, generally followed by 'routine reassurance' but no offer of psychological treatment (M. R. Clark et al. 1994; McCormick et al. 1992).

Many people complaining of disorientation welcome the somatic approach, since a physical diagnosis not only provides social legitimation of their complaint and protection against allegations of moral or emotional weakness (Locker 1981; Pollock 1993; Stacey 1986), but also offers the hope and reassurance that the underlying cause of the dizziness can be identified and controlled by medical science. However, disillusionment with this type of management can ensue once the limitations of the somatic model become apparent. Sally describes the uncertainty and frustration which result when the somatic model is adopted, but proves unable to provide definite confirmation or exclusion of a physical problem, effective physical treatment, or adequate reassurance, information and advice:

> He [the medical specialist] put me through a CAT scan and a caloric test which I vomited violently to. X-rays, hearing tests – my hearing is supposed to be fine. He did all those tests and he said he really couldn't say what it was. He couldn't give me an exact diagnosis. He put me on [betahistine], which did nothing, and I am the kind of person I have got to feel I am doing something constructive otherwise I don't think it is going to sort itself out, I have got to do something. So I tried that, and I left it a couple of years because he said, 'A couple of years and it should compensate'. So I waited a couple of years and it didn't compensate. So I went back to him, I pushed to see him and he sent me through most of the tests again. . . . In all the tests put together I was slightly off the range. Only by 1 per cent, 2 per cent, in sort of worrying areas. There was obviously a problem there so it did prove physically something. But the next time it was more within the regular range. They couldn't even say to me 100 per cent 'No, you haven't got a tumour'. Nobody would commit themselves 100 per cent and say you are OK. . . . I came away feeling, 'Nobody seems able to help me. They have washed their hands of me. They can't give me a specific diagnosis, therefore what can I do?' Whereas if I have as much knowledge as possible then maybe I can do more about it.

The psychic model

Patients whose complaints of disorientation are referred to a psychiatrist or psychologist encounter a corresponding determination to identify a psychosocial aetiology. Freud (1924) was among the early clinicians who noted that agoraphobia often developed following attacks of vertigo with accompanying anxiety, but he claimed that vertigo was caused by unsatisfactory sex (due to the practice of 'coitus interruptus'), while mild chronic dizziness was due to masturbation. Freud and other psychoanalysts later suggested

that agoraphobia might be caused by a fear of temptation and desire in public places, or could be a defence against anxiety (Snaith 1968). Weiss (1935)
likened the open squares which can provoke phobia to the castrated mother
(thus explaining the instinct to place statues and fountains in squares), and
interpreted fear of going down streets or tunnels as a manifestation of the
female castration complex – a symbolic expression of the inability to pene-
trate the vagina (i.e. tunnel). Katan argues that the street can play a number
of symbolic roles in agoraphobia: 'Thus street and bridge would symbolize
the penis at one phase of the treatment of my woman patient, and at a later
period would mean the bedroom, and street traffic would then equal
parental intercourse' (1951: 49).

In more recent times, attacks of dizziness and nausea believed to be of
psychogenic origin are most likely to be attributed to panic, and traced to
catastrophic interpretations of physical sensations, 'anxiety sensitivity' or
'fear of fear', and/or a psychophysiological propensity to over-arousal and
hyperventilation (Chambless and Gracely 1989; Clark 1986; Klein and
Gorman 1987; McNally and Lorenz 1987). The therapist may also explore
the relationship of feelings of disorientation in public places to lack of independence, or anxiety about the possibility of physical danger (Beck 1985;
Goldstein and Chambless 1978).

In contrast to the physical treatments for disorientation, some psychological therapies have the potential to empower the individual by supporting
efforts to understand and deal with their beliefs and feelings about disorientation. However, this advantage is partly undermined if clients are first
implicitly required to discount the subjective reality of their own sensations
of dizziness and physical imbalance – particularly if these appear to persist
even when a positive mental attitude has been achieved. Moreover, admission that there is a psychological element to the disorientation tends to result
in any physical aspects being overlooked:

> Clare   If you tell them [the doctors] you get panic attacks, they'll look
> at you a bit strange, they'll think the rest of your symptoms are all
> just psychosomatic, (*sarcastically*) which is just fine, and they'll just
> refer you to a counsellor or whatever and put you on tranquillisers.

All three women quoted in this chapter had been prescribed psychoactive
medication, which they rejected quite quickly as undesirable and ineffective.
All had also tried various psychological therapies, which were only partially
successful. Sally and Clare found it difficult to decide whether to attribute
the limited success of psychological therapy to only partial psychological
recovery, or to an unresolved physical problem:

> Sally   Well, I am trying to do various therapies and things, generally
> only trying to sort this stuff out, emotional stuff out, and up until I
> came here [specialist hospital where she was given diagnosis of

vestibular disorder] I wasn't sure how much was anxiety. So it is general therapy, and hoping that as a result of that that I wouldn't have as many physical symptoms of things like the vertigo. . . . I don't think anything helped the dizziness because I haven't sorted any of it out. Well, not enough of it anyway. Obviously, I have changed a lot, but I haven't come to a point where I can say, 'Yes, I feel OK', 'No'. So it is hard for me to determine how much the dizziness has been affected.

Clare   [talking about most recent psychological therapy of six tried] It's a humanistic sort of therapy, she's not so much like the other ones, it's not very clinical, I feel she's more like a friend. We sort of – yeah – my panic attacks have improved slightly so, I mean, I know how to (actually, I don't) but I mean, in certain circumstances I don't know how to cope with them and some I do . . .

Interviewer   Is it helping with the dizziness?

Clare   Hmm. No. No, no, no. I mean, the dizziness is a result of panicking or the travel sickness, and that doesn't go away, so nothing is going to help that basically.

The psychosomatic versus somatopsychic debate

Each of the unidimensional (somatic and psychic) approaches has undoubtedly contributed significantly to our present understanding of the experience of disorientation, and a unidimensional therapy can have a successful outcome in cases where a simple and remediable physical or psychological cause can be identified. However, the reduction of disorientation to purely physical or wholly psychological factors presents many individuals with an artificial forced choice between the somatic and psychic models, with the result that important aspects of their experience remain unexplained and untreated. Converging evidence from psychologists and psychiatrists, neurologists and otolaryngologists, points to an extensive covariance between symptoms of organic balance system dysfunction and signs of anxiety, panic and agoraphobia (e.g. D. B. Clark et al. 1994; Eagger et al. 1992; Jacob et al. 1989; Sullivan et al. 1993; Yardley et al. 1995). Yet this research is often simply interpreted as evidence of co-morbidity, and our cultural tradition of dualist thinking, combined with the socio-historical division between physical and mental health care, perpetuates the theoretical segregation of the somatic and psychic aspects of disorientation. Indeed, research on psychological factors in disorientation can too easily degenerate into an attempt to establish the proportion of cases of dizziness which are 'organic' rather than 'psychogenic', or a debate about whether psychological problems are the cause or the consequence of symptoms of physical disorientation. These questions are far from neutral in terms of their moral implications; deviations from normal behaviour for which no somatic explanation is provided inevitably carry a social penalty, since psychological problems are considered less 'real' and more blameworthy than physical deficits (Pollock 1993).

The contradictions and uncertainties produced by the opposition between somatic and psychic models of disorientation are manifest in the way in which Clare explains her disorientation:

> I think that maybe it stems from the fact that I get travel sickness a lot, or motion sickness. Anything I ride on I feel sick, and then it goes on to nausea, and I get panic attacks, so I get dizzy spells and palpitations and everything that goes along with that . . . I couldn't like tell the difference between the nausea and the dizziness, it's very difficult to tell the difference between those two things, so when I said dizziness it sort of meant nausea, and the nausea sort of meant my stomach (so they fixed my stomach) but obviously I'd feel dizzy from my panic attacks.

In a penetrating analysis of the partly analogous phenomenon of chronic pain, Jackson (1994) notes that the dualist conception of physical sensations as emotionally neutral deprives sufferers of a language to convey their experience of pain (or here, dizziness) as a state of both physical *and* emotional distress. The inability to define or communicate the experience further contributes to their distress, and so they are forced to resort to the unsatisfactory discourses available to them in order to (mis)represent their problem to themselves and to others.

Another effect of the somatic versus psychic debate is to create a compelling incentive for sufferers to validate their complaints with 'objective' evidence that their disorientation is associated with physical impairment or disability. In the first excerpt from Sally's account, she stresses that the tests 'did prove physically something'. Elizabeth opens her account of disorientation with the authentication of a physical diagnosis, backed up by descriptions of physical disability:

> I suffered what was diagnosed as severe viral labyrinthitis last year which incapacitated me to such an extent that I was not able even to turn over in bed without total loss of balance. Obviously I couldn't walk, felt too nauseous to eat, losing two stones in weight, and spent months suffering dreadful vertigo. A brain scan and hospital tests revealed nothing.
>
> About three weeks into the illness I began suffering anxiety attacks. I became frightened to sit up, to move, to eat and even walk. I saw a psychiatrist who diagnosed general anxiety and I was put on Librium and then anti-depressants, neither of which I am taking now. I have been receiving stress counselling . . .
>
> Still when I walk or stand I feel off balance, and my body literally locks with fear. When I walk along the road the sensation is as though I

am walking on a tightrope. I'm making myself take two 'drunken' walks a day in the hope my body will finally get the message that it's not that bad!

I take on board all the advice I've had about stress and anxiety management which have helped me to cope. But at the end of the day, if I could improve my balance I know the anxiety would go. . . . At one stage I began to think I had simply inherited my mother's anxiety, then I began to agree with the 'experts' that it was all down to stress. They're factors but I'm sure there is more to it and I know my lack of balance is the key.

Elizabeth's letter explicitly highlights the extent to which her conceptualisation of disorientation was influenced by 'expert' opinion, but the accounts of the other women are also permeated by terminology and debates which seem to echo the dualist concepts and concerns of the 'expert' models. For example, when asked what she believed to be the causes of dizziness, Clare entered into a disquisition which clearly reflects the psychic versus somatic debate:

Stress. And also, I read in a book recently that 90 per cent of phobias, whatever, come from the disorders of the middle, inner ear, whatever, and I was reading this book and it's really interesting, and I think maybe they do, because lots of instances where I feel dizzy have nothing to do with my being scared of anything, or, you know, I'm feeling perfectly relaxed when I'm feeling dizzy so it can't be my, you know, [anxiety]. . . . You see the danger is, I'd like to say that it's a disorder of the inner ear but that's, because, people when they're not feeling well they want to attribute it to something that is physical, that gives a sort of explanation or an excuse for something that is maybe within you. And so maybe it's an excuse, I don't know, but I believe in it. . . . I'm sure it's got a lot to do with the mind too though, because I know that if I'm really happy or something I don't think about my dizziness.

By openly entertaining the possibility that the dizziness is due to anxiety, these women attempt to demonstrate a rationality and open-mindedness which anticipates, and itself seems to refute, any tacit accusation that they may be emotionally unbalanced. A similar discursive function is served by Elizabeth's candid admission that she had developed anxiety attacks (*after* the onset of dizziness), and by the avowals made by all the women that they accepted and benefited to some extent from psychological therapy – and yet still remained symptomatic. In addition, Elizabeth maintains her psychosocial integrity by distancing herself from her weak body, emphasising that it is her *body* that 'locks with fear' and must be persuaded that 'it's not that bad'. Both Sally (see first quotation) and Elizabeth are eager to stress their socially laudable determination to 'do something constructive' about their problem. But while one function of these women's accounts must naturally have been to construct a defensible social position, they also seem to express a profound and uncomfortable subjective uncertainty about how best to characterise and hence proceed with their disorientation. This is revealed by the incessant oscillation between the somatic and psychic models, which is linked to the issue of how the problem of disorientation can be controlled. For example, despite her fervent desire to be provided with a definitive categorisation, Sally expressed ambiguous feelings about which model was preferable:

> I know dizziness, vertigo, whatever, can obviously, a lot of people believe it can be caused by deep-rooted hang-ups and all this sort of thing. It has just been diminished really, 'As long as you sort your head out you will be alright'. . . . I wanted someone to tell me, someone who knew to say to me 100 per cent, 'This is what it is, this is what is causing your dizziness. This is what it is, this is anxiety.' As long as I know, if it is physical. All I wanted was an answer and so nobody, before I came here anyway, had said to me for sure, so I just kept pushing, I pushed as far as I can go. And in some ways I kind of feel, you know, when you said, 'It probably is mainly physical', relief partly, but on the other hand, I almost wanted it to be purely anxiety, because there are things I can do about it, there wouldn't be a physical problem (as opposed to a psychological problem) which could be permanent.

The dilemma faced by these women is whether to position themselves as a passive and defective body in the hands of the doctors, or to try to assert a more constructive role – which also entails embracing personal responsibility (and blame) for their apparent weakness, and their inability to meet social expectations for emotional and physical competence and self-control. The purpose of the ecological–constructionist analysis developed in the second half of this chapter is to offer a radically different perspective on disorientation, which invalidates this dilemma by challenging both the dualism of the mind–body dichotomy, and the individualistic emphasis on personal (physical or mental) deficiencies.

AN ECOLOGICAL–CONSTRUCTIONIST ANALYSIS OF DISORIENTATION

The phenomenology of disorientation

Disorientation is not an internal state, like pain, but arises in the course of interactions between an individual and their environment. Someone who feels disoriented is uncertain about their relationship to the environment, and hence their capacity to act appropriately. It is therefore possible to avoid disorientation – but only at the unacceptable cost of abandoning attempts to interact with the environment. The following analysis examines the parallels and links between the psycho-social and perceptual–motor aspects of this debilitating state of uncertainty and helplessness.

The visual, somatosensory and vestibular systems are all involved in the perception of orientation and self-motion. Disorientation occurs whenever there appears to be ambiguity or incongruence in the perceptual information detected by the three systems (Brandt and Daroff 1979). This may be provoked by physiological dysfunction; for example, impairment of one of the vestibular organs generally leads to some degree of transient disorientation. Alternatively, the disorientation may be linked to some perceptually unusual or confusing attribute of the physical environment (Crampton 1990), such as the strange vertical motion of the 'ground' on board a ship or in an elevator, or the illusion of self-motion associated with large-scale movement of the visual scene – for instance, at the cinema, or when watching flowing water, passing traffic, or moving crowds (Yardley 1994a).

Perceptual disorientation is inevitably accompanied by some degree of physical incompetence, since without accurate knowledge of orientation and self-motion it is impossible to properly control posture or accomplish any kind of co-ordinated activity. A vestibular disorder may therefore not only produce a strong sensation that the world is spinning around, but may also reduce an adult's confident upright gait to staggering, falling, crawling, or even complete immobility (as well as triggering a host of ancillary symptoms ranging from sweating and nausea to vomiting). Heights and wide open spaces can elicit a milder degree of perceptual disorientation and a less dramatic increase in postural instability (Brandt et al. 1980; Bles et al. 1980). At the level of perceptual–motor functioning, this is because vision is normally utilised to control the constant, minute postural adjustments necessary to maintain balance. Even a slight forward sway results in a perceptible looming of nearby surfaces, but when looking into the horizontal or vertical distance the movement of the visual scene resulting from a small degree of body sway is below the threshold for detection. This creates a perceptually ambiguous situation in which an increased level of sway is detected (and controlled) by means of the somatosensory and vestibular systems, but the visual system does not register self-motion.

Although the preceding brief account of some perceptual–motor factors contributing to disorientation focuses on the material aspects of dizziness and postural control, it differs in important respects from reductionist, materialistic explanations for disorientation. A key difference is that the ecological account characterises disorientation as arising at the interface between the individual and their environment, whereas reductionist analyses typically attempt to pinpoint unitary physical causes of disorientation, located either inside the individual (i.e. physiological impairment) or in the environment (i.e. sensory stimuli). Disorders and environments which predispose to disorientation can certainly be identified, but it has not proved possible to establish an exact correspondence between internal or external 'stimuli' and the 'response' of disorientation. The interactive, functional nature of disorientation cannot be reduced to such simple, physical cause–effect relations. The extent to which an individual with a particular degree of vestibular impairment experiences disorientation will depend upon whether they are attempting to move vigorously, and whether they are in a familiar or perceptually unusual environment. Similarly, the potentially disorienting features of a certain environment may be entirely negated by the perceptual–motor skills, experience or activities of a particular individual (Yardley 1992); for example, the orienting skills of athletes and dancers help them to tolerate and counteract the disorienting effects of artificial vestibular stimulation. Indeed, it is only through activity that the disorientation produced by a vestibular disorder can ultimately be overcome. If activities which initially provoke dizziness (e.g. head movements, which stimulate the vestibular system) are repeated then central adaptation occurs and the symptoms gradually subside – in just the same way that sailors eventually conquer seasickness and gain their 'sealegs' after prolonged exposure to the motion of the sea. The prolonged mild disorientation which commonly follows vestibular disorder in Western populations may therefore be partly a product of our relatively sedentary modern lifestyle; in former times the luxury of avoiding vigorous activity (and thereby indefinitely retarding adaptation) was not an option. Persistent vertigo may also be maintained by cultural conventions which discourage adults from engaging in the activities which children still naturally employ to develop their orientation capabilities, constantly hopping and dancing, swinging around lamp-posts, turning somersaults, or balancing on narrow walls.

By placing the emphasis on dynamic relations rather than essential causes, the ecological account thus provides a description of material functioning which is compatible with, and complementary to, phenomenological and social constructionist analyses. In a reductionist materialistic account, psychosocial factors can only play a secondary role as responses to a physically determined level of disorientation. But if activities and environments are central to the generation (and amelioration or prevention) of disorientation, then the psychosocial aspects of these activities and environments assume a fundamental aetiological significance. This is no simple psycho-somatic or somato-psychic relationship, but a profound and intricate interactive bond between the material and discursive aspects of disorientation, which creates and reproduces the condition and preconditions, meaning and implications of disorientation.

Disorientation disrupts the relationship between self and environment at such a fundamental level that it can undermine the basis for meaningful activity. Grisby and Johnston (1989) have described the 'depersonalisation' and feelings of unreality that can be provoked by vestibular disorder, while Skelton-Roberts (cited in Fewtrell and O'Connor 1994) found that nearly half of a sample of individuals identified as suffering from depersonalisation reported dizziness or vertigo. Shaffer (1979: 79) has characterised disorientation as a '"primal terror" – the fundamental emotional experience with the ability to naturally maintain one's balance in opposition to gravity and to integrate vestibular input'. He suggests that childhood experiences of disorientation (for example, learning to ride a bike) may have a comparable impact to early experiences of overwhelming sexual or destructive impulses. In literature, the term vertigo is used not only to describe reactions to abrupt discontinuities in perceptual–motor experience (for example, when entering the virtual realm of 'cyberspace' in the books of William Gibson), but also as a symbol for states of radical uncertainty, and even the complete loss of self-identity. For instance, in 'The approach to Al-Mu'tasim' (1991) Borges writes that in the quest for enlightenment, it is necessary to traverse a mythic sea named 'Vertigo', which precedes a final sea called 'Annihilation'.

Phenomenological and philosophical analyses of the meaning of disorientation consistently identify vertigo as the experience of incoherence and irrationality associated with an existential apprehension of the multiple possibilities for being (or, worse still, not-being) which we must confront. In his analysis of (height) vertigo in *Being and Nothingness* (1986: 29–32), Sartre argues that although vertigo first announces itself as a fearful awareness of the arbitrary and destructive power of external forces (e.g. that the earth at the edge of the precipice might crumble), the defence against this fear is to attempt to exert control (e.g. to take special care in walking). Yet the thought that one *ought* to act in a certain way simultaneously implies the awareness that one *might not* act in that way. Thus, the state of vertigo and anguish stems from awareness of the indeterminate gulf between the present and future self, and uncertainty about one's own future behaviour. In her analysis of addiction, Ronell draws on Heidegger to make a very similar point; 'the experience of Being-possible is an experience of total powerlessness – powerlessness or fascination, or heady vertigo' (1989: 44). The state of vertigo is also a recurrent theme in Lyotard's *Libidinal Economy* (1993). Again, vertigo is interpreted as the joint reaction of mind and body to the awareness of multiple possibilities – or rather, according to Lyotard, the multiple 'incompossibilities' which unitary concepts or entities are unable to contain.

Since disorientation entails doubt about the relationship between self and environment, the context of disorientation is clearly crucial to the experience. In the following section I will consider the ways in which the phenomenological experience of disorientation may be shaped by the compound influence of its material and discursive context.

The context of disorientation

Loss of control is not well countenanced in modern Western society, which is imbued with the ideal of individual autonomy, and the desire to rise above and subdue nature (Gordon 1988). This preoccupation with individual control is reflected in attitudes to health, in particular our readiness to assign personal responsibility, first for the social sin of becoming ill, and then for the social duty of overcoming the effects of illness (Radley 1993). It is also reflected in attitudes to control of the body (Scheper-Hughes and Lock 1987). The dominant view in our culture is that 'a morally upright life begins with, and is inseparable from, a balanced, upright posture: a body standing upright, firm and steady in its gait' (Levin 1985: 270). This attitude to postural control is embedded in our very language (Lakoff and Johnson 1980); in the uniformly positive metaphoric connotations of the terms 'rise', 'upstanding', 'unbowed', 'erect', and the negative associations of 'crawl', 'prostrate', 'brought low' and 'fallen'. Indeed, vertigo is indexed in *Roget's Thesaurus of English Words and Phrases* (Kirkpatrick 1987) as part of a cluster of terms which includes not only 'illness' but also 'weakness', 'impotence', and 'inadequacy'.

People prone to disorientation are intensely aware of the normative expectations for control, and consequently learn particularly to fear and avoid any situation in which their weakness might be betrayed. Being seen to lose control is cited by sufferers from disorientation as a major concern and the reason for a coping strategy of 'phobic' avoidance and self-imposed restriction of activity (Pollard and Frank 1990; Telch et al. 1989; Yardley 1994b). For example, asked about the reactions to her disorientation of family and friends, Clare's response centred almost entirely around anticipated and perceived stigmatisation:

Interviewer   How did your family react at all?

Clare   No, they were sympathetic but not very understanding. I mean, obviously if you had not experienced it, you can't really understand what it feels like, so they couldn't understand what it was. I mean, it's easy for someone to tell you to relax, but to actually do it is different. I mean, they tried, but after a while it seemed like they were a bit annoyed. . . . 'Oh, it's all in your mind, it's your imagination, you should relax,' basically that I was a hypochondriac basically, in short.

Interviewer   And how about friends and so on?

Clare   Again, I didn't tell a lot of my friends when I was suffering, or a lot of people. I didn't tell, I was very quiet about it, every time I was having a panic attack I would be looking normal, but feeling very tense inside, so a lot of people didn't know. But the people that did know would ask me 'How are you?' basically everybody would tell me to relax, which didn't help. . . . They wouldn't like – I guess

> the bottom line is you don't want to look weak, or you don't want
> to look like you're suffering in any way. You want to seem, I don't –
> yeah that's what it is, you don't want them to disapprove of what
> you're feeling, because people don't tend to like people that are not
> fine, and also they get, people (I find) get uncomfortable, they don't
> know how to react when someone is in that state, so – you don't.

The modern Western emphasis on maintaining control is not dominant in
all cultures. For instance, Douglas (1970) describes a tribe where possession
by the tribal divinity was traditionally signalled by shaking and staggering
around in a giddy trance. Significantly, it was only when a member of this
tribe converted to Christianity that that individual became afraid of fainting
and falling down during the sacrifice to the divinity. Indeed, even within
Western society there are sub-cultures which celebrate loss of mental and
physical control, explored through such media as trance-like music and
dance, fun-fair rides and perceptually confusing visual displays, and drugs
which alter perceptions and consciousness. Transgressing the boundaries of
control forms a popular theme of 'alternative' or 'youth' cultures, and is
sometimes self-consciously justified by reference to other cultures in which
altered states have been valued and respected. For example, the band self-
styled 'The Shamen' draw on the work of the author Terence McKenna to
define the role of the shaman as a beneficent 'agent of evolution' who uses
psychedelic drugs to 'dissolve boundaries' in order to achieve higher states
of awareness and knowledge:

> a shaman is someone who has . . . risen outside, above, beyond the
> dimensions of ordinary space–time . . . stepped outside the confines of
> learned culture, and of learned and embedded language, into the domain
> of what Wittgenstein called 'the unspeakable', the transcendental pres-
> ence of the other.
>
> (Lyrics from the 1992 hit single *Re-Evolution*)

The theme of transgressing the limits of normality is often explicitly linked
with the state of disorientation. For example, the long-running adult comic
book series titled 'Vertigo' is devoted to the hyper-real imaginative worlds of
magic, science fiction, and horror, while the 'Vertigo' record label markets
techno music, characterised by rapid repetitive rhythmic beats which are
designed to encourage and support a dance-induced euphoric high, as the
following description explicitly acknowledges: 'the epitome of techno is the
frenetic, overwhelming blur of NOW rushing through the body, the moment
just before launching yourself over vertiginous waterfalls of abandonment'
(*New Musical Express*, 10 December 1994, p. 33).

This affirmative attitude to loss of control is espoused by only a small
section of the Western population (who are frequently vilified by the majority), and hence disorientation is sanctioned only in extremely restricted con-

texts, such as at a fairground, 'rave' or festival. Moreover, there are clearly important differences between disorientation which is deliberately self-induced, whether by dance, drugs or dazzling displays, and sudden attacks of vertigo and dizziness which were neither anticipated nor desired. Nevertheless, these cross-cultural comparisons serve to illustrate that the negative experience of disorientation may be partly culture-specific, in so far as it is created by the predominant modern Western terror of failing to maintain self-control.

To the extent that disorientation is implicated in agoraphobia, evidence for partial cultural specificity is provided by two studies which suggest that agoraphobia has a much lower incidence in India than in Western society (Chambers et al. 1986; Raguram and Bhide 1985), and is restricted mainly to well-educated middle-class urban males. Of course, *many* cultural and material differences are likely to have influenced the observed difference in the incidence of diagnoses of agoraphobia in India and in Britain; for example, the gender bias may be attributable to the norm that Indian women are not generally expected to leave the home. In the cultural production of agoraphobia, changes in social mores may be linked with changes in diagnostic and therapeutic practices. A sociological explanation for the appearance of agoraphobia in the Western world in the late nineteenth century has been proposed by de Swaan (1981), whose account explains the link with dependence on the family and fear of sexual temptation suggested by many psychotherapists. He notes that in the early part of the nineteenth century the woman's domesticity was an indication of her husband's social, economic and erotic status; bourgeois women were therefore virtually prohibited from going alone into the streets, which were depicted as thronged by uncouth destitutes who might threaten or seduce her. This explains how the street may have become the focus for repressed fears and sexual fantasies. However, when social restrictions on women's liberty were eased later in the century, the lack of independence which had formerly been encouraged was medicalised by the emerging therapeutic professions as a sign of anxiety.

Further evidence for cultural diversity in the significance of disorientation is provided by Low (1994), who has documented how the meaning of 'nervios' (a syndrome in which dizziness is a prominent symptom) varies in different regions of Costa Rica. In urban Costa Rica, complaints such as 'I lost myself' or 'I could not tell where I was, I was so dizzy and confused' articulate the disorientation caused by dislocation of traditional social ties, and function as a plea for social support. However, in rural Costa Rica *nervios* expresses the distress of mind and body caused by chronic poverty, hunger and exhaustion. Interpreted from a fatalistic perspective, the experience of being out of control is characterised as a physical state triggered by the inevitable stresses of life, thus absolving both sufferer and others of guilt for the condition. In contrast, in the English-speaking Caribbean *nervios* is stigmatised as a lack of balance, attributable to excesses such as emotionality or alcohol abuse.

Some authors identify modernism with the rhetoric of control, and postmodernism with the rhetoric of disorientation. For example, Smith writes that selfhood is at risk from a 'postmodern orientation . . . [which] is dizzy and disoriented' (1994: 408), while Michael (1994) suggests that the modern self is discrete, controlled and has a powerful sense of place, whereas the postmodern experience is one of fragmentation, radical discontinuity, and dislocation in time and space. Yet this is an over-simplification, since there are tensions and contradictions within (post) modern capitalist society which give rise to the simultaneous creation of a tendency towards fragmentation and a need for control. Lyotard notes that the rigid rules and categories that modernism and capitalism attempt to impose can simply serve to intensify the experience of incompatible being; hence, 'the strictest theoretical articulation may give rise to vertiginous passages, and capital in its very rigidity may give rise to jouissance' (1993: 258). An opposite perspective is offered by Sampson (1981), who argues that there is an invidious inverse relationship between rhetorical demands for self-control and the potential for real control. Indeed, he asserts that the growth in society's demands for self-control parallels a decrease in the possibility of material control by the individual, upholding the social order by promoting virtual (i.e. mental) rather than material change as the solution to dissatisfaction. Douglas also draws attention to the close link between social control of the individual and a normative ideal of self-control, commenting that 'the full possibilities of abandoning conscious control are only available to the extent that the social system relaxes its control on the individual' (1970: 110).

Some of the earliest analysts of modern capitalism, in particular Georg Simmel and Walter Benjamin, highlighted the way in which modern spaces and technologies frequently combine physical and social dislocation. Benjamin noted that forms of mass transport such as trains, and mass gatherings such as the world exhibitions and the Parisian arcades, create an entirely novel social situation in which the individual is exposed to the gaze of numerous strangers (Frisby 1985). In these new environments:

> Shopping ceases to be a quick visit down the street amidst neighbours and becomes a more organised expedition into more anonymous public spaces where certain standards of dress and appearance are deemed appropriate. The individual is increasingly on display as he/she moves through a field of commodities on display.
>
> (Featherstone 1991: 173)

Likewise, Langman (1991) suggests that, in modern capitalist society, basic emotions such as existential anxiety are translated into a failure of consumption, while successful impression management becomes the equivalent of moral integrity in a world where functional relations with strangers must not be disrupted by subjective feelings. According to this view, the shopping mall falls within Goffman's definition of a 'total institution' – a concentration camp where the chains are forged of commodities and control is exerted by the glance of other shoppers. In combination with the self-consciousness and alienation caused by proximity to strangers, the bright colours and lighting, the constant movement and novelty, produce heightened arousal and a dream-like state of derealisation. Although this enhanced level of stimulation can be experienced as enjoyable entertainment, Simmel observed that:

> Here [in the city] in buildings and in educational institutions, in the wonders and comforts of space-conquering technique, in the formations of social life and in the concrete institutions of the state is to be found such a tremendous richness of crystallizing, depersonalized cultural accomplishments that the personality can, so to speak, scarcely maintain itself in the face of it.
>
> (Simmel 1971: 338)

Indeed, Simmel suggested that agoraphobia was a modern pathology resulting from an inability to cope with this level of stimulation, or to maintain the inner barriers of intellectual detachment – even callousness – needed to cope with constant exposure to strangers.

These situations have, from the first, typically incorporated passive motion of the body and/or perceptually confusing visuo-spatial characteristics: large edifices constructed from iron and glass; huge painted panoramas and photographic montages designed to *trompe l'œil*; moving stairways and lifts (which were first employed in exhibitions and department stores). The trend towards the creation of ever more perceptually confusing environments has continued in more recent times. In large supermarkets, hotels and shopping malls, perception of orientation in space is perturbed by the multilevel open layout, with its heights and vistas, reflecting surfaces and moving crowds, escalators and transparent elevators. In modern wide-screen cinemas a silent and immobile audience is effectively captured by the torrent of perpetually moving visual images, while the advent of 'virtual reality' technology promises a more completely absorbing illusion, and a form of motion sickness hitherto experienced only by pilots training in flight simulators. Driving on fast, busy roads is a task which demands accurate perception and complete control, yet the strong and unusual motion cues produced by rapid accelerations and constant velocities, the bright, flowing road markings or stream of passing lights, can provoke perceptual confusion and motion sickness not only in children but also in people with marginally deficient orientation capabilities (Page and Gresty 1985). The safer alternative is to become a passenger on trains, buses and planes, but always at the cost of submitting to increased social scrutiny and a further loss of control over one's environment, identity and destiny.

The discursive and material aspects of this progressive transformation of the modern world are inextricably linked. Elevators and escalators were introduced partly for the functional purpose of controlling movement of public, but were also appreciated as a way of providing entertainment and crowd display (Benjamin 1978; Pursell 1994). Moreover, such public and passive forms of self-motion have far-reaching implications for the way in which we construe ourselves; while individuals submit to the physical manipulation of their bodies, they are enjoying (or enduring) a form of commodification which alienates them from themselves and others, and simultaneously couples their living bodies to the inorganic world. As Kvale has observed:

> The labyrinthine and self-reflecting postmodern space, as in the new hotels, makes it difficult for the body to be oriented in space. This post-modern space may be seen as a symbol of the inability of consciousness to grasp the larger, global, multinational and decentralized communication networks of a postmodern society.
>
> (Kvale 1992: 39)

Hence the (post) modern world is characterised by spaces and activities which are fundamentally alienating and disorienting, and which simultaneously impose passivity and demand self-control. The chronic impotence associated with disorientation can therefore be understood as a phenomenon which is maintained by socially constructed imperatives and environments. The individual suffering from dizziness is trapped between the rhetoric of modernity and the experience of postmodernity; on the one hand, the exhortation to maintain self-control and, on the other, an environment in which it is difficult to exert control.

CONCLUDING COMMENTS

In this chapter I have tried to show how the material and discursive aspects of disorientation can be considered in inter-relation. In order to do so I have sampled and intercalated very different types of research: sociological analyses of modernity and psychophysical studies of postural control; questionnaire surveys of symptomatology in panic disorder and phenomenological interpretations of the meaning of vertigo; psychoanalytic explanations for phobia and cross-cultural comparisons of attitudes to disorientation. While this approach provides a welcome liberation from the constraints of any single perspective, one major disadvantage of such eclecticism is that within the space of a short chapter it is impossible to begin to do justice to the epistemological, methodological or empirical intricacies of any of the diverse forms of research which are cited. Some may find the apparently cursory and superficial nature of the resulting analysis unsatisfactory, and the abrupt shifts in theoretical perspective disorienting. My justification is that it may sometimes be useful to try to distinguish the wood from the trees – to step back and take a broad, imaginative view of a topic. The ample reference list is intended to allow the interested but sceptical reader to determine for her or himself the plausibility or insubstantiality of the foundations on which this account of disorientation has been constructed.

Of course, the particular perspective on disorientation I have presented above is only one of many that could provide valid and interesting insights. To give just one example, an equally compelling and relevant story could be told about the role of arousal: the sociological and psychophysiological reasons why some people seek out both vestibular and social stimulation and revel in sensations of danger and abandon, while others fear and avoid arousing situations; the neuroanatomical links between vestibular and autonomic centres in the brainstem; and the symbolic implications of reaching for the 'dizzy heights', whether of metaphysical awareness or social ambition, and whether by climbing mountains or taking drugs. The aim of this particular illustration was simply to show that a rich, multi-layered understanding may be attained by simultaneously exploring several interlinked aspects of the phenomenon.

A second legitimate concern of many people working in the field of health and illness will relate to the practical utility of this account – whether it can actually benefit people with disorientation. My belief is that an ecological–constructionist approach to disorientation could help to alleviate their experience in two ways. First, the emphasis on the intimate links between the physical and psychological aspects of the experience is intended to encourage a shift in clinical focus away from the futile debate about primary aetiology and towards a more potentially fruitful examination of how both aspects of disorientation might be simultaneously addressed by therapy (see Yardley and Luxon 1994; Yardley and Hallam 1996). The second function of an ecological–constructionist analysis is to show that many of the problems attributed to the individual sufferer can be seen as wider problems of society, manifested both in attitudes, social relations and the constructed environment. Accordingly, it may be necessary not only to determine whether features of the immediate context of the individual (e.g. occupational demands, family expectations) are contributing to their difficulties, but also to consider what preventative measures can be implemented at the level of society at large. These might include: disseminating information about disorientation in order to reduce the ignorance, passivity and stigma associated with it; publicising the concept and value of adult perceptual–motor 'fitness' as a supplement to the more familiar notions of cardiovascular and muscular–skeletal fitness; providing socially and physically safe therapeutic micro-environments to support the exploration requisite to overcoming uncertainty and disorientation; advising town-planners and designers on how to minimise the alienating and disorienting aspects of new buildings and forms of transport; and, perhaps most importantly, contributing to a discourse which highlights the reciprocity between mind and body, and questions the origin, function and consequences of the modern capitalist obsession with self-control.

REFERENCES

Barany, R. (1907) *Physiologie und Pathologie des Bogengangsapparates beim Menschen*, Vienna: Deuticke.

Barlow, D. H., Vermilyea, J., Blanchard, E. B., Vermilyea, B. B., DiNardo, P. A. and Cerny, J. A. (1985) 'The phenomenon of panic', *Journal of Abnormal Psychology* 94: 320–328.

Beck, A. T. (1985) 'The agoraphobic syndrome', in A. T. Beck, G. Emery and R. L. Greenberg (eds) *Anxiety Disorders and Phobias: A Cognitive Perspective*, New York: Basic Books.

Benjamin, W. (1978) *Reflections: Essays, Aphorisms, Autobiographical Writings'*, in P. Demetz (ed.), New York: Schocken Books.

Bles, W., Kapteyn, T. S., Brandt, T. and Arnold, F. (1980) 'The mechanism of physiological height vertigo: II. Posturography', *Acta Otolaryngologica* 89: 534–540.

Borges, J. L. (1991) *Fictions*, Paris: Calder Publications.

Brandt, T. and Daroff, R. B. (1979) 'The multisensory physiological and pathological vertigo syndromes', *Annals of Neurology* 7: 195–203.

Brandt, T., Arnold, F., Bles, W. and Kapteyn, T. S. (1980) 'The mechanism of physiological height vertigo: I. Theoretical approach and psychophysics', *Acta Otolaryngologica* 89: 513–523.

Chambers, J., Yeragami, V. K. and Keshavan, M. S. (1986) 'Phobias in India and the United Kingdom', *Acta Psychiatrica Scandinavia* 74: 388–391.

Chambless, D. L. and Gracely, E. J. (1989) 'Fear of fear and the anxiety disorders', *Cognitive Therapy and Research* 13: 9–20.

Chambless, D. L., Caputo, G. C., Jasin, S. E., Gracely, E. J. and Williams, C. (1985) 'The mobility inventory for agoraphobia', *Behaviour Research and Therapy* 23: 35–44.

Clark, D. B., Hirsh, B. E., Smith, M. G., Furman, J. M. R. and Jacob, R. G. (1994) 'Panic in otolaryngology patients presenting with dizziness or hearing loss', *American Journal of Psychiatry* 151: 1223–1225.

Clark, D. M. (1986) 'A cognitive approach to panic', *Behaviour Research and Therapy* 24: 461–470.

Clark, M. R., Sullivan, M. D., Fischl, M., Katon, W. J., Russo, J. E., Dobie, R. A. and Voorhees, R. (1994) 'Symptoms as a clue to otologic and psychiatric diagnosis in patients with dizziness', *Journal of Psychosomatic Research* 38: 461–470.

Crampton, G. H. (ed.) (1990) *Motion and Space Sickness*, Boca Raton: CRC Press.

de Swaan, A. (1981) 'The politics of agoraphobia', *Theory and Society* 10: 359–385.

Douglas, M. (1970) *Natural Symbols*, London: Barrie & Jenkins.

Eagger, S., Luxon, L. M., Davies, R. A., Coelho, A. and Ron, M. A. (1992) 'Psychiatric morbidity in patients with peripheral vestibular disorder: a clinical and neuro-otological study', *Journal of Neurology, Neurosurgery and Psychiatry* 55: 383–387.

Eaton, W. W. and Keyl, P. M. (1990) 'Risk factors for the onset of diagnostic schedule/DSM-III agoraphobia in a prospective, population-based study', *Archives of General Psychiatry* 47: 819–824.

Featherstone, M. (1991) 'The body in consumer culture', in M. Featherstone, M. Hepworth and B. S. Turner (eds) *The Body: Social Process and Cultural Theory*, New York: Sage.

Fewtrell, D. and O'Connor, K. (1994) *Clinical Phenomenology and Cognitive Psychology*, London: Routledge.

Freud, S. (1924) 'The justification for detaching from neurasthenia a particular syndrome: the anxiety-neurosis', in E. Jones (ed.) *Collected Papers*, vol. 1, London: International Psycho-analytical Press.

Frisby, D. (1985) *Fragments of Modernity: Theories of Modernity in the Work of Simmel, Kracauer and Benjamin*, Cambridge: Polity Press.

Goldstein, A. J. and Chambless, D. L. (1978) 'A reanalysis of agoraphobia', *Behavior Therapy* 9: 47–59.

Gordon, A. G. (1986) 'Otoneurological abnormalities in agoraphobia', *American Journal of Psychiatry* 143: 807.

Gordon, D. R. (1988) 'Tenacious assumptions in modern medicine', in M. Lock and D. R. Gordon (eds) *Biomedicine Examined*, Dordrecht: Kluwer Academic.

Grisby, J. P. and Johnston, C. L. (1989) 'Depersonalization, vertigo and Ménière's disease', *Psychological Reports* 64: 527–534.

Guye, A. (1899) 'On agoraphobia in relation to ear-disease', *Laryngoscope* 6: 219–221.

Jackson, J. (1994) 'Chronic pain and the tension between the body as subject and object', in T. J. Csordas (ed.) *Embodiment and Experience: The Existential Ground of Culture and Self*, Cambridge: Cambridge University Press.

Jacob, R. G., Lilienfeld, S. O., Furman, J. M. R., Durrant, J. D. and Turner, S. M. (1989) 'Panic disorder with vestibular dysfunction: further clinical observations and description of space and motion phobic stimuli', *Journal of Anxiety Disorders* 3: 117–30.

Jacobson, G. P., Newman, C. W. and Kartush, J. M. (eds) (1993) *Handbook of Balance Function Testing*, St Louis: Mosby Year Book.

Katan, A. (1951) 'The role of "displacement" in agoraphobia', *International Journal of Psychoanalysis* 32: 41–50.

Kirkpatrick, B. (ed.) (1987) *Roget's Thesaurus of English Words and Phrases*, London: Penguin.

Klein, D. F. and Gorman, J. M. (1987) 'A model of panic and agoraphobia development', *Acta Psychiatrica Scandinavia* 76 (suppl. 335): 87–95.

Kvale, S. (1992) 'Postmodern psychology: a contradiction in terms?', in S. Kvale (ed.) *Psychology and Postmodernism*, London: Sage.

Lakoff, G. and Johnson, M. (1980) *Metaphors We Live By*, Chicago: University of Chicago Press.

Langman, L. (1991) 'Alienation and everyday life: Goffman meets Marx at the shopping mall', *International Journal of Sociology and Social Policy* 11: 107–124.

Levin, D. M. (1985) *The Body's Recollection of Being*, London: Routledge & Kegan Paul.

Linstrom, C. J. (1992) 'Office management of the dizzy patient', *Otolaryngologic Clinics of North America* 25: 745–780.

Locker, D. (1981) *Symptoms and Illness: The Cognitive Organization of Disorder*, London: Tavistock.

Low, S. M. (1994) 'Embodied metaphors: nerves as lived experience', in T. J. Csordas (ed.) *Embodiment and Experience: The Existential Ground of Culture and Self*, Cambridge: Cambridge University Press.

Lyotard, J-F. (1993) *Libidinal Economy*, London: Athlone Press.

130   Lucy Yardley

McCormick, M. S., Primrose, W. J. and MacKenzie, I. J. (1992) *A New Short Textbook of Otolaryngology*, London: Edward Arnold.

McNally, R. J. and Lorenz, M. (1987) 'Anxiety sensitivity in agoraphobics', *Journal of Behavioral Therapy and Experimental Psychiatry* 18: 3–11.

Michael, M. (1994) 'Discourse and uncertainty: postmodern variations', *Theory and Psychology* 4: 383–404.

Noyes, R., Clancy, J. and Gravey, M. J. (1987) 'Is agoraphobia a variant of panic disorder or a separate illness?', *Journal of Anxiety Disorders* 1: 3–13.

Page, N. G. R. and Gresty, M. A. (1985) 'Motorist's vestibular disorientation syndrome', *Journal of Neurology, Neurosurgery and Psychiatry* 48: 729–735.

Pollard, C. A. and Frank, M. A. (1990) 'Catastrophic cognitions and physical sensations of panic attacks associated with agoraphobia', *Phobia Practice and Research Journal* 3: 3–18.

Pollock, K. (1993) 'Attitude of mind as a means of resisting illness', in A. Radley (ed.) *Worlds of Illness*, London: Routledge.

Pursell, C. (1994) *White Heat: People and Technology*, London: BBC Books.

Radley, A. (ed.) (1993) *Worlds of Illness*, London: Routledge.

Raguram, R. and Bhide, A. V. (1985) 'Patterns of phobic neurosis: a retrospective study', *British Journal of Psychiatry* 147: 557–560.

Ronell, A. (1989) *The Telephone Book: Technology, Schizophrenia, Electric Speech*, Lincoln: University of Nebraska Press.

Sampson, E. E. (1981) 'Cognitive psychology as ideology', *American Psychologist* 36: 730–743.

Sartre, J-P. (1986) *Being and Nothingness*, London: Methuen.

Scheper-Hughes, N. and Lock, M. M. (1987) 'The mindful body: a prolegomenon to future work in medical anthropology', *Medical Anthropology Quarterly* 1: 6–41.

Schneier, F. R., Fyer, A. J., Martin, L. Y., Ross, D., Manuzza, S., Liebowitz, M. R., Gorman, J. M. and Klein, D. F. (1991) 'A comparison of phobic subtypes within panic disorder', *Journal of Anxiety Disorders* 5: 65–75.

Shaffer, M. (1979) 'Primal terror: a perspective of vestibular dysfunction', *Journal of Learning Disabilities* 12: 89–92.

Sharpe, J. A. and Barber, H. O. (eds) (1993) *The Vestibulo-Ocular Reflex and Vertigo*, New York: Raven Press.

Shulman, I. D., Cox, B. J., Swinson, R. P., Kuch, K. and Reichman, J. T. (1994) 'Precipitating events, locations and reactions associated with initial unexpected panic attacks', *Behaviour Research and Therapy* 32: 17–20.

Simmel, G. (1971) *On Individuality and Social Forms*, D. N. Levine (ed.), Chicago: University of Chicago Press.

Smith, M. B. (1994) 'Selfhood at risk: postmodern perils and the perils of postmodernism', *American Psychologist* 49: 405–411.

Snaith, R. P. (1968) 'A clinical investigation of phobias', *British Journal of Psychiatry* 114: 673–697.

Stacey, M. (1986) 'Concepts of health and illness and the division of labour in health care', in C. Currer and M. Stacey (eds) *Concepts of Health, Illness and Disease*, Leamington Spa: Berg.

Sullivan, M., Clark, M. R., Katon, W. J., Fischl, M., Russo, J., Dobie, R. A. and Voorhees, R. (1993) 'Psychiatric and otologic diagnoses in patients complaining of dizziness', *Annals of Internal Medicine* 153: 1479–1484.

Telch, M. J., Brouillard, M., Telch, C. F., Agras, W. S. and Taylor, C. B. (1989) 'Role of cognitive appraisal in panic-related avoidance', *Behaviour Research and Therapy* 27: 373–383.

Weiss, E. (1935) 'Agoraphobia and its relation to hysterical attacks and to traumas', *International Journal of Psychoanalysis* 16: 59–83.

Yardley, L. (1992) 'Motion sickness and perception: a reappraisal of the sensory conflict approach', *British Journal of Psychology* 83: 449–473.

—— (1994a) *Vertigo and Dizziness*, London: Routledge.

—— (1994b) 'Contribution of symptoms and beliefs to handicap in people with vertigo: a longitudinal study', *British Journal of Clinical Psychology* 33: 101–113.

Yardley, L. and Hallam, R. (1996) 'Psychosocial aspects of balance disorders', in A. Bronstein, T. Brandt and M. Woolacott (eds) *Clinical Aspects of Balance and Gait Disorders*, London: Edward Arnold.

Yardley, L. and Luxon, L. M. (1994) 'Rehabilitation for dizziness', *British Medical Journal* 308: 1252–1253.

Yardley, L., Beech, S. and Weinman, J. (1996) 'Deconstructing accounts of dizziness: the question of causation and control', paper presented at the Third International Interdisciplinary Qualitative Health Research Conference, Bournemouth.

Yardley, L., Britton, J., Lear, S., Bird, J. and Luxon, L. M. (1995) 'Relationship between balance system function and agoraphobic avoidance', *Behaviour Research and Therapy* 33: 435–439.

Chapter 7

The relationship between representational and materialist perspectives

AIDS and 'the other'

Hélène Joffe

INTRODUCTION

In this chapter, I show that lay and medical scientific explanations of AIDS contain similar elements. Both sets of explanations are underpinned by the need to protect the positive identity of the in-group and the self. Both are also influenced by the tacit assumptions of the culture. The theory of social representations is chosen in order to examine the links between scientific 'facts' and lay explanations. The theory is located within the broad rubric of social constructionism, but places more emphasis on the non-verbal realm than other social constructionist theories. The inherent focus upon people's behaviours and their symbolic rituals, in social representations theory, affords it an intrinsic capacity to integrate the material and representational elements of phenomena such as AIDS.

The chapter draws upon my empirical study of lay and medical scientific explanations of AIDS. Having provided a broad outline of the method of study used, I go on to delineate the relevant aspects of social representations theory, and the theory's relationship to the materialist–representational debate. A central mechanism within this theory is 'anchoring'. This mechanism refers to the process whereby people who are faced with the task of thinking about a new phenomenon, such as the arrival of AIDS, draw upon representations which they have of seemingly similar phenomena. Since AIDS was 'anchored' to previous mass, incurable illnesses, I look at the associations carried by such illnesses, according to historians. I argue that all such illnesses have been linked to a sense of 'otherness', which includes foreign nations, out-groups within a society, and practices which are deemed perverse. Once this research has been examined, I move on to look at lay thinkers' responses to questions concerning the origin and spread of AIDS, and then to medical scientists' theories of origin and spread. I investigate reasons for the resemblance that is found between the two sets of theories, and then return to the discussion of the role of material practices in representations of phenomena such as AIDS.

By way of introduction to the empirical study which I conducted in the early 1990s, I will provide a summary of the method (see Joffe 1996a for a fuller account). Both lay and medical scientific representations of the origin and spread of AIDS were examined. Lay representations were gleaned by way of semi-structured, depth interviews with sixty Britons and South Africans. The sample was chosen in accordance with a strict set of criteria to ensure comparability across cultures and groups. A basic criterion for selection was that respondents were young, urban adults with a high level of education. Half of the respondents were British and half South African. In each of the two countries, the sample was composed of white and black heterosexuals of both genders, and of gay men.

The interview was designed to elicit social representations of the origin and spread of AIDS in the respondent's own country. The primary focus was on the following topics: where HIV/AIDS originated, how HIV/AIDS spreads, which group(s) may be worst affected by AIDS in the respondent's own country, the respondent's personal sense of risk in relation to HIV/AIDS. Each transcribed interview was coded using Textbase Alpha, a computerised system for coding data which provides both a qualitative and a quantitative database. The program was employed to generate details of the themes and processes evident in the interviews of individuals, sub-groups and the total sample.

There has been a proliferation of systematic media and health policy analyses related to AIDS (e.g. Wellings 1988; Alcorn 1989; Herzlich and Pierret 1989; Kitzinger and Miller 1991; Beharrell 1992; Berridge 1992; Farmer 1992). While the majority have not been conducted within an explicitly representational model, they examine the prominent features of the social context in which lay thinking had been formed in the early 1990s and constitute a useful component of a social representational analysis. In addition to utilising these studies, I draw on my own systematic analysis of the ideas which circulated in the social context to which lay thinkers had been exposed, at the time of being interviewed.

THE MATERIAL–REPRESENTATIONAL DEBATE

In contradiction to the tacit assumptions of modern culture, the representations created of a phenomenon such as AIDS by medical scientists carry many similar elements to those created by lay thinkers. The practices of medical science are viewed as value-free and objective. Yet the 'material facts' generated by medical science contain the social values and emotional content which are usually attributed to lay thinking. The similarities relate to a similar set of motivations which drive scientific and lay thinking. In a line of thought conceived by Lévi-Strauss, anthropologists and sociologists suggest that while modern science and 'myth' appear to be fundamentally different, both are attempts to order the chaos in the perceived relation of men to nature. Approaching the issue from a different angle, psycho-dynamic strands of thought offer clarification of this rather abstract notion: people – be they scientists or lay thinkers – are motivated to control the sense of anxiety that a change in the social environment evokes. Changes such as the arrival of a mass, incurable illness re-evoke the sense of fear and insecurity experienced in the first years of life, a period in which infants have little control over their worlds (see Joffe 1996b).

Influenced by anthropological, psycho-dynamic and sociological notions, social representations theory, originated by Moscovici in 1961, is a highly specific and appropriate way of conceptualising the processes which drive 'mythical' thinking, linking it directly to the world of science. In my view, precision in relation to this link is crucial to the material–representational debate and this chapter examines the processes involved in the circulation of ideas between medical science and lay thinking. Among psychological theories, the social representational paradigm is rare in that it views the relationship between material practices and representation in an integrated manner. A classic study within the social representations field illustrates this point. Jodelet (1991) studied members of a French village who housed mentally ill lodgers. Jodelet observed material practices or rituals of exclusion operating in these homes: the clothes of the lodgers were washed separately and their eating utensils were kept apart from those of family members. The villagers enacted these rituals to keep themselves apart from the lodgers and to protect their identity. Despite the fact that lodgers had been willingly taken in, obviously without conscious dread of contagion, the villagers were representing madness as contagious through ritualistic practices. Material practices and representations are not separable: by observing the material practices of the villagers it is concluded that representations of mental illness contain primordial beliefs concerning contagion.

These findings stand in contrast to, and have the potential to add a dimension to, the majority of discourse analytic studies, with their inherent bias towards the socio-linguistic and communicative aspects of ideas about health and illness. Jodelet's findings also challenge mainstream health psychology's propensity to operate in a stimulus-response model: the material aspects of health and illness are seen to exist independently of, and prior to, the discursive level. Instead, social representations theory views material practices as perceivable solely within the realm of representation.

SOCIAL REPRESENTATIONS THEORY

Social representational theory, as a particular reading of social constructionism, is a powerful tool for explaining the relationship between scientific and lay ideas about mass, incurable illness. The theory defines the precise way in which knowledge circulates in a society. It delineates the processes which are at work when thoughts about, and explanations of, a social phenomenon (such as AIDS) develop. The term 'social representation' refers to two notions which are interlinked. First, it refers to the *content* of people's ideas about a phenomenon in much the same vein as the 'lay explanation' or 'common sense' theory, which refers to people's understanding of aspects of their social environment. It goes beyond this, concerning itself with the *processes* by which these contents are shaped. A central process relates to the interplay of science and common sense. The origin of many social representations, including representations of AIDS, is in the interplay between science and 'common sense': 'We take the *transformation* of scientific knowledge to be a fundamental aspect of common sense' (Moscovici and Hewstone 1983: 99). Scientific knowledge is assimilated primarily by way of the mass media: 'The revolution in communication has allowed the diffusion of images, notions and vocabularies that science keeps inventing. They become an integral part of the intellectual baggage of the lay person' (Moscovici and Hewstone 1983: 104). Had the media not passed information from the medical domain to society at large, AIDS would have concerned only a few thousand people, at most, for quite some time. Mass communication brought AIDS to the awareness of social actors and crystallised people's ideas concerning AIDS (e.g. see Herzlich and Pierret 1989).

While not all knowledge originates in the sciences (see Duveen and Lloyd 1990), knowledge of illness – at least in contemporary Western culture – originates in the medical sciences: AIDS was initially identified by medics and subsequently brought to the attention of the masses by way of the mass media. I will argue that the processes which are operative in the earliest moments of medical scientific thinking are similar to those which take place in lay thinking. Since scientists and lay thinkers are initially under-equipped to deal with new phenomena, social representations theory advocates specific mechanisms which they use as tools to integrate these phenomena into a known, safe world-view. In the early period of discovery, the process of 'anchoring' (Moscovici 1984), akin to a cultural form of the more cognitive categorisation process, is brought into play. Unfamiliar concepts are compared and interpreted in the light of phenomena which are already understood. Unwittingly, the meaning of seemingly similar phenomena is imposed on to new phenomena: AIDS is imbued with the ideas formerly associated with other mass, incurable illnesses. This explains, at least in part, why the response to such illnesses has been so similar historically. Cultural memories are re-evoked when the new illness is assimilated.

In social representation formation, the process termed 'objectification' works in tandem with 'anchoring', transforming the abstract links to past ideas which anchoring sets up, into concrete mental content. Abstract knowledge is made conceivable within everyday discourse by way of the more concrete devices of image, symbol and metaphor (Wagner et al. 1995). This process differentiates social representational theory from traditional discourse analysis since it deals with meaning which is generated outside of texts – such as visual imagery and ritual. Before providing the flesh of the study of AIDS, approached within the social representational paradigm, the likely 'anchors' and 'objectifications' for AIDS must be explored.

A HISTORY OF LINKING EPIDEMICS WITH 'THE OTHER'

What 'anchors' and 'objectifications' have been used by scientists and lay thinkers to understand mass, incurable disease in the past? Mass, incurable illnesses – from syphilis to cholera, from the Black Death to leprosy – have been linked to 'otherness' both historically and cross-culturally. 'Otherness' includes: (1) out-groups within the society, (2) people from other continents, and (3) practices which are deemed alien and perverse within the culture. The response to syphilis, when it began its sweep through Europe in the fifteenth century, provides the now classic example: 'It was the "French pox" to the English, *morbus Germanicus* to the Parisians, the Naples sickness to the Florentines, the Chinese disease to the Japanese' (Sontag 1989: 47). In nineteenth-century Western culture, syphilis was also identified with black women and with prostitutes, as well as with unbridled sexual practices (Gilman 1985). Cholera was termed 'Asiatic Cholera' in the first of the large-scale epidemics in Britain in 1832. It was connected with dirt and with excessive drink and passion (Morris 1976). In the United States, poliomyelitis – often proclaimed to be a mass, incurable illness which did not elicit a link to 'otherness' – was, in fact, associated with Jewish and Italian immigrants and with dirty practices prior to the change in its image which came about through the popularisation of Franklin D. Roosevelt's paralysis from it in 1921 (Rogers 1992). Typhus was imagined to have been brought into Britain in 1847 by refugees from the Irish famine (Morris 1976). Leprosy and many other mass, incurable illnesses have been 'anchored' and 'objectified' within this triad of foreigner, out-group and alien practice.

Traditionally, that which science names is deemed to be 'fact' or 'material reality', whilst the media and lay thinking are regarded as drawing on the more mythical elements of knowledge (see Comaroff 1982), entering the fantastical with greater ease and relish. The historical chronicles which document the tendency to 'otherise' epidemics are not always clear as to *who* links the epidemic with the 'other' – whether it was medics or the 'masses' and the mass media (once it had been invented) who did so. Identification of, and differentiation between, these agents of thought allows one to map the circulation of ideas in a society. Social representations theory draws a distinction between what it terms the 'reified' universe of science and the more 'consensual' universe of the mass media and lay thinking. While different interpretations of the dichotomy between these worlds exist within the theory, I propose to show that the two universes contain similar thought processes, especially when they seek to explain or to represent a phenomenon that is new to a society. The extent of the dichotomy between 'scientific fact' and 'lay fantasy' is diminished once it can be shown that there is a great degree of commonality between 'reified' and more 'consensual' thinking, and that knowledge moves in a distinct pattern from one to the other, motivated by similar concerns. Having shown that there is a history of linking mass, incurable illness with the 'other', I turn to examining lay and medical ideas about a contemporary mass, incurable illness.

STUDYING THE SPECIFIC FORMS WHICH 'OTHERISATION' TAKES IN REPRESENTING AIDS

The rationale for the study

I will focus on a study which I conducted within the social representational paradigm concerning the origin and spread of AIDS in Britain and South Africa. Prior to considering the findings, I will furnish the rationale for the chosen methodology (see 'introduction' for a synopsis of the method). Since social representations theory assumes that the representations which circulate in the social environment of the individual form the backdrop against which lay thinking occurs, the content of individual thinking is sampled in parallel with the content of the mass media, scientific concepts and, less commonly, other societal institutions. The way in which one examines social representations of the origin and spread of AIDS depends upon the very way in which the notion 'social representation' is conceived. One definition of social representations views them as 'consensual' or shared beliefs (see Jaspers and Fraser 1984; Potter and Litton 1985; Fraser 1994). If one operates within this definition, then the extent to which a representation is shared in the population allows one to determine whether it is a 'social' representation or not. However, I operate within an alternative definition of the 'social' in the social representation. This is in keeping with Moscovici's (1988) definition thereof, and relates to a far wider conceptualisation (see Kaes 1984; McGuire 1986): a representation is 'social' in that it refers to a social phenomenon; originates in a social context; guarantees the possibility of social exchange and communication; constitutes a social reality for members of a society which can influence individual behaviour; is social in function; and is shared by some members of certain groups. Within this delineation, a methodology must be chosen on the basis that it taps the social processes which feed representation formation, interaction and transformation. The need to examine these processes outweighs the quest to ascertain what proportion of a population shares one or other representation. Within this framework, lay thinkers are not regarded as members of a democratic opinion group, waiting to be canvassed, but as containers of chunks of social thinking. By subjecting the representations found in a limited number of institutions and groups to close and systematic examination, one taps into a wide set of thinking in a given society. The necessity of a systematic mode of study relates to being faithful to one's data, to openness to the scrutiny of other researchers, and to striving to gain a sense of the typicality of certain themes and the idiosyncrasy of others. The version of social representations theory which is being utilised in this study does not aim to satisfy the criteria of 'good science' which psychology has imported from the natural sciences.

This type of research is driven by the comparative methodology which has been developed within the discipline of anthropology: sampling is based upon the researcher's hypotheses concerning where differences and similarities may lie within a sample. Cross-cultural, inter-group work is an ideal way of revealing the extent to which ideas are constructed differently within different societies and groups. It has the capacity to reveal whether widespread responses to a social phenomenon such as AIDS exist, or whether trends are different in different cultures and groups.

Lay thinking about the origin and spread of AIDS

Representing the origin of AIDS in terms of a foreign continent

When asked where AIDS originated, respondents in my study linked it with a continent with which they did not identify: over three-quarters of the *white* respondents, in both the British and South African samples, thought that AIDS *originated in Africa*, while an even greater proportion of *black* respondents, in both samples, thought that it *originated in the West*. This representation of the origin of AIDS is in keeping with the historical trend found in relation to other mass, incurable illnesses, and demonstrates the process of 'anchoring' a threat by associating it with 'the other'. Of course the way in which this finding is presented rests upon the assumption that the white people in the sample (be they British or South African) do not identify with Africa, and, similarly, that the black people do not identify with the West. With few exceptions, the interviews are shot through with evidence of this style of identification. The extracts which follow provide an indication of this tendency.

Representing the spread of AIDS in terms of out-groups

Representing AIDS in terms of 'the other' is further demonstrated in responses to a prompt concerning the spread of HIV/AIDS. A third of both the British and the South African samples explicitly deny that HIV/AIDS affects their in-group, as demonstrated in excerpts from both countries:

> It is like word association, isn't it. I think about AIDS, I think of drug use, I think of decadent Stars, I think of homosexuals. I very rarely think of heterosexuals when I think about it . . . when I think about it . . . usually it belongs more to people in the white community. . . . It is just the way

I've been trained I suppose. Because they tend to do more, I don't know.
Their sexuality seems more like perverse.

(British black heterosexual male)

In South Africa we do have immorality but we do have people who stick
to their principles – the blacks.

(South African black heterosexual male)

These respondents indicate that they deny the link between the in-group
and the spread of AIDS. Similarly, in relation to direct questions concerning
their personal risk, over two-thirds of the members of both the British and
South African samples (excluding those with HIV/AIDS) state that their
own chances of contracting HIV are below average. Differences between the
groups are not significant: gay people and heterosexuals, whites and blacks,
males and females, are equally likely to deny personal vulnerability.

Representing the spread of AIDS in terms of alien practices

The anchoring of AIDS to 'otherness' is symbolised or 'objectified' in terms
of the association of AIDS with various 'perverse' or 'deviant' practices.
Over two-thirds of both the British and South African samples mention at
least one of the following five factors in association with contracting HIV:
aberrant sexuality (including bestiality and promiscuity); *tribal rituals*
(including cannibalism and incest); *'Third World' conditions* (including a lack
of Western medicine and overcrowded living conditions); *unhygienic practices*; and *the practices of uneducated people*. One half of this group *combine*
at least two of the five factors, arriving at a heady combination which I term
the 'sin cocktail'. The sin cocktail involves the combining of two or more
'aberrant' practices, over-generalising the extent to which they are practised,
and linking them to specific groups. The following extracts from the interviews indicate this process. They are responses to the questions: 'Where did
HIV/AIDS originate?' and 'How does HIV/AIDS spread?'

Monkeys in Africa. I think that was what I heard and that was passed
through God knows what to get through. I've heard some extreme stories about how it reached our shore [much laughter]. Which I care not
to utter. . . . It was just meant to be bestiality, I suppose. . . . I could
probably imagine it would be something like their tribe in Africa would
probably be more prone to that sort of thing. . . . If a man caught it
and he had sex with his wife and someone came along, I don't know
how these tribes work so I don't know the moral judgement you place
on them. Someone could come along and pay some money and have sex
with his wife and then he could take it back to his country and give it to
his wife.

(British white heterosexual male)

The respondent tells a story in which AIDS originates in a monkey on a foreign continent, and reaches the British shore by way of animal–human sexual contact as well as a Western man's engagement in the tribal ritual of wife-lending. The objectification of AIDS in practices which take place on a foreign continent is not a mechanism used by Westerners alone, as the following account from a black South African's interview demonstrates:

> As I heard it started in England. . . . It started between a monkey and a person after a person intercoursing with a monkey . . . after the person is intercoursing with the monkey he never washed and he went to his partner. Then they intercoursed. Then the partner couldn't hold herself, went and intercoursed with someone else and that is how it spread. He never washed before going to soccer and so AIDS was transmitted to people . . . because in soccer they sweat. Then after getting that sweat he touch me with it and then I've got AIDS.
>
> (South African black heterosexual male)

The accounts presented are typical of the range of issues which arise in the broader data set. They illustrate a remarkable symmetry: both white and black people imagine 'the other' to be aberrant in terms of its sexual rituals, and this is seen to spread, and often to cause, HIV/AIDS. Many lay thinkers appear to create a boundary between a 'pure' self and a polluted, polluting 'other'. I turn to examining medical scientific thinking with regard to HIV/AIDS.

Medical scientific thinking on the origin and spread of AIDS

The lay thinking appears fantastical – a mythical level which stands in opposition to objective 'scientific facts'. This idea is symbolised or 'objectified' in health campaigns, which present the prevailing lay 'myths' concerning a particular health issue alongside the scientific 'truths'. Such campaigns leave their audience in no doubt as to which of the two ways of thinking is the more desirable. Yet it is instructive to investigate the unfolding of the world of apparent 'facts', of 'material realities', at the time that the 'lay myths' were developing. An investigation of the medical scientific ideas that existed in the early stage of the discovery of the AIDS pandemic shows that the link between foreigners, out-groups, aberrance and disease does not originate in the psyches of private individuals. It is drawn, at least in part, from the medical and media representations of AIDS, which interact with historically-conferred collective thinking.

From the very moment that scientists recognised the illness, they linked it to an out-group. The earliest account of what was later termed AIDS (in the American journal *Morbidity and Mortality Weekly*, 5 June 1981) referred to the set of symptoms which had been observed as Gay Related Immune Deficiency (GRID) because the symptom-holders were all gay. American medics initially perceived the newly-discovered illness in terms of its relationship to gay identity.

Until late in 1983, when AIDS was found to be caused by a virus, the fact that AIDS had principally affected homosexual men prompted medical scientists in search of a cause to look for distinctive features related to homosexual practice (Wellings 1988). An article in the *Lancet* (1982), for example, postulated that the drug butyl nitrite ('poppers'), widely used in the American homosexual community, might impair the body's immune system (Geodert, Neuland, Wallen et al. 1982). A further article in the *Lancet* (Lacey and Waugh 1983) posited that homosexual coitus causes immunosuppression. In fact, when the viral component of AIDS was discovered, talk of practices which led to immune overload temporarily faded from the medical literature. However, the link between the 'homosexual lifestyle' and AIDS lingered in the media and in lay chatter. The terms in which an event is initially anchored has consequences for the social representations which subsequently develop. AIDS was anchored, by medics, to the practices of gay men rather than to other factors. Homosexuality and promiscuity were not seen merely as facilitators of the spread of AIDS, but as a potential cause of it.

The medical representation of AIDS in terms of 'otherness' went beyond making the link to a single out-group and to its 'deviant' practices. It was compounded by the association made with additional out-groups, practices and foreign peoples. The link between AIDS, voodoo practices and Haitians entered prestigious American medical journals in the early eighties, and then flowed between the mass media and the lay worlds. Farmer investigated the line of medical thinking which associated AIDS with voodoo practices and concluded: 'North American scientists repeatedly speculated that AIDS might be transmitted between Haitians by voodoo rites, the ingestion of sacrificial animal blood, the eating of cats, ritualized homosexuality and so on – a rich panoply of exotica' (1992: 224). The 'sin cocktail' that I discovered in lay people's accounts of the origin and spread of AIDS is not profoundly different from this 'panoply of exotica' evident in medical scientists' theorisation of AIDS.

The Haitian and homosexual links do not complete the picture. The link between AIDS and 'otherness' also exuded from medical reports, which claimed a link between Africa, Green monkeys and AIDS: the Green monkey theory became popularised in 1985 when two Harvard professors isolated an HIV-like virus from wild Green monkeys. Many newspapers published stories related to these findings in 1985 (Vass 1986), linking the Green monkey theory to Africa. Sections of the medical world appear to have reached a consensus in relation to this link. A haematologist from an eminent Cambridge department wrote in *Nature* (Karpas 1990: 578): 'There is now little doubt human AIDS began in Africa. Not only is the disease widely spread in central Africa, but only in Africa are the monkey species naturally infected. . . . Although the first such virus was isolated from the macaque, that animal was probably infected in captivity with . . . the African sooty mangabey monkey.' Karpas suggests that the cross-species transfer of an HIV-like virus may be related to the sexual habits of the people of the large African lakes: these people are injected with monkey blood to induce them to intense sexual activity.

The status of the African origin as 'fact' is a testimony to the extent to which this medical anchor for AIDS has lived on in the collective imagination. The Green monkey theory is one among a number of accounts of the origin. In the scientific literature, the African Green monkey is not unanimously assumed to harbour a precursor to HIV that crossed the species barrier. For example, hypotheses concerning a laboratory origin appear in the mainstream scientific literature (Chirimuuta and Chirimuuta 1989). However, I will return to this issue, since a relativistic view – a view which advocates that each sector of a society advocates different representations of a phenomenon, and that none carry any more weight than others – carries as many problems as the realist view which has dogged the social and natural sciences.

I have shown that the representations which existed in the medical, scientific and lay worlds early in the AIDS pandemic, contained the link between AIDS and 'otherness'. I will now suggest reasons for this similarity. The empirical literature, which challenges the tacit assumption that scientific facts originate in a way that is different from lay ideas, provides a useful starting point. Many empirical studies (e.g. Bloor 1976; Latour and Woolgar 1979; Collins 1985) have shown that scientific 'facts' are produced in a manner akin to the production of knowledge in other spheres. Having conducted a closely observed study of how a 'fact' is established in a laboratory, Latour and Woolgar are convinced that 'a body of practices widely regarded by outsiders as well organised, logical, and coherent, in fact consists of a disordered array of observations with which scientists struggle to produce order' (1979: 36). This body of practices is imbued with the qualities of logic and coherence by the worlds inside and outside of the laboratory. It is regarded as being beyond the scope of sociological study – 'facts' have a quality which places them beyond the scope of historical and temporal considerations. Latour and Woolgar focus on the way in which apparently logical processes of reasoning can be construed as 'practices of interpretation'. Having observed laboratory life over a two-year period, no evidence of differences from common sense reasoning was found. Even the act of falsification, usually regarded as a cornerstone of the scientific method, was found to be far from straightforward. It involved a process of negotiation, with scientists asking one another 'what do we accept as a negative answer?' (ibid.: 158). Other rhetorical aspects which influenced the fact-building process included adherence to claims on the basis of who made them. Latour and Woolgar argue that 'having an idea' or solving something previously mysterious is the outcome of a complex debate in which social factors are highly visible. Yet the 'fact' which this process produces bears no trace of its social construction. It is seen as an independent entity which has a quality of being 'out there'. Latour and Woolgar's central point is that ' "out-there-ness" ' is the *consequence* of scientific work rather than its *cause*' (ibid.: 182). So scientists construct knowledge of the material world, rather than 'facts' pre-existing scientific endeavour, awaiting to be discovered.

The social aspects involved in the scientific 'discovery' of AIDS – the way in which Western scientists initially linked the symptoms to various forms of 'otherness' – corroborates Latour and Woolgar's finding that fact-building is equivalent to social construction. An observation concerning early representations of AIDS in South Africa and in Britain demonstrates that medical science is highly interconnected with social values. What could be more scientific, more value-free and objective than tables containing statistics which report the prevalence of AIDS? Yet like the origin theories, such tables speak to a representational universe, to a specific way of anchoring and objectifying the illness. The way in which a population is divided into groups by the official statistical tables reflects the manner in which the epidemiologists deem it logical to represent the population. This is well demonstrated by the fact that the early British tables did not include a racial division of the population, whilst the South African tables followed the four-way racial division ('Black', 'Coloured', 'Asian', 'White') constructed by the apartheid regime (which was still in power). Bearing in mind the salience of the racial category in apartheid South Africa, the four-way division can be construed as a reflection of a representation in which race is a central feature. Epidemiology is influenced by social construction, rather than being 'objective'.

The material basis of AIDS was framed through a lens which contained a culture-specific outlook, in combination with the motivation to protect the identity of that culture (explored below), rather than through objective, value-free practices. However, Latour and Woolgar's claim to the overriding similarity between the scientific and lay processes of knowledge production overlooks the intention of scientists to utilise formalised procedures. Such intentions are less pervasive in lay thought (see Garfinkel 1967). Perhaps a model which differentiates what happens at the point of assimilation of new ideas, from the later point of accommodation of these ideas, would be able to grasp the complexity of knowledge production. I would suggest that lay and scientific knowledge production operate similarly when a phenomenon is new to a society, but that the processes that come into play after assimilation, at the point of accommodation, differ. This is not surprising since knowledge undergoes change in the light of new information.

I have demonstrated the similarity of the reactions to AIDS in the 'reified' and 'consensual' universes, showing that it was linked to 'the other' when people initially constructed their 'facts'. I have introduced the notion of 'anchoring' which goes some way to explain why this historical pattern of response to epidemic illness has repeated itself: scientists and lay thinkers carry forward ideas about previous mass illnesses when they are compelled to explain seemingly similar phenomena. However, there is still a question to be asked concerning why mass, incurable illness was initially 'anchored' to otherness, historically. Social representations theory has proposed that a central purpose of representation is to defend against threat (Kaes 1984; Moscovici 1984; Joffe 1996b) and the way in which epidemics get pushed out on to an 'other' corroborates this hypothesis. The fundamental dynamic, when faced with a crisis, is to form representations of the crisis which protect the positive identity of the in-group. Linking AIDS with out-groups, foreigners and 'perverse' practices is such a representation. Since it is firmly established that group identity forms a component of self-identity (Tajfel and Turner 1979), the process of linking epidemics with the 'other' sustains a positive self-identity. The motivation to forge a positive sense of identity explains why groups ascribe to representations in accordance with the identities which require protection. The black–white divide, within both the British and the South African samples, concerning representations of the origin, spread and risk of AIDS, provides evidence of the identity-protective process, as does the Western scientists' proclivity to link the origin of the spread of HIV/AIDS with non-Western nations and with out-groups within Western societies.

Both scientists and lay thinkers act to protect a positive identity when they represent AIDS. The focus on the parallel processes which are at work in the scientific and lay spheres has not yet allowed me to touch upon the influence which scientific ideas have on lay thinking. There can be no contention that AIDS was initially 'discovered' in the world of medical science. Consequently, lay thinkers must have learned of the illness via assimilation of what were originally scientific ideas. However, I use the term 'lay thinkers' to imply the active nature of human assimilation of information. This mollifies the supposition that since medics linked AIDS to the 'other' in their 'factual' findings, lay people passively followed suit. Rather than adhering to the 'cause–effect' model, it can be argued that, while lay thinkers negotiate the meaning of ideas which are transmitted from the scientific world (via the mass media), the range of meanings is constrained by the set of ideas to which they are exposed. Whereas, to my knowledge, medics attempting to explain the spread of HIV did not suggest African bestiality as a form of contact between Green monkey and human, it does not require a huge leap to imagine how this re-presentation of scientific thinking occurred. Scientific talk of the simian HIV-like virus approximating the human one, and Karpas's sexually-based theories, lend themselves to re-presentation in lay minds. The forces of the unconscious may be less restrained, leaving the unconscious level of fantasy to exert itself with greater force in lay thought, as the theories of bestiality suggest.

A lay representation of AIDS was initially shaped by ideas which originated in medical science. Yet the scientific ideas interact with the stock of representations which surround lay thinkers in their social environment. Such representations are evident in expressions such as 'avoiding someone like the plague', in jokes and in actions such as sipping from a different part of the rim of a glass which someone else has used. The form taken by a medical scientist's representation of AIDS is not only influenced by the shared concern to avoid the danger of contagious disease, it is also dependent on the forces of history, and of mass-mediated and lay ideas. So ideas circulate, rather than being passed in a linear fashion, from one sphere to another.

DISCUSSION

This chapter has focused on the parallel processes of 'otherisation' in lay and Western scientific representations of AIDS. This has been interwoven with an account of how medical knowledge presents as 'natural' that which is actually a culturally constituted representation. I hope to have shed light on the motivations which inform the specific representations. Lay thinkers share with scientists a motivation to find security and order in the face of anticipated chaos, a desire to protect themselves from the impact of the crisis. Representing AIDS in terms of 'otherness' diminishes people's perception of its potential threat to the in-group and the self, thereby safeguarding a positive sense of identity. This correlates with high self-esteem.

The chosen representation of AIDS is not merely useful to the individual, it is also socially useful in that it maintains a sense of that which is normal and desirable in a given culture. The similarity of the responses of scientists and lay thinkers to mass, incurable illness is attributable to the way in which the interests of the dominant groups in a society become seamlessly incorporated into the set of tacit assumptions concerning what the 'material facts' are (see Comaroff 1982). Certain interests shape what come to be viewed as 'material facts'. Social interests are imbibed by lay people while they witness the media representing scientific ideas.

Once we recognise that socially and emotionally based interests and motivations shape 'material facts', rather than believing that they are constituted by 'natural' laws, we realise that the material facts are not 'out there' awaiting to be discovered, but are constructed within a representational process. We are also alerted to the flimsy nature of the division that is believed to exist between the 'material' and the 'representational'. Traditional discourse analytic theories and social representational theories view this issue in a similar vein. The two theories also share convictions concerning the social regulatory and identity forming aspects of representation/discourse. The idea that there is a breakdown in the hierarchy of knowledge, that the ideas of 'experts' and non-experts both have validity and are mutually reinforcing, is a further point of commonality. Furthermore, both theories have the potential to show that the ideas which emanate from science do not carry 'equal' status to those of lay thinkers. Scientists have more power in defining an issue. A relativist understanding of the origin of AIDS, in which all explanations are imagined to carry equal weight, overlooks the role that dominant groups play in forging thought in a society. Scientists define the 'anchors' and 'objectifications' in which illness is couched. Others take up their stances in relation to this interpretation.

While traditional discourse analytic theories and social representational theories share a number of features, social representations theory is more appropriate to the project of embracing the material aspects of a phenomenon. There is a tendency in the discourse analytic literature to advocate that since 'being' can only be experienced through socially constructed verbal discourses, all that lies outside of verbal discourse has little significance. Participant observation of non-verbal behaviour, referred to in the Jodelet study, provides good grounds for de-centring from verbal discourse. Unfortunately, the study reported in this chapter does not pay sufficient homage to this method. While social representationalists recognise the value of non-verbal data, they often collect data which resemble the texts utilised by discourse analysts.

Implied within the idea of re-presenting something is a division between different types of knowledge: scientific ideas are re-presented by the mass media and then re-presented by lay thinkers. However, the concept of 're-presentation' can be perceived in a different way. Perhaps contained within the very notion of re-presentation is the implication that there is a thing 'out there' to be looked at and assimilated. Something is being presented again, in a different form. Even though I have argued that material practices are only perceivable within the realm of representation, I am not willing to accept the idea that everything which lies outside of verbal discourse has little relevance. It is important, at least, to consider whether AIDS could have been linked to homosexual practices such as anal sex even if this material practice had played no role whatsoever in the spread of HIV.

If we are to gain a fuller understanding of the social construction of AIDS, we need to recognise that the material practices which are implicated (and which may, indeed, lead to the transfer of illnesses) exist outside the realm of representation, but that as soon as they are represented they are used towards certain ends. Dehumanisation, expressed in accusations of animal-like (avaricious, promiscuous) sexuality, sex with animals, eating one another as some animals do, is certainly a way in which dominant groups have denunciated out-groups throughout history.

CONCLUDING COMMENTS

In this chapter I have used an empirical study conducted within a social representational rubric in order to show that the 'panoplies of exotica' invented by scientists to explain the origin and spread of AIDS have their counter-part in the 'sin cocktails' fantasised by lay thinkers. The process of pushing epidemics out on to the 'other' is widespread. It is not specific to certain groups or cultures. I have examined reasons for the similarity of the proces-ses of thought formation which operate in the scientific and lay realms. A process of social construction operates in both realms, rather than the diver-gent processes of scientific fact formation and the lay invention of 'myths'. The process of anchoring operates in both universes: the self is protected against the shock of the discovery of a new, potentially fatal, illness by drawing on a set of ideas which live on from the past, and which allow the individual to push responsibility for the illness on to outsiders. Beyond these parallel processes, the way in which knowledge circulates determines that scientific ideas provide the range of ideas that lay thinkers are able to take up. Yet the emphasis is upon the *circulation* of knowledge, since medical ideas about AIDS are not simply imbibed by lay thinkers in a linear fashion. Lay thinking and the forms of thought that occur in other non-scientific institutions influence the ways in which scientists construct AIDS. South African epidemiologists' construction of the AIDS statistics in terms of racial categories provides a concrete symbol (or 'objectification') of the influence of apartheid on medicine.

I hope to have conveyed that it is useful to maintain a distinction between the 'material' and the 'representational', even though they operate in an inte-grated manner. The relativism which can result from removing the distinc-tion between the 'material' and the 'representational' contains a danger. It can erode the sense of reality which an experience – such as the experience of illness or that of potentially catching an illness – has for an individual. Yet this danger has to be weighed up in relation to the risks inherent in pre-senting certain 'material facts'. Since we know that natural and social scien-tific research is interest-based, rather than value-free, it is useful to think of research in terms of value positioning. Precisely because the 'material facts' which we report are used in a value-laden way, we need to be careful about the 'facts' we re-present, both as social scientists and as medics.

The 'facts' which health professionals choose to convey have consequences. The early national AIDS campaigns in Britain and in South Africa drew upon epidemiological, rather than virological, medical 'facts'. AIDS was con-structed in terms of the potentially affected groups, and of risk groups, from the very inception of the media campaigns. If the campaigns had followed a more virological way of depicting AIDS – perhaps images of an HIV under a microscope – a wholly different representation of AIDS would have devel-oped. Those who devised the campaigns may have feared that lay people would find it difficult to relate to the viral images: images which are not only devoid of humans, but are linked to the reified universe of science. However, by adopting the 'risk group' model, in preference to the viral one, they con-veyed a very problematic set of social values. The chosen 'anchors' and 'objectifications' communicate messages concerning which people are impure and polluting, as well as imparting ideas concerning which people and what practices should be avoided. An image of a virus would have been hard-pressed to dispatch information concerning 'deviance' and 'deviants'.

I am not suggesting that symbols of a virus should have been utilised in AIDS campaigns. I present this idea only to illustrate that the 'facts' which health professionals present to the public have social consequences. Denegation of the 'other' in social representations of AIDS is the forerunner of the stigmatising acts, the rituals (material practices) of exclusion (such as gay-bashing), which such representations produce. This shows that representation can be the antecedent of material practice. This finding challenges the tacit assumption of much research in the health and illness field, that material aspects of health and illness exist independently of, and prior to, the representational level. The representation has other material consequences for the representor. Imagined immunity to AIDS leaves one physically vulnerable to its transmission, since the realm of representation leaves one with a sense that there is no need to utilise material barriers. By highlighting the material and representational facets of AIDS, one invites a complex strategy for dealing with its spread. The relevant professionals are challenged to contain both the viral epidemic and the epidemic of representations which cast AIDS out on to the 'other'.

REFERENCES

Alcorn, K. (1989) 'AIDS in the public sphere: how a broadcasting system in a crisis dealt with an epidemic', in E. Carter and S. Watney (eds) *Taking Liberties: AIDS and Cultural Politics*, London: Serpent's Tail.
Beharrell, P. (1992) 'AIDS and the British press', in J. E. T. Eldridge (ed.) *Getting the Message*, London: Routledge.
Berridge, V. (1992) 'AIDS: history and contemporary history', in G. Herdt and S. Lindenbaum (eds) *The Time of AIDS: Social Analysis, Theory and Method*, Newbury Park, CA: Sage.
Bloor, D. (1976) *Knowledge and Social Imagery*, London: Routledge & Kegan Paul.
Chirimuuta, R. and Chirimuuta, R. (1989) *AIDS, Africa and Racism*, London: Free Association Books.
Collins, H. M. (1985) *Changing Order*, London: Sage.
Comaroff, J. (1982) 'Medicine: symbol and ideology', in P. Wright and A. Treacher (eds) *The Problem of Medical Knowledge: Examining the Social Construction of Medicine*, Edinburgh: Edinburgh University Press.
Duveen, G. and Lloyd, B. (1990) 'Introduction', in G. Duveen and B. Lloyd (eds) *Social Representations and the Development of Knowledge*, Cambridge: Cambridge University Press.
Farmer, P. (1992) *AIDS and Accusation: Haiti and the Geography of Blame*, Berkeley: University of California Press.
Fraser, C. (1994) 'Attitudes, social representations and widespread beliefs', *Papers on Social Representations* 3: 13–25.
Garfinkel, H. (1967) *Studies in Ethnomethodology*, New Jersey: Prentice-Hall.
Geodert, J. J., Neuland, C. Y., Wallen, W. C., Greene, M. H., Mann, D. L., Murray,

C. F., Strong, D. M., Fraumeni, J. F. and Blattner, W. B. (1982) 'Amyl nitrite may alter T-lymphocytes in homosexual men', *Lancet* i: 412–415.

Gilman, S. (1985) *Difference and Pathology: Stereotypes of Sexuality, Race and Madness*, Cornell: Cornell University Press.

Herzlich, C. and Pierret, J. (1989) 'The construction of a social phenomenon: AIDS in the French press', *Social Science and Medicine* 29: 1235–1242.

Jaspers, J. M. and Fraser, C. (1984) 'Attitudes and social representations', in R. M. Farr and S. Moscovici (eds) *Social Representations*, Cambridge: Cambridge University Press.

Jodelet, D. (1991) *Madness and Social Representations*, Hemel Hempstead: Harvester Wheatsheaf.

Joffe, H. (1996a) 'The shock of the new: a psycho-dynamic extension of social representational theory', *Journal for the Theory of Social Behaviour* 26: 197–219.

—— (1996b) 'AIDS research and prevention: a social representational approach', *British Journal of Medical Psychology* 69: 169–190.

Kaes, R. (1984) 'Representation and mentalisation: from the represented group to the group process', in R. M. Farr and S. Moscovici (eds) *Social Representations*, Cambridge: Cambridge University Press.

Karpas, A. (1990) 'Origin and spread of AIDS', *Nature* 348 (13 December): 578.

Kitzinger, J. and Miller, D. (1991) *In Black and White*, Medical Research Council Working Paper no. 27, in association with the Glasgow University Media Group.

Lacey, C. J. N. and Waugh, M. A. (1983) 'Cellular immunity in male homosexuals', *Lancet* ii: 464.

Latour, B. and Woolgar, S. (1979) *Laboratory Life: The Social Construction of Scientific Facts*, Beverly Hills, CA: Sage.

McGuire, W. (1986) 'The vicissitudes of attitudes and similar representational constructs in twentieth-century psychology', *European Journal of Social Psychology* 16: 89–130.

Morris, R. J. (1976) *Cholera 1832: A Social Response to an Epidemic*, London: Croom Helm.

Moscovici, S. (1984) 'The phenomenon of social representations', in R. M. Farr and S. Moscovici (eds) *Social Representations*, Cambridge: Cambridge University Press.

—— (1988) 'Notes towards a description of social representations', *European Journal of Social Psychology* 18: 211–250.

Moscovici, S. and Hewstone, M. (1983) 'Social representation and social explanations: from the "naive" to the "amateur" scientist', in M. Hewstone (ed.) *Attribution Theory: Social and Functional Extensions*, Oxford: Basil Blackwell.

Potter, J. and Litton, I. (1985) 'Some problems underlying the theory of social representations', *British Journal of Social Psychology* 24: 81–90.

Rogers, N. (1992) *Dirt and Disease: Polio before FDR*, New Jersey: Rutgers University Press.

Sontag, S. (1989) *AIDS and its Metaphors*, London: Allen Lane.

Tajfel, H. and Turner, J. (1979) 'An integrative theory of intergroup conflict', in W. G. Austin and S. Worschel (eds) *The Social Psychology of Intergroup Relations*, Pacific Grove, CA: Brooks/Cole.

Vass, A. (1986) *AIDS: A Plague in Us*, St Ives, Cambs: Venus Academia.

Wagner, W., Lahnsteiner, I. and Elejabarrieta, F. (1995) 'How the sperm dominates the ovum: objectification by metaphor in the social representation of conception', *European Journal of Social Psychology* 25: 671–688.

Wellings, K. (1988) 'Perceptions of risk', in P. Aggleton and H. Homans (eds) *Social Aspects of AIDS*, London: Falmer Press.

Chapter 8

Discourses and sexual health
Providing for young people

Roger Ingham and Denise Kirkland

INTRODUCTION

Our intention in this chapter is to present some material which relates sexual conduct amongst young people to the various ways in which the area is talked about, written about, discussed and described. We draw on a variety of sources, including our own transcripts of taped interviews with young people and adults, debates in the House of Lords, government publications, and others. Since the field of research into social aspects of sexual conduct is relatively new (as indeed is the discursive approach itself), much of what we say needs to be regarded as speculative. Some of our readers may regard some of what we say as being obvious. If this is the case, we can assure them that others would not have the same reaction; very recently one of us heard a very eminent psychology professor remark, at the end of a conference on young people, that he 'always thought that psychology was about the way people behave, not about the way they talk'. But it is the very wide variation in the ways that people do talk about, and think about, sex that makes a discursive approach so necessary.

Leaving aside the rather difficult issue of whether we could get past ethical committees in order to make direct observations of young people engaging in sexual activity, the professor did have a point. There is a tendency in some discursive writing to overlook the 'real world'; nothing is able to be tied down. In the 'real world', however, young people do get pregnant, they do transmit and acquire sexually transmitted diseases (STDs) of various kinds, they do agonise over aspects of their relationships and sexual dealings, and so on. The issue is one of how we should go about researching and accounting for these material outcomes, and it is our contention that recent research into sexual health has begun to demonstrate the high (actual and potential) utility of a discursive approach to the area.

A discursive approach helps to illuminate the constrained nature of agency, drawing attention, on the one hand, to the power of constraining influences of social discourses and, on the other, to the potential that people have – albeit to a limited extent – as autonomous agents. Prevalent discourses constrain to some extent what is possible, or at least readily available, for people to think, say and do. Yet, nevertheless, each of us retains some autonomy to resist (Foucault 1979, 1984b) or 'challenge' any discursive position. We are agents with some element of choice regarding how certain areas will be 'treated' in social settings. At the very least, in the arena of sexual behaviour, we must resolve the 'dilemmas' raised by the competing and often contradictory claims of the different discourses about sexual behaviour (for a general discussion of dilemmatic thinking, see Billig et al. 1988). Throughout this chapter we will explore, through examples of actual discussions, texts and accounts, what some of the underlying discourses are, and how they are used to change legislation, to affect what resources are made available and where, and to explain, account for, and challenge, people's behaviour.

This theoretical understanding does, of course, have methodological implications. Most of the primary research reported in this chapter has used qualitative interviews, with the probability that participants in such research are presenting themselves in certain ways for the benefit of the interviewer (a challenge for all self-report research, since of course 'subjects' can equally present themselves in certain ways when filling in questionnaires). However, such self-presentation reflects assumptions, shared experiences and 'obvious' (taken-for-granted) positions which contrast them with others. The advantage of interviews over questionnaires is that these assumptions, etc. are presented in more detail, are contextualised and, on occasion, can be challenged, all of which assist in the search for 'explaining' variation. Our view is that discourses operate at many levels, are complete or fragmentary, and have material consequences, which are not always the consequences intended by participants in the discourse.

Throughout the chapter, we will be drawing on material collected during the course of various research projects conducted by the first author and collaborators, as well as drawing on the work of others where appropriate. To avoid repetition, the four main Southampton-based projects are summarised here:

(a) The Economic and Social Research Council (ESRC) project (Ingham, Woodcock and Stenner), in which over 200 young people aged between 16 and 25 years old were interviewed in detail about aspects of their sexual conduct and risk-taking (see, for example, Ingham et al. 1991; Ingham et al. 1992; Woodcock et al. 1992a,b; Ingham 1994).

(b) The Health Education Authority (HEA) project, which was designed to explore sex education initiatives in non-school settings in various parts of the UK. The study involved between ten and twelve detailed interviews in each of eight sites with staff from a range of agencies, including health, education, social services, youth service, voluntary organisations, and so on. For reasons of confidentiality, the sites selected cannot be identified, and the full report (Ingham et al. 1994) has not been published by the HEA (but see Ingham et al. 1997).

(c) The House of Lords analysis, in which Diane Stevens has conducted detailed analyses of the transcripts of the debates held in the House of Lords during the revisions to the Education Act in as far as it deals with sex education in schools. This involved ninety-three columns of *Hansard*[1] drawn from four separate occasions when various amendments were considered (10 May, 13 May, 21 June and 6 July 1993).

(d) The parents' interviews – Denise Kirkland has recently interviewed a number of parents of teenagers regarding their own views on sexual health, what they feel their children should know, and so on. This work is, as yet, unpublished.

All interviews in each of the projects were tape-recorded and have been fully transcribed.

To anticipate the end point, sexual health outcomes ultimately rest on the shared actions of two (or more) people engaging in sexual activity. Research conducted over the last decade or so suggests that what this shared action will be is not at all easy to predict, and is influenced by many different aspects of prior history of the participants, as well as their subsequent (and consequent) reactions to events. We aim to illustrate, through some selected examples, the ways in which different discourses operate at different levels, and how these might have effects on material outcomes. These 'material outcomes' include not only effects on the 'body' (a key theme in other chapters) such as the inception of an unintended pregnancy or transmission of disease and consequent undesired bodily changes, but also provision (or lack) of health services for young people, the acquiring (or not) of interactional competence, the provision (or not) of appropriate education, or the very 'material' siting (or not) of condom machines.

We first outline some pervasive discourses of sexuality identified in research over the last decade, then discuss the interaction of discourses with policy development in the arenas of health and education, and the impact on service provision, before moving on to consider the operation and effects of discourses in more intimate settings, first within the family environment, and ultimately (perhaps crucially?) with the dyad – the potentially sexually active couple.

DISCOURSES OF SEXUALITY IN SOCIETY

Wendy Hollway (1984), in an influential article on gendered subjectivities, identified three main social discourses about sexual behaviour; she termed these: the *male sexual drive* discourse (in which it is assumed that males have a need for regular sexual gratification, and it is the female's role in life to provide it); the *have–hold* discourse (in which the aim of young women is actively to obtain and hang on to a young man for the purposes of child-rearing and protection); and the *permissive* discourse (in which sexual pleasure can be experienced by either sex for its own sake, and there is no assumed obligation on either side to enter any other form of commitment). She has discussed the implications of these different discourses for the perception of gender difference and power relations, and the production of subjectivities.

More recently, Danny Wight (in press) found evidence that all three discourses were recognisable amongst young working-class men from a particular Glasgow estate, though they were not identical as reported by Hollway. Wight added a fourth discourse – *not interested* – which applied to many of the younger males in his sample, and which persisted with some older interviewees. He also observed transitional interaction with discourses over time, drawing attention to the 'dynamic' nature of these discourses; young men seemed to draw on different discourses to describe their behaviour, and expectations, depending on time and circumstance, for example, as 'one of the lads' or when settling down and starting a family.

Wight (in press) prefers the term *predatory* to Hollway's *male sexual drive*, since he found little evidence in his young men's talk of any form of 'biological essentialism' (of the 'need for sexual release' often cited as the genesis of the drive). He stresses instead the social demands experienced by many of the young men from their peers, pointing out that

> within this discourse heterosexual intercourse is fundamental in asserting one's masculinity, and physical sexual pleasure is of less importance than the opinions of one's male peers . . . the challenge is to seduce a woman, and the less accessible she is the greater one's esteem if successful.

The other major development proposed by Wight expands Hollway's *have–hold* discourse by the addition of *romantic*. The impact of this addition is to recognise that men, as well as women, can 'take up' positions as subjects within the discourse – in Hollway's original chapter she implies that women are the subjects within this discourse with men the objects, in contrast to the male sexual drive discourse. Wight points out that 'perhaps half' of his young men recognised that at some stage, possibly when they were somewhat older, a traditional loving relationship would be sought. He also points out that some men switched in their accounts between the object and subject positions within this romantic discourse.

Obviously, much more could be written (and much more enquiry needs to be conducted) regarding these societal discourses of sexual relations, their origins in the media and elsewhere, under what circumstances people are more and less likely to 'locate themselves' (or 'be located') within one or more of them, and so on. Their impact on gender relations and personal and social identities is profound; this has been clearly pointed out both by Hollway, based on her limited number of interviews with articulate and reflexive men and women in the early 1980s, as well as more recently by the WRAP authors with a wider (age and class) range of respondents (Holland et al. 1991, 1992, 1994).

For the present, these outlines must serve as a backdrop to our more specific analyses, where it will be seen that sometimes, but not always, they inform the content of the texts and transcripts under scrutiny.

DISCOURSES AND POLICY

In the Foucauldian sense, discourses operate in part through the institutions of society (for example, Foucault 1984a) and there have been some fascinating analyses of the ways in which sexual activity has been publicly discussed and controlled in the UK over the past two centuries (for example, Weeks 1981, 1985). However, the level of public debate has reached new heights over the past ten to fifteen years since the acknowledgement in the early 1980s of AIDS as a very 'material' threat to the health of the nation. Two key institutions relevant to sexuality in the UK are the National Health Service, and the education system.

Health policy

In 1992, in the White Paper *The Health of the Nation* (HotN), the Government set targets to reduce teenage conception rates (the UK has one of the highest rates in Europe), and to reduce the incidence of gonorrhoea (as an indicator of probable infection levels of HIV) by the year 2000. As a result of this White Paper, many sexual health intervention initiatives have been led by medical and health care providers.

Although it is of course grossly inappropriate to stereotype all health personnel and initiatives, nevertheless, there is some indication of a fairly consistent approach to the area within health settings. Not surprisingly, the dominant discourse stresses the negative aspects of sexual activity; indeed, the opening section of the Department of Health's *Key Area Handbook on HIV/AIDS and Sexual Health* (a companion volume to the HotN White Paper) starts off by saying: 'Rewarding personal and sexual relationships promote health and well-being. However, sexual activity can also have undesired results such as unwanted pregnancies and the transmission of HIV and other sexually transmitted diseases' (Department of Health 1993: 7). The majority of the rest of the document is concerned with the need for increased services aimed at reducing these negative effects of sexual activity, and pointing to the advantages of healthy alliances (collaborations within and between agencies and sectors).

Our HEA study revealed some quite interesting variations between those staff employed in mainstream health settings and those involved in more community based, or outreach, work (some of whom were paid from health service finance as providers, whilst others were paid through Social Services departments, voluntary organisations, charities, churches, and others). The former were primarily motivated by the national targets of reducing conceptions amongst young women and the reduction of STDs, whilst the latter had more wide-ranging objectives for their work, as illustrated by the following examples:

> I aim to access the disadvantaged and young people to improve choices or empower them to make informed choices about their sexual health . . . ultimately to ensure that they can discuss sex and practise safer sex.
>
> (outreach worker)

> If you feel good about yourself you will not put yourself under threat.
>
> (community development worker)

What became apparent from these interviews was that the target of achieving healthy alliances, and thereby (in theory, at least) making adequate provision for young people's needs, is hindered by the varying discourses surrounding the issue. When specifically discussing their experiences of, and hopes for, alliances, many respondents pointed to the difficulties of working harmoniously together when the different parties involved had such varied agendas. Although many of the specific aims of individual respondents, some of which are cited above, could be regarded as essential prerequisites towards achieving the more objective targets of the funders, little effort appears to have been made in any of the sites to work through this process of integration. There were various reasons for this, but a lack of mutual understanding of what each other was trying to achieve was a major one. In many ways, these key players are speaking different languages (engaging in different discourses?) with alliances providing little in the way of translation.

Even within the higher tiers of health service management, there was evidence of some disagreement regarding the appropriate ways of approaching the area. A somewhat vivid example was provided by the respondent (echoing others) who reported:

> I've been requested by fellow managers to take down posters with condoms on them because it made them feel physically sick, and they will say so at senior meetings of managers; they are not embarrassed to say so, in fact they feel quite noble.

These different discourses not only affected the ways in which people talked about what they were trying to achieve, but also the types of provision which they felt to be relevant. Generally, health-oriented staff emphasise service provision with an implicit understanding that, if sufficient services are available, then they will be used. Whilst we would not wish for one moment to doubt the need for improved sexual health services for young people, it is clear that services which simply make contraception more easily available do not address the wider issues identified by the outreach workers. To take a simple example, the new purchaser–provider model within the health service involves the inclusion of service specifications into contracts. In many that we have seen, little attention is paid to the actual quality of the interactions between clients and staff (in terms of increasing self-esteem, improving assertiveness, increasing choice, challenging dominant gendered discourses, or whatever); rather, the outcome measures tend to be based primarily on numbers of clients using the service, and how long they have to wait to be seen. This reliance on quantitative forms of assessment also, of course, places the outreach workers at a severe disadvantage when competing for resources.

The dominant discourses within health service staff are very reminiscent of certain models within health psychology, such as the Health Belief Model and some applications of the Theory of Reasoned Action. (Indeed, it is tempting to suggest that the views of health service staff may well be affected by their attendance at psychology modules during their training.) The notion of individual rationality contained in these models places emphasis on the individual 'doing the right thing' so long as he or she has adequate knowledge and perceives sufficient threat. For example, one senior health purchaser remarked:

> At the end of the day it is your choice or my choice what you do with your life and whether you do or you do not have a sexually transmitted disease.

Such ways of understanding lend themselves to information-giving and service-provision approaches. The risk is that these do not pay adequate attention to the social contexts in which risk-taking behaviour occurs, nor to the evidence that few young people place their early sexual experiences within a medical and health care discourse.

So, varying discourses can lead to varying policy responses to the challenges posed by threats to 'sexual health' leading to varying provision of services. However, we also came across some examples where differing discourses led to the same intervention, but for quite different reasons. In one site, a full-time project worker was funded by a local authority to establish contact with gay men (and men who had sex with men) in the area, to provide support, to assist in overcoming stigmatisation and prejudice and to ensure that adequate provision was made for their sexual health needs. The project worker described at length how the funding had been forthcoming, not as a direct result of the authority following national guidelines about priorities, nor out of genuine acceptance of 'alternative' lifestyles. The clinching argument, he suggested, arose from the data from a needs assessment which suggested that the area contained a number of married men who covertly frequented gay bars and clubs. As he put it:

poor married men might spread the plague to their nice little heterosexual wives.

In sum, the varied discursive approaches within these sites can be understood with reference to the following three dimensions:

- *Power, control and agenda setting* – mainstream providers have a top-down approach to needs assessment, whereas voluntary agencies and community-based workers place greater emphasis on the perceived needs of the groups they serve. Health professionals generally have adequate funding to employ full-time workers and are more commonly represented on formal alliances and decision-making bodies.

- *Female heterosexuality and male homosexuality as the 'problems'* – the White Paper emphasis on achieving specific targets has led to a concentration on these, and has had an effect of diverting attention away from the wider contexts. Thus, for example, a focus on pregnancy – hence the female – fosters an impression of negative (young) female sexuality and obscures the dyadic nature of sexual activity – the role of the heterosexual male partner 'disappears' from the account. (Of course, a study of the controversy raised by the efforts of the Child Support Agency (CSA) might illuminate more of the complexity of discourses in this arena.) Similarly, work with gay men tends to be problem-centred rather than sexuality-centred. Having said this, however, some health professionals recognise that the roots of the 'problems' lie elsewhere, and that unplanned conceptions and STDs reflect wider social issues, but feel obliged (because of the dominant health discourse) to concentrate their efforts on relatively small-scale single-agency solutions.

- *Empowerment versus damage limitation* – most mainstream health (and education) workers conceptualised sexual health initiatives as a form of damage limitation rather than seeing the benefits of a sexual education in its own right. Community development workers, on the other hand, with their focus on empowerment, attempted to treat sexuality in its entirety rather than just focusing on problematic outcomes.

Finally, a brief word about a couple of other issues related to health discourses and sexual conduct. First, some, if not many, health authorities have responded to the White Paper targets by increasing the availability and accessibility of Family Planning Clinics (through having sessions after school hours, for example). Whilst this is to be welcomed, discussions with young people make it clear that, since they have no intention of starting a family just yet, these are not suitable places to visit to obtain advice and/or contraception; the more generic term 'Young People's Drop-in Centres', which offer a range of services, was generally felt to be more appropriate (Cooper et al. 1992). Second, we have avoided the temptation to attempt a definition of the term 'sexual health'. We hope that we have been able to demonstrate that the range of ways in which the term is interpreted amongst those working in the field has implications as to the sort of initiatives which are felt to be appropriate; selecting one particular definition runs the risk of restricting the ways of thinking about the issues involved.

Education policy

Given the problems that many young people face in accessing appropriate health services (through lack of available and/or suitable facilities, fears regarding confidentiality, and so on) a great deal of attention has been placed on school-based sex education. Whilst there has long been debate regarding what should and should not be covered in such classes, the recent increased public discussions of sexual matters has forced serious reconsideration of the area. Assuming that coverage does indeed have some impact on young people (although this may be a presumptuous assumption! – see, for example, Kirby et al. 1994), then the ways in which policies are implemented will have material outcomes on the ways in which young people relate to the issues involved; the processes involved in arriving at policies then become of major interest.

Between the late 1980s and 1993, maintained schools were required to have a written policy on sex education, but this policy could be simply that the area was not covered in the school (other than some coverage of the biological aspects of HIV and reproduction in the Science Core Curriculum). In 1993, a new Education Act was introduced; this contained over 500 amendments to the earlier Act, with some of these relating to sex education. What appeared to lead to this detailed reconsideration of the latter were two conflicting pressures on government. On the one hand, there was pressure from many quarters that it was insufficient to leave it to individual school-governing bodies to decide on whether sex education should be included, given the concerns about teenage conception rates and HIV/AIDS. On the other hand, there were some small but effective lobby groups who wished to retain the right to withdraw their children from sex education altogether, and they argued that this was not possible whilst coverage was included in the core curriculum.

The eventual outcome of the debate was to prohibit the teaching 'as part of the National Curriculum in Science, of any material on AIDS, HIV, and other sexually transmitted diseases, or any aspect, other than biological aspects, of human sexual behaviour' (Department for Education 1994). Instead, sex education, within a suitable moral framework which stresses family values, was to be included as a compulsory – but not core curriculum – subject, but parents would have the right to withdraw their children from some or all of the relevant classes if they requested so in writing (although there is no provision to take into account the students' wishes, nor to exempt them from parental right of withdrawal even if they are over 16 years of age). Governing bodies are required to draw up policies, and to make these available to parents for their information. Throughout the guidelines, it is made clear that the government regards parents as the major source of education regarding sex and related matters, and that school programmes are designed to support the parents' endeavours. This is somewhat in contrast with Isobel Allen's findings which report that 96 per cent of parents actually want schools to take the lead in sex education (Allen 1987).

Although the transcripts of the discussions through which each and every school-governing body arrives at their policies would be a truly fascinating source of discursive material, this would be a rather large project, and, in any event, gaining access may be difficult. The debates in the House of Lords are, however, public documents, and it is likely that the issues raised therein reflect, in varying degrees, those covered in meetings of governing bodies. Accordingly, Diane Stevens' analysis will be briefly summarised.

Some common themes emerged throughout, including the recognition that action was required in the face of the threats of HIV and unplanned conceptions, that sexual activity cannot be separated from a moral/value framework, that close liaison between schools and parents was important, and that the right of withdrawal should apply both to primary- and secondary-school-aged children. However, beyond these issues, two very distinct discourses could be identified in the course of the debates about withdrawal from classes at the secondary level. The first, which we shall call Discourse A and supporting the non-withdrawal option, can be summarised as *Promiscuity is the problem, education is the solution*, whereas the second, Discourse B, supporting the right of withdrawal, is *Education is the problem, morality is the solution*. Some brief examples of the arguments used to support these positions are provided.

In relation to Discourse A, we use the term 'promiscuity' with a dose of irony. There were fairly frequent references to the perceived dangers of non-intervention, although no speaker really defined exactly what they meant. A common rhetoric was to highlight the possible dangers, and then to suggest that providing the facts to everyone was a preferred option. For example, Lord Addington argues, in effect, that promiscuity is, and always has been, a problem:

> In our society everything from coffee to cars is sold through sex appeal. Sexuality is part of our art and culture. We cannot avoid it. . . . Therefore let us provide the facts . . . I cannot think of any period in history when abstinence has been the social norm . . . I suggest that a more realistic approach is to provide information.
>
> (21 June 1993: cols. 128–9)

Following from this, others argued that some sex education, however limited, is better than the 'rumour' of the playground:

we must be realistic and recognise that however bad the teaching of sex education may be in the classroom, it will probably be better than the murky sex education of the playground. We cannot isolate or insulate our children from the stuff they pick up in the playground or behind the bicycle shed . . . we cannot withdraw children from that, and withdrawal from the classroom may mislead children into thinking that everything they learn in the playground is acceptable. For that matter, withdrawing . . . may mislead parents into thinking that their children are unsullied by the grubby half-truths of the playground.

(The Lord Bishop of Guildford, ibid.: col. 130)

Whilst others highlight the apparent results of ignorance:

[after citing figures on teenage conceptions] I do not know how many of those single women became pregnant out of ignorance. . . . I am certain, however, that far more of those young people became pregnant out of ignorance than they did out of a desire to obtain a council house.

(Earl Russell, 6 July 1993: col. 1313)

and the consequent need for information:

we have no right . . . to deny children information which it may be essential for them to have to lead happy and healthy lives. Unless they have information and knowledge, they can fall into the trap of temptation which surrounds them. The temptations are far more powerful than the equipment that they have to resist them.

(Lord Houghton of Sowerby, ibid.: col. 1306)

Concerns were also expressed regarding the abilities and/or willingness of some parents to replace adequately what would be missed were children removed from school sex education classes, either in terms of access to 'up-to-date' information:

the amendment seeks to create a situation in which information . . . about HIV and AIDS . . . should be from their parents, from newspapers and from playground gossip. . . . Their information would not come from formal and informed sources at school. I believe this to be – particularly today – an extremely dangerous amendment.

(Lord Eatwell, 21 June 1993: col. 131)

or of an alternative source against which to evaluate family circumstances:

I am concerned that teachers may be gagged in helping children who may be abused by their own parents. Teachers may provide the only opportunity which the children will have of confiding in a trusted adult. . . . What happens if the abusing parents withdraw their children from sex education?

(Baroness Masham of Ilton, 6 July 1993: col. 1308)

Other arguments in favour of this approach drew on data from other countries, making links between the availability (or lack) of sex education and rates of teenage conception and HIV. These advocates suggested that 'lifesaving' information should be given at every opportunity, and reported research which demonstrated that the vast majority of parents want schools to take the lead in provision of sex education, not least because they find it a difficult topic to discuss with their offspring. The impracticalities involved in withdrawing young people from sex education, especially when taught as a cross-curriculum subject, were also pointed out in a number of contributions. The lack of increase in rates of HIV infection when compared with some earlier predictions was attributed to the success of increasing sex education within schools. Strangely, the views of young people themselves were referred to in very few contributions, but those that did raise this issue did so (with one exception) in support of more comprehensive coverage.

Speakers in support of Discourse B covered generally similar issues but with differing emphases and assumptions. Thus, for example, concerns were raised about possibly misleading and amoral material being used in schools:

[discussing material used in sex education] I should like to support [the amendments] because I am among many of your Lordships who were angered when we discovered that what we thought as over-explicit AIDS education had somewhat surreptitiously appeared in the science curriculum for 11-year olds. . . . [a particular manual] reveals that there is still an element, perhaps a strong element, in our teaching fraternity that wishes to discuss some aspects of sex education with children whose age indicates that they may not be ready for them.

(Lord Pearson of Rannoch, 21 June 1993: col. 127)

I want to paint a scenario where two parents – mother and father – ask to meet the person designated as responsible for their child's education. I suppose, for the purposes of the scenario, that they take an instant dislike to him or her and decide to embark on their child's sex education in the home, so as to immunise their child against the exposition that they attribute to the individual they distrust, justly or unjustly, rightly or wrongly, and which will circulate among other children as I described. Are they to be denied this right? It is no use preaching that the family is the natural unit of a healthy society and then doing something calculated to undermine it. . . . The needle, not normal sex, is the major source of AIDS.

(The Earl of Halsbury, 10 May 1993: col. 1099)

These comments regarding the supposedly inappropriate nature of some sex education material (the extent of which is never clarified) were often associated with an assumption that there is a direct causal relationship between the material received and subsequent behaviour. For example:

On the question of information, surely the fact is that when children are informed and learn at school, they imbibe knowledge for the future. But information on the kind of sex education that is being given in schools today is not just information; it encourages them to act on it. It affects their moral outlook, their moral behaviour and their conduct in general. . . . It is not just information; it is an encouragement to promiscuity.

(Baroness Elles, 10 May 1993: col. 1103)

We should all be concerned about the decline in the personal behaviour of our young people, but could it be a result of some insensitive sex education that has been taking place for years in our schools?

(Baroness Blatch, 6 July 1993: col. 1319)

Within Discourse B, one solution to this state of affairs is to increase the checks on schools by enabling parents who feel uncomfortable to withdraw their children, and, in cases where the withdrawal option is not taken up, simply the threat of such would be sufficient to restrain the more 'adventurous' schools. However, others had more straightforward solutions:

I believe that the *real* answer for dealing with AIDS and other sexually transmitted diseases is for the Government to take their courage in both hands and *tell* citizens that, if they want to avoid those diseases, they should be chaste before marriage and faithful within it [our emphases].

(Lord Ashbourne, 10 May 1993: col. 1106)

Whilst further support recommended learning from the USA:

the only bright thing on the horizon comes from correspondence I received from America which says that there is a group there which has become aware of the fact that the kind of sex education that I have just read out . . . is counter-productive. A new movement has sprung up and is gaining momentum, as far as I can see. It is described as the abstinence movement. . . . It is said that: 'American schoolchildren are learning the A to V of a new kind of sex education – A for abstinence and V for virginity'. . . . Students are being told to 'just say no'. In California teenagers following a course called Sex Respect chant a 'chastity pledge' – 'Do the right thing! Wait for the Ring!' . . . It emphasises traditional family values, and the benefits of idealism and self-discipline. We copy so much that comes from the United States, so would it not be a good idea to copy some of that instead of some of the stuff that I have read out earlier?

(Lord Stallard, 21 June 1993: cols. 124–5)

Speakers drew on a variety of devices to justify, or 'warrant', their claimed special expertise in the area (see Antaki (1985) for further discussion of such 'warranting' devices). These included being a parent, being a grandparent, being an ex-teacher, being a school governor, being a Christian, having been young once themselves, being an ex-nurse, being a 'reasonable' person, and so on. However, data from actual research very seldom got a mention (although, one of the present author's papers was cited, albeit to advance a position which he does not support!). Charitable organisations were, when it suited the speaker, denigrated to the status of 'lobbyists' and part of the to-be-feared 'AIDS industry'; this included the Sex Education Forum, an umbrella body which includes a large number of religious and similar organisations amongst its membership.

A further feature of many of the contributions to the debate related to the notion of 'normality'. Thus, the spirit of the quote cited earlier – 'the needle, not normal sex, is the major source of sex' – recurred from time to time, with 'normality' being clearly associated with one male and one female within a stable family relationship, akin to the 'have–hold' discourse discussed above.

We could obviously discuss at length the assumptions and models of human conduct which are implicit, and sometimes explicit, in this debate. Our aim, however, has been to reveal something of the wide variety of ways of talking about sexual activity and how these link in with the supposed function of, or need for, sex education. The provisions of the Act came into force in summer 1994, so it is rather too early to make any confident statements about their material impact. (A project has recently started in Southampton specifically on the issue of the relationship between parents, teachers and governors, and will explore their mutual understandings, the level of contact, and related issues.) However, there are some early indications that the threat of withdrawal is already having an effect on school policies. The practicalities of withdrawal from specific classes appears to be reducing the enthusiasm for cross-curricular approaches, as well as the degree to which schools will include some of the more 'controversial' topics which might attract unwanted publicity. Further, in a context in which greater freedom has been given to parents to select between schools, there is the additional threat of a student being removed from a school altogether. As one of our respondents (a Personal and Social Education teacher) in the HEA study told us:

> the image of the school is important – we are competing – every youngster who comes into our school is carrying money with them . . . you lose 10 students, you lose £10,000, half a teacher.

This whole issue needs to be set against a backdrop of what we know about young people's stated needs and wishes for school-based sex education. Various studies (for example, Woodcock et al. 1992a; Evans et al. 1994) have revealed overwhelming support for earlier and more comprehensive coverage of the non-biological aspects of relationships and sexual activity, including consideration of issues related to homosexuality, abortion and sexual abuse.

Many young people refer to the frequency with which they are confronted with such issues in the media (often in a sensationalist manner), and yet have little opportunity, if any, to explore and discuss their own reactions (or, in our terms, to be offered alternative discourses). How these young people talk is far removed from the fact and information (and morally) based discourses which permeated the House of Lords debates.

DISCOURSES AND FAMILIES

Much of the discussion in the House of Lords debates was based on the assumption that any interventions within schools would be supportive of, and supplementary to, treatment of the topics within family settings. As pointed out above, however, there was some division of opinion amongst the contributors regarding the extent to which parents would indeed provide this support. Some speakers clearly had in mind parents who were linked with, or sympathetic to, organisations like the Conservative Family Campaign, Family and Youth Concern, the Brethren, certain other religious or cultural groupings, and so on, and were confident that a clear moral and value framework would be provided. Others, however, were less confident, making reference either to the stresses that some parents faced in coping generally, let alone in being able to deal with value frameworks, or pointing to the difficulties reported by parents and young people in discussing some of the less biological areas related to sexual activity and relationships.

There has not, to date, been much research on the specific topic of how sexual issues are discussed within families (but see Friday 1979; Arcana 1981; Apter 1990). Some of our previous research does touch on the area, and points to some promising avenues for future research endeavours. Ideally, analysis of actual conversations between parents and young people would be obtained, but such data would not be easy to collect. We are therefore reliant on accounts from one side or the other; these are derived from different families, and a nice study for the future would be to discuss issues with different members of the same families.

Our ESRC project interview protocol, which collected data from young people about a large range of issues, did include some coverage of how the respondents felt they had been influenced by their parents and/or step-parents. Not surprisingly, there was quite wide variation in the level of 'factual' information reported to have been gained from parents, as well as the ease with which the topic could be discussed (with a majority of respondents reporting that it was 'not easy', 'very embarrassing', and so on). Perhaps of more relevance within a discursive context, however, were the parents' values as reported by our respondents. Some, although not many, referred quite explicitly to having acquired a sense of moral values (in some cases, but not always, based on religious beliefs) which they felt had influenced them strongly – specific discussions of sex did not need to have occurred in these families, since 'it was always understood' that sex and marriage were inseparable. Others reported a less specific morality based on respect for others and themselves which they felt had been influential in a general sense in how they related to others, how able they felt to say what they wished, and related issues.

On the issue of the extent of specific discussions regarding sex, a number of varied discursive contexts were described (overall, substantially more young women reported discussing issues with their mothers than did young men with either mothers or fathers). Detailed analyses of these are ongoing; so far four contexts have been identified. These include the *moralistic*, in which sexual activity is placed in a particular moral and value framework which discouraged any form of sexual activity prior to marriage, *general negativity*, in which some mothers were reported as having described sex in very negative terms, stressing the pain (physical and/or emotional) involved, the *laissez-faire*, in which parents were described as appearing to not take any interest in what their children did in regard to relationships and/or sexual activity, and the *realist–humanist*, in which parents were described as accepting that their children would engage in sexual activity, and emphasising the need for adequate protection against conceptions and/or STDs. For the young women, this meant ensuring that they were on the pill, or knew how to get and use condoms, whilst for some of the young men, this involved little more than warnings (usually from their fathers) about taking care to 'not get any girls into trouble' (this advice also featured in the *laissez-faire* approach).

Obviously, there were variations within these reported contexts, with combinations and/or fragments of discourses being reported either simultaneously or at different times during the young person's development. Of particular interest, of course, for the present chapter, is the possible impact that these different approaches to 'treating' sex within the family had on the sexual activity (the material outcome) of the young people concerned. Detailed analyses of these possible effects are currently being carried out, but an initial consideration would suggest that what we call the realist–humanist approach was associated with a rather later age of first sexual intercourse as well as higher use of contraception. It would, however, be too simplistic to attribute any direct causal link here, since many other features may distinguish the families which were described in the various different ways.

It is interesting to note, however, that some research in the Netherlands has identified a strong association between early relations within families (as described by young people) and subsequent risk-taking in sexual contexts, with those reporting that their parents were approachable and having time for them adopting rather lower levels of risk-taking (van Zessen and Zijlmans 1993). These authors speculate that communication competence is a key variable which serves to link these factors.

Other relevant research adopting a cross-national approach was conducted by Jones et al. (1986, 1988). Comparing over thirty developed countries on various measures, they reported a strong association between what they call 'sexual openness' and rates of teenage conceptions, with more 'open' countries having the lower rates. More recently, the British national survey on sexual behaviour and attitudes (Johnson et al. 1994) reported that the manual social classes generally hold less permissive attitudes towards pre-marital sexual activity than do those from non-manual classes, and yet rates of teenage conceptions are considerably higher amongst the manual social class. From these different sources, a general picture is emerging that greater 'openness' in talking about sexual activity does appear to lead to the adoption of 'safer' practices.

Further work is needed in order to understand how this comes about, but Thompson's (1990) analysis of teenage girls' accounts of 'sexual initiation' is relevant here. She found two predominant accounts. In the first, young girls tended to describe first intercourse as something that 'just happened' (pp.343 ff.). Thompson shows how the accounts of this group of girls indicate a level of sexual naiveté that makes this description unsurprising – they simply had no experience, expectation *or language* with which either to understand the event at the time, or to describe it later. In contrast the 'pleasure narrators' of the second story 'from earliest childhood . . . seem to take sexual subjectivity for granted' (pp.350 ff.). Thompson suggests the source of this expectation of pleasure is in the support of parents and friends who 'believe in pleasure' and 'think masturbation and childhood sexuality are good omens, not sins' (p.350). They tended to engage in sexual experiences in a spirit of experimentation and pleasure seeking, and, most relevant here, were able to express their own sexual preferences, and to say 'no' as well as 'yes' (p.351).

It might seem a simple matter to modify childhood experience, but Thompson notes that whilst the majority of mothers believe they 'should' talk to their daughters about sex, for most it is no trivial undertaking. On the whole, according to the girls' stories, mothers limited the talk to 'the facts of life' or became entangled in 'judgmental no-win' arguments (p.354). Whilst the latter *may* lead to delay of first coitus it is also likely to contribute to first coitus being an experience of the 'first story' kind.

Thompson's 'first story' echoes another preliminary finding of ours which also relates to the 'general negativity' often associated with sex. Whereas in some cases this appeared to have an effect of delaying sexual initiation, in other cases it appeared to have the opposite effect (Kirkland and Ingham, in preparation). Thus, 'fear' of sex, whilst not cited as a reason for their earliest activities, seemed for a number of respondents to be an adjunct to 'getting it over with', for example:

I was always scared of doing it for the first time really . . . frightened me . . . I always thought it hurt always dunno why – people turned round and said 'Oh it does hurt' and I think that's what frightened me.
(female, 16 years old at the interview, a few months after first intercourse)

As well as young people talking about their recollections of the ways in which their parents discussed sex and related matters, and the possible effect this had on them, Kirkland has recently been discussing with some parents their approaches towards these areas with their own children. She reports great variety of discourses even within this relatively small sample of middle-class and fairly well-educated parents.

A number of the parents stressed how important they felt it was to place sexual activity within a wider and more caring context, and to try to be open with their children, for example:

> I say . . . 'it's part of life . . . and before you come to sex there's learning to like yourself, and other people, and considering others' . . . cos I said sex isn't just 'Oh wham bam thank you ma'am'.
>
> (female, about 40 years old)

> My husband and him, they'd be sat in the room chatting, or if we're out for a ride different things would crop up, and Chris would feel quite able to say . . . and I mean when he started having wet dreams he said, 'Oh, mum' . . . and I said, 'Oh' (I saw him with the sheet) I said, 'Oh you had a wet dream' . . . 'Ooh you're growing up!'
>
> (female, about 40 years old)

On the other hand, some of these parents advocated at least delay in addressing some topics, often drawing on the notion of 'childhood innocence':

> I don't believe that you should push information before they're ready for it. It's difficult to judge but I think . . . some people are much more innocent than others aren't they?
>
> (female, about 40 years old)

However, a recurring theme was the *lack* of any actual talk, or of things being left unsaid:

> There was something on the television recently . . . somebody was said to be 'having it off' with somebody, and our youngest one sniggered a bit, she knew exactly what it meant. Well, she, she seemed to know exactly what it meant anyway, she sniggered and er . . . and . . . em . . . nothing much was said about it.
>
> (male, mid-forties)

This area of the 'unspoken' seems to generate a general air of mystification, or in the words of one informant, of 'taboo':

> My mother had the problem of bringing up two boys and she found it extraordinarily difficult to discuss . . . in fact . . . I think we have to say we had no sex education at home . . . whatsoever . . . and whilst in a way that triggers in you a desire not to have that experience repeated in

your own children . . . it equally makes the subject a bit taboo sometimes.

> (male, about 40 years old)

Such mystification is pervasive in discussions (or lack of discussion) of sexuality (Lee 1983). It is not clear whether mystification should be counted as a
discourse in its own right (focusing on the maintenance of 'innocence', the
subject of sex as 'taboo'), or whether it is more appropriately considered as
embedded in other discourses. As 'taboo' it is perhaps a persistent feature of
the male sex drive discourse, with constant references to the 'unspoken' or
'unspeakable' ('know what I mean?!' nudge, nudge!) but is not always present
with the have–hold discourse. Alternatively, it might be a 'symptom' of the
fragmented and incomplete nature of 'sexual' discourses. Notice that the
surface content of the have–hold discourse is primarily about relationship
rather than sex.

As with the reports from the young people, the issue of embarrassment
came up amongst the parents, for example:

> Perhaps I should have asked . . . but perhaps they might be just too
> embarrassed to tell me?

> (male, mid-forties)

Interestingly, the parents never directly attributed the source of embarrassment to themselves.

DISCOURSE AND THE DYAD

Whatever the historical and preceding contextual discourses, the critical discussion about sexual health (and pregnancy outcome) is dyadic at the time
immediately prior to copulation. This is when the state of contraception
should be known, and STD protection (use of condom, femidom, etc.) must
be negotiated. This analysis refers, of course, only to the most obvious
'material' outcomes of sexual intercourse. There are many other personal
and interpersonal implications of coitus, and of non-coital sexual conduct,
which have impact on life outcomes, self-respect, and other more or less
'material' issues just a few of which are touched on below. It is illuminating
that research projects, funded through the 1980s and 1990s in a search for
interventions relevant primarily to HIV transmission and teenage pregnancy, have consistently increased our awareness of these less easily 'measurable' outcomes. For example, new researchers are often discomfited by the
prevalence of accounts of child sexual abuse in interview accounts of young
men and women's sexual histories.

Whatever outcomes we are concerned with, the data suggest that adequate discussion fails to occur, especially amongst the younger age groups.
Given the diverse and often fragmentary nature of the various discourses

around sexuality this is perhaps not surprising. In the sexual dyad, even where discussion does occur, discourses may be in conflict. The following example is provided by a single woman in her mid-thirties with dependent children, and draws on an argument based on 'taking care of ourselves' to support her insistence on condom use with a new partner. He apparently raised many counter arguments, and the outcome was reported as being very damaging for the relationship:

> It has spoilt the whole thing. [Interviewer: Because it introduced an element of conflict?] Because, you know we had to stop, and like do this like negotiation and we got, not exactly into a debate about, you know, whether you should . . . look after, you know, whether you could actually protect yourself from life, or whether you should just . . . I mean he gave the indication that he would, he respected my wishes, and it was all right . . . so I mean that seemed to be all right, and I thought he'd accepted it and it was all right, and accepted my argument, I mean we'd take care of ourselves and, I just felt I couldn't take the risk . . . but when I went to stay with him . . . then I think his true feelings came out that . . . he just thought that it, it wasn't . . . he just didn't like it. And I think . . . yeah, I think that was a serious handicap, yeah, to the relationship.
>
> (female, mid-thirties)

On the other hand, both discussion, *and action*, relating to a discourse of safe sex may be suppressed – in this account, apparently losing out to 'male sex drive':

> I planned to use them, and they were in my coat, only four metres away, but still, it's four metres. You are in somebody's bed, and you want to do it and you are both in a certain state, and I was afraid for the moment that she would say 'Ho, wait a minute', and that she would suddenly realise what the hell she was doing.
>
> (Dutch male, 22 years old)

And indeed it can be the case that any kind of discussion, especially, but not only, about sexual aspects of the encounter, is simply considered irrelevant:

Interviewer   Did you know the woman well?
Man   No, I met her that night.
Interviewer   How was the experience?
Man   Fine.
Interviewer   Did you have an orgasm?
Man   Yeah.
Interviewer   Did she have one?
Man   Gee, I'm not sure . . . I guess so.

Interviewer   But you're not sure. Is there a way you could have found
        out?
Man   Hmmm . . . I don't know.
Interviewer   You could have asked her, couldn't you?
Man   Asked her? I hardly knew her name!
        (Radio interview, quoted in Zilbergeld *Men and Sex*, 1980: 182)

Although there is often little discussion *in advance of* coitus, informants
often report considerable reflection *after* the event, and these aspects of
accounts tend to be constituted in terms of the societal discourses we discussed above. For example, analyses of the reasons provided by young people for their first ever sexual experiences point clearly to the powerful impact
of these different ways of 'discoursing' sexual relations, and what it means
to be a man or a woman. What 'boys' (or girls) 'expect' reflects the male sex
drive discourse:

> I knew he expected it more than I did. Boys always seem to don't they
> (*laugh*) always seem to.

> (female, 16 years old)

And here we see a relationship 'tested' against the expectations of the
'have–hold' discourse:

> I liked him obviously, but . . . I couldn't see myself for the rest of my life
> with him.

> (female, 19 years old)

There is a further aspect of this analysis which helps to justify importance
being placed on evaluation of the encounter. Our ESRC transcripts included
sections on our respondents' reactions to their early experiences. In many
cases, especially amongst those younger at first intercourse, women reported
considerable regret at events (men quite often did as well, but normally in
terms of purely physical aspects of the events) (Ingham et al. 1991). This
regret was frequently described in terms of the contrast between what they
had expected of first intercourse (the background discourse?) and their
experience. For example:

> . . . I always believed it would be someone I loved first [time], and it
> wasn't, so I felt a bit out of order for that, so I cheated myself more than
> anything, nobody else.

> (female, 16 years old)

And another:

> I regretted it, I really did. I thought, 'Oh God, this is not the way to lose
> it' . . . you are supposed to lose it in a meaningful relationship you know.
> You're supposed to do it after you've known a guy five months, six

months, you know. There's me on my one night stand, pissed as hell, and lose it in someone else's bedroom, you know. I thought 'great, well done'.

(female, 17 years old)

What characterises both of these examples is not only the apparent loss of self-esteem and the self-blame which occurred, but also a reference to some imagined circumstances under which sexual activity *should* occur, which seems to draw on some variant of the *have–hold* or *romantic* discourse. However, close reading of the transcripts, as well as material gathered from interviews with young men, suggests that, in many cases, the self-blame is simply inappropriate.

CONCLUDING COMMENTS

In this chapter we try to draw together information from a number of studies related to a variety of topics concerned with sexual health, in order to understand the discursive implications of the research findings. Perhaps one of the most obvious outcomes is to highlight that, whilst researchers such as Hollway and Wight have identified some dominant discourses of sexuality (and these certainly figure in the accounts we have collected), none the less the discursive life of the informants in our studies seems far more complex, and often more fragmentary, even than the first sight of the three or four dominant discourses might suggest.

Of course the studies we cite, and the preliminary conclusions we have reported here, are subject to the usual limitations of qualitative research, in that we are trying to identify important discursive themes relevant to a wide audience whilst drawing on the accounts of a relatively few individuals (though our total number of informants is in the hundreds). Furthermore, there is not space in one book chapter to give an adequate account of the sexual life history of even one of our informants, let alone to do justice to all of them.

At another level, we have not addressed some of the 'meta-discourses' often brought to bear on a social analysis of topics such as sexuality. Unlike many sociological perspectives, we have not considered issues of class, nor have we considered the extent or influence of patriarchal hegemony, as feminist theorists might. It is not that we discount the influence of such 'grand narratives' but rather we have sought to 'tease out' some of the material effects of the more immediate, though often partial and fragmentary, discourses evidenced in the texts and transcripts we have analysed. We do not doubt that these in turn may be influenced by, and influence, the meta-discourses – and each other. Our view is not that discourses can be identified once and for all, packaged up, and labelled. But rather that a discursive analysis helps us to identify key themes and processes at work in society now – albeit these themes and processes are in a continuous state of flow and flux, movement and change.

Additionally, as we have indicated above, some of the analyses presented here are preliminary, and further work is in progress in some of these areas. Nevertheless, we argue that it is useful to introduce some of the discursive themes which we are beginning to find, and to show how they are relevant both to social policy, and to professional, personal and family lives.

First, this brief overview has provided a few examples of how discourses around sexuality, amongst young people, in families, and in the broader community, tend to have little or no direct health content.

At the same time, we have introduced a few examples of how discourses of sexuality can and do have material effects. They appear in discussions in Parliament and affect (and effect) legislation. Through that legislation they effect change in institutions; the legislation changes how sex education is implemented in schools, how sex-related services are delivered by health care providers and, of course, which research topics get academic funding.

Within institutional settings, services are delivered to people who arrive with diverse, and often fragmented, discourses about sexuality, derived from widely varying family backgrounds, and of course (though there's no space for examples here) from other sources such as friends and/or the media. We suggest that this diversity should affect how the services are delivered (albeit remembering that the providers of services often have similarly diverse and fragmented discourses about sexuality) – but it is not so clear that it always does. There are, however, some material effects of recognition of this need – for example, the move towards provision of 'drop in' centres for health care provision and opportunities for counselling support for young people.

Finally, sexual conduct does seem to be discursively constituted and construed, as evidenced by the words people use when they reflect on, describe, explain, or justify their sexual behaviour. However, the discourse does not always seem to be adequate to the task in hand, as in the case of young women being unable to 'tell' of their experience of first intercourse. Even when participants are more mature and articulate, the discovery of conflicting discourses between partners can lead to unsatisfactory outcomes. More often it seems people are quite unaware of how their partner 'construes' the situation, or perhaps they assume they share a common understanding (though our informants' accounts suggest this is often discovered later to be a mistaken assumption).

Conflicting discourses seem also to compete within individuals, as with our young Dutchman, who preferred to ensure the continuance of the sexual episode in preference to pausing to ensure his and his partner's protection from STD transmission. Furthermore, despite holding to some discourse that includes the notion that you 'should' wait until you have known your partner for several months before considering sexual intercourse, many young women seem swayed (by some alternative interpretation of the situation? by pressure from their partner? or by some irresistible biological drive?) to accede to intercourse much earlier in a relationship than they report having intended.

In sum, whilst discourses of sexuality have been identified, and warrant the label 'discourse' in that they recur in accounts from diverse informants from diverse locations, they are often inadequate, contradictory and fragmented, leading to unexpected and often undesirable (and undesired) material outcomes whether they meet in Parliament, the classroom, the parking lot, or in bed.

NOTE

1 *Hansard* is the official report of the proceedings of the British Houses of Parliament and is published daily during parliamentary sessions by Her Majesty's Stationery Office (HMSO). The reports are numbered by column, not page.

REFERENCES

Allen, I. (1987) *Education in Sex and Personal Relationships*, Research Report 665, London: Policy Studies Institute.

Antaki, C. (1985) 'Ordinary explanation in conversation: causal structures and their defence', *European Journal of Social Psychology* 15: 213–230.

Apter, T. (1990) *Altered Love: Mothers and Daughters during Adolescence*, Hemel Hempstead: Harvester Wheatsheaf.

Arcana, J. (1981) *Our Mothers' Daughters*, London: Women's Press.

Billig, M., Condor, S., Edwards, D., Gane, M., Middleton, D. and Radley, A. (1988) *Ideological Dilemmas*, Bristol: Sage.

Cooper, P., Diamond, I. and High, S. (1992) 'Quality measures in family planning: services and provision in Wessex; report and recommendations', Winchester: Wessex Regional Health Authority.

Department for Education (1994) *Education Act 1993: Sex Education in Schools*, circular no. 5/94, London: DfE.

Department of Health (1992) *The Health of the Nation*, London: HMSO.

—— (1993) *The Health of the Nation Key Area Handbook: HIV/AIDS and Sexual Health*, London: HMSO.

Evans, D., Ingham, R. and Roots, B., (1994) *Sex Education in Salisbury: Report of an evaluation project in Salisbury schools*, Health Commission for Wiltshire and Bath.

Foucault, M. (1979) *The History of Sexuality. Volume I: An Introduction* (trans. Robert Hurley from *Histoire et la sexualité*, Paris: Gallimard 1976), London: Allen Lane.

—— (1984a) 'Madness and civilisation', in P. Rabinow (ed.) *The Foucault Reader*, Harmondsworth: Penguin.

—— (1984b) 'On the genealogy of ethics: an overview of work in progress', in P. Rabinow (ed.) *The Foucault Reader*, Harmondsworth: Penguin.

Friday, N. (1979) *My Mother, My Self: The Daughters' Search for Identity*, London: Fontana.

Holland, J., Ramazanoglu, C., Sharpe, S. and Thomson, R. (1991) 'Between embarrassment and trust: young women and the diversity of condom use', in P.

Aggleton, G. Hart and P. Davies (eds) *AIDS: Responses, Interventions and Care*, London: Falmer Press.

—— (1994) 'Power and desire: the embodiment of female sexuality', *Feminist Review* 46: 21–38.

Holland, J., Ramazanoglu, C., Scott, S., Sharpe, S. and Thomson, R. (1992) 'Pressure, resistance, empowerment: young women and the negotiation of safer sex', in P. Aggleton, G. Hart and P. Davies (eds) *AIDS: Rights, Risk and Reason*, London: Falmer Press.

Hollway, W. (1984) 'Gender difference and the production of subjectivity', in J. Henriques, W. Hollway, C. Urwin, C. Venn and V. Walkerdine *Changing the Subject*, London: Methuen.

Ingham, R. (1994) 'Some speculations on the concept of rationality', in G. Albrecht (ed.) *Advances in Medical Sociology: A Reconsideration of Health Behavior Change Models*, vol. 4, Greenwich, CT: JAI Press.

Ingham, R., Jaramazović, E. and Stevens, D. (1994) *Sex Education in the Community: A Feasibility Study*, London: Health Education Authority.

—— (1997) 'Constraints in the development of sexual health alliances', in P. Aggleton, P. Davies and G. Hart (eds) *AIDS: Activism and Alliances*, London: Taylor & Francis.

Ingham, R., Woodcock, A. and Stenner, K. (1991) ' "Getting to know you . . . ": young people's knowledge of their partner at first intercourse', *Journal of Community and Applied Social Psychology* 1(2): 117–132.

—— (1992) 'The limitations of rational decision-making models as applied to young people's sexual behaviour', in P. Aggleton, P. Davies and G. Hart (eds) *AIDS: Rights, Risk and Reason*, London: Falmer Press.

Johnson, A. M., Wadsworth, J., Wellings, K. and Field, J., with Bradshaw, S. (1994) *Sexual Attitudes and Lifestyle*, Oxford: Blackwell Scientific.

Jones, E. F., Forrest, J. D., Silverman, J. and Torres, A. (1988) 'Unintended pregnancy, contraceptive practice and family planning services in developed countries', *Family Planning Perspectives* 20: 53–55, 58–67.

Jones, E. F., Forrest, J. D., Goldman, N., Henshaw, S., Lincoln, R., Rossoff, J. I., Westoff, C. F. and Wulf, D. (1986) *Teenage Pregnancy in Industrialized Countries*, New Haven, CT: Yale University Press.

Kirby, D., Short, L., Collins, J., Rugg, D., Kolbe, L., Howard, M., Miller, B., Sonenstein, F. and Zabin, L. (1994) 'School-based programs to reduce sexual risk behaviors: a review of effectiveness', *Public Health Reports* 109(3): 339–360.

Kirkland, D. and Ingham, R. (in preparation) *Fear of Sex as a Motivating Factor for Intercourse* (provisional title).

Lee, C. (1983) *The Ostrich Position: Sex, Schooling and Mystification*, Trowbridge: Writers and Readers Publishing Cooperative Society Ltd.

Rabinow, P. (ed.) (1984) *The Foucault Reader*, Harmondsworth: Penguin.

Thompson, S. (1990) 'Putting a big thing into a little hole: teenage girls' accounts of sexual initiation', *The Journal of Sex Research* 27(3): 341–361.

van Zessen, G. and Zijlmans, W. (1993) *Contactgerichten en Casanova's. Levensloop, identiteit en veilig vrijen*, Utrecht: NISSO.

Weeks, J. (1981) *Sex, Politics and Society: The Regulation of Sexuality since 1800*, London: Longman.

—— (1985) *Sexuality and its Discontents: Meanings, Myths and Sexualities*, London: Routledge & Kegan Paul.

Wight, D. (in press) 'Beyond the predatory male: the diversity of young Glaswegian men's discourses to describe heterosexual relationships', in L. Adkins and V.

Merchant (eds) *Sexualising the Social: Power and the Organisation of Sexuality*, London: Macmillan.

Woodcock, A. J., Stenner, K. and Ingham, R. (1992a) 'Young people talking about HIV and AIDS: interpretations of personal risk of infection', *Health Education Research: Theory and Practice* 7: 229–247.

—— (1992b) ' "All these contraceptives, videos and that . . . ": young people talking about school sex education', *Health Education Research: Theory and Practice* 7: 517–531.

Zilbergeld, B. (1980) *Men and Sex*, Glasgow: Fontana.

Chapter 9

Discourses of pregnancy and childbirth

Anne Woollett and Harriette Marshall

INTRODUCTION

In this chapter we examine critically discourses of pregnancy and childbirth, drawing on two main sources of accounts. The first comprises booklets distributed to pregnant women at antenatal clinics and which hence have an official status. These were *The Baby Book* (1988) whose editors and advisors identify themselves as medical practitioners and *The Pregnancy Book* (1984) published by Health Education Council, which draws on the research of social scientists as well as medical practitioners. The other major source of accounts comprises interviews about their pregnancy and childbirth with women from a variety of social and cultural backgrounds living in the UK. They included Asian women who participated in a study of parenting in a multi-ethnic community, described more fully in Woollett and Dosanjh-Matwala (1990) and Woollett et al. (1995) and with white women interviewed as part of a study of the expectations and experiences of women expecting twins (Woollett and Clegg 1989). Asian women were interviewed by an Asian psychologist and the interviews were conducted in the women's preferred language. All were tape-recorded, and then transcribed and translated if necessary. Extracts from the booklets and the interviews are used to illustrate the analysis.

These sources are analysed using social constructivist and discursive approaches to identify general themes, differences and contradictions as well as omissions in accounts (Potter and Wetherell 1987; Banister et al. 1994). Two major discourses are identified: medical/biological discourses which are drawn on in the booklets addressed to women and in the accounts of women themselves, and psychological discourses which position women's embodied experiences of pregnancy and childbirth within the experiences of individual women, the meanings of pregnancy, and women's relations with partners.

Biological–medical accounts draw on a variety of interrelated discourses such as 'monitoring health/normality', 'detection of abnormality' and 'medical intervention' with the expressed purpose of delivering 'healthy' babies.

In doing so, pregnancy and childbirth are presented as both 'natural' and 'normal' biological and physiological events, and as 'illness' requiring medical management and intervention. Psychological accounts draw on a variety of discourses which position in terms of women's identities, lives and development. Biological–medical and psychological accounts, and the discourses on which they draw, are contrasted with the accounts of feminists and researchers taking the perspective of women, and those of consumer groups such as the National Childbirth Trust (NCT). These position pregnancy and childbirth as embodied experience with social and cultural significance, and resist the regulation of women's readings of their childbearing bodies. Lastly we draw on diverse discourses to examine the ways in which nausea and sickness are constructed.

BIOLOGICAL–MEDICAL DISCOURSES

Monitoring normality/health

The predominant discourses of pregnancy and childbirth position them as biological and medical events. This incorporates a variety of different and, at times, contradictory accounts. One account views pregnancy as a 'normal/healthy state' and antenatal care as monitoring 'normality/health'. Bodily changes in pregnancy and childbirth are taken as being part of a 'normal' unfolding of a physical process which is marked by physiological changes such as the cessation of menstruation, nausea and sickness, increases in women's weight and size, and the movement of the fetus. This account is employed in *The Pregnancy Book* (1984), which starts by delineating women's 'sexual organs' and the process of conception and physiological changes in pregnancy, using drawings of a diagrammatic, disembodied mother and baby (pp. 2–6, 9–12). Pregnancy and childbirth are taken to be essentially 'healthy' and antenatal care is portrayed as monitoring progress, as in the following extract (p. 27):

> Throughout your pregnancy you will have regular check ups. . . . This is to make sure that both you and the baby are fit and well, to check the baby is developing properly. . . . These check ups also give you a chance to get answers to the questions and worries that are bound to crop up at different stages of your pregnancy.

As this extract illustrates, the emphasis is on 'checking' with medical procedures constructed as essentially facilitatory, providing health professionals with the information to be sure that everything is going 'well' and to address women's questions and concerns. Women draw on this account of monitoring normality/health, as in the following extracts from interviews with Asian women expecting their first child:

Interviewee   All they did was to check your weight, take blood samples, check your tummy, check your blood pressure. Mostly they used to check my weight because I didn't put on too much weight. . . . They were worried about why I wasn't putting on weight so I had to have a lot of scans to see if the baby was normal.

Interviewer   What were the hospital visits for?

Interviewee   To have everything checked, to see if everything's alright. Well blood test and they checked the baby with that machine to hear the heart beat. And scans. I had a urine test every time.

However, many women find that their antenatal care does not deliver knowledge or reassurance and it is difficult to obtain the results of tests, as in the following extracts from two Asian women:

Interviewer   What were the tests for?

Interviewee   Don't know why we had the tests. I never asked for the results. There probably wasn't anything wrong with me so they didn't tell me. They don't give you the results of the tests unless there is anything wrong: you have to ask. They could be a bit more helpful. They could tell you rather than wait for you to ask because some Asians there they don't know how to speak and they won't push for anything.

Women recite off lists of tests, but as in these extracts, there was often little engagement with the process and little detailed knowledge of what the results might signify, as Reid (1990) reported. While some women complained that they wanted more information and argued that women need to be assertive, others left things to the medical professionals, assuming they would be told if something was wrong.

Regulating normality

A closer examination of accounts of antenatal care suggests that tests are used not only to 'monitor normality', but have a more regulatory role. They would seem to be used normatively, to make comparisons with what are considered biological and physiological 'norms' about pregnancy and childbirth. Taking as an example women's weight gain, the booklets provided for pregnant women in some respects present a relaxed line on this. For example, *The Pregnancy Book* (p. 40) gives information about average weight gain, which suggests 'normal' variability rather than a set of norms:

An average total weight gain in pregnancy is 22–28 lbs, or 10–12.5 kg. But weight gain varies a lot from woman to woman. It is not usually anything to worry about, but if you are concerned, talk to your doctor or midwife.

However, this relaxed presentation is undermined by using women's weight gain as an indicator of 'normality', with greater or lesser weight gain given as a reason for doing further tests, as in the case of the woman in an earlier extract who was given a scan because she was not gaining 'sufficient weight'. Another woman reports that it was discovered she was pregnant with twins after she was sent for a scan 'because I was too large for dates'. This implies that weights are being compared with a 'norm', in spite of any lack of evidence about the universal appropriateness of such norms or their predictive value (Oakley 1979; Reid 1990; Raphael-Leff 1991; Phoenix 1990).

Comparing women against a set of 'norms' implies that there is a right way in pregnancy, and contradicts statements about all pregnancies being different and there being no rules. Women draw on biological–medical discourses in their accounts of bodily changes and increasing weight in the later months of pregnancy, as Wolkind and Zajicek (1980) report, and as in the following extracts from interviews:

> The pregnancy was fine, my health was OK, but I had put on too much weight.

> I got a lot heavier. I used to get tired a lot, even when sweeping a room.

However, closer examination suggests that women's accounts position weight gain largely in terms of their identities and sense of themselves and its impact on their lives. Weight gain and bodily size were often discussed in terms of women's ability to do everyday things such as getting to sleep, look after older children and fulfil their domestic roles, as in the following extract:

> I think because it was my second and I had him [first child], he was about one and half, it was difficult to attend to him, like give him a bath, especially in the later months. Sometimes I had trouble feeding him. I used to feel really tired by the end of the day, and it was difficult to bend over and give him a bath.

Some of the women expecting twins discussed the ways in which the weight of two babies could accentuate other problems, as in the following extract:

> I feel uncomfortable. And when I'm in the bath, and things like that. I can't get out. And getting up from lying down is awkward. I wasn't very happy at all with my figure at the beginning. I really saw myself as being maternal, the mothering figure. When I started changing shape and everything I really didn't like it at all.

In this extract, the woman expresses dissatisfaction with her 'mothering figure'. Wolkind and Zajicek (1980) also found that women disliked their pregnant shapes, even when they were pleased to be pregnant. The booklets provided at the antenatal clinic emphasise the importance of eating well in pregnancy, but do not address women's embodied experiences as they get larger and fatter, even though these are issues of major concern to women (Wiles 1994).

Health and illness

Within biological–medical accounts, pregnancy and childbirth are constructed as both 'health' and 'illness'. While acknowledging their 'normality' and 'naturalness', pregnancy and childbirth are treated and managed as potentially problematic, and hence as 'illness'. 'Normality' and 'health' come to be defined only in retrospect (Hewison 1993). The booklets provided for pregnant women have sections labelled 'problems' which range from 'normal/healthy' symptoms such as morning sickness and tiredness to more medically significant problems such as swollen ankles and pre-eclampsia. The potentially problematic nature of childbirth is used to argue for the benefits of hospital delivery:

> The advantage of a hospital birth is that both expertise and equipment are on hand in case they are needed. If something goes wrong during labour (and no-one can be 100 per cent sure that it won't) then you don't have to be moved. A Caesarean delivery, for example, can be done on the spot if need be. In the same way, if there is anything wrong with the baby when it is born, hospital facilities can be life saving. The baby can be cared for immediately without vital time being lost in a journey to hospital.
>
> *(The Pregnancy Book* 1984: 19)

While the risks of 'normal delivery' are emphasised, those associated with medicalised childbirth are either not discussed or are presented in terms of 'disadvantages' rather than risks, as in the case of epidurals:

> Also since you can no longer feel your contractions, the midwife has to tell you when to push rather than you doing it naturally. This means it can take longer to push the baby out.
>
> (ibid.: 50)

Feminist researchers and consumer groups such as the National Childbirth Trust are critical of the ways in which pregnancy and childbirth are constructed and managed as if they were illnesses – that is, being largely hospital-based and with the routine use of drugs and surgical procedures (Stoppard 1995; Oakley 1979; Kitzinger 1990). They are also critical of the depersonalisation of pregnant and birthing women, as 'bodies' or 'reproductive systems', arguing that this is used to justify medical views of women's passivity and their exclusion from decision-making processes (Oakley 1980; Hewison 1993).

This tension between pregnancy and childbirth as 'illness' and 'health', and ideological struggles between biological–medical discourses and those of feminist and consumer groups over the nature and management of pregnancy and childbirth, are also found in women's accounts. Women distinguish between aspects of pregnancy which they see as needing to be medically managed and 'normal/healthy' symptoms of a pregnant body. In the following interview, a woman expecting twins makes a clear distinction between a medical account and her own account of pregnancy:

Interviewer   How do you think your pregnancy went?

Interviewee   It depends. If you take it clinically, medically, it was wonderful. Otherwise it was bloody awful. I complained every day about it. Because I was so well with [first child] I didn't know one could be so ill when one is pregnant. I just didn't expect it. I was sick for the first 4 months, then I had pain in the ribs . . . I couldn't eat and couldn't walk. I couldn't sleep in the end. I just couldn't enjoy myself at all. Clinically it was OK: I didn't have to go into hospital, and I didn't have high blood pressure, swollen ankles, anaemia, what else didn't I have. . . . But I felt awful.

Women are committed to childbirth as 'normal' and 'natural' but also to the delivery of 'safe and healthy' babies and hence to medical intervention if and/or when things 'go wrong'. In many respects they express themselves in language similar to that used in the booklets provided at antenatal clinics, as in the following extract from a woman hospitalised prior to the birth of her twins:

I feel I am happy here [in hospital], because if anything goes wrong, I'm here. At home there's no-one. They are at school, and my husband's out at work, and I'm frightened that they'll come so quick there will be no one to help me.

The tensions between childbirth as 'health' and 'illness' can also be seen in accounts of pain and its management. Accounts which position childbirth as 'natural/healthy', construct pain as a 'normal' accompaniment to a 'natural' function whose outcome is welcomed, rather than as signal of 'illness' which needs to be managed by means of medical intervention, such as anaesthesia. While pain is unpleasant, the avoidance of pain is not the main objective for many women, especially those who are more informed, who have non-medical strategies for coping with pain or who express a desire not to 'miss out on' the experience of childbirth (Green et al. 1990), as in the following extract from a woman expecting twins:

The only picture I get [about delivery] is that I want to have a natural birth, and not a Caesarean. I want to see everything and I don't want to be knocked out and then wake up half an hour later.

In contrast other women constructed pain as interfering with their own and their partner's enjoyment of childbirth and expected doctors to provide pain relief for childbirth as they would for 'other illnesses' (Green et al. 1990; Woollett et al. 1983):

> I wanted assurance that they weren't going to let me suffer. I don't want to suffer more than I have to. . . . They give pain killers when they decide you are in too much pain, not when you decide you are in too much pain. . . . What worries me about childbirth is that I don't like to give up control of my body to someone else, and the minute you go into hospital that's what you do.

As the woman in this extract argues, agreeing to pain relief means that women's control over their deliveries is given over to medical professionals. Not losing control is an issue for some women and first-time mothers are somewhat less likely to report having felt in control than mothers having subsequent children (Green et al. 1990). But control operates in complex ways and it is often not easy for women to reach decisions with which they are comfortable, as in the following extract from an interview with an Asian woman:

> I couldn't speak English so they called a woman to explain that I had to give birth. I was very frightened at first, my husband was at work and I wanted them to wait for him. The woman [interpreter] said it might be too late by then and she wasn't sure whether she was going to be available later on. The doctors said they weren't forcing me to give birth and it was my decision. But then I thought in my heart that if I said no I might cause a problem for the baby and myself. So I said they should do whatever their hearts tell them to do.

Detection of abnormality and medical intervention

The rationale for 'monitoring normality/health' in pregnancy and childbirth is to detect abnormality and to intervene medically to ensure the delivery of 'healthy babies', as argued in *The Pregnancy Book* (p. 31):

> Just having your blood pressure checked, though it only takes two minutes, would be worth going – and waiting – for, because like the other checks done at the clinic, it tells you that your pregnancy is going well. If it shows that all is *not* [their emphasis] well, then something can be done about it straightaway.

Biological–medical accounts assume that medical intervention is of benefit for mothers and babies, even though the scientific evidence for such benefits is sometimes lacking (Schwarz 1990), as is recognised in a recent Department of Health report (1993: 9):

It has to be acknowledged that some of the interventions of recent years, for example fetal heart monitoring, have gained acceptance because of the assumption that they would increase the likelihood of a safe outcome. It is important that benefits are proven rather than assumed.

Moreover, the medical interventions available are limited: in pregnancy medical management often does not go beyond monitoring (albeit by means of some highly sophisticated techniques). Interventions such as bed rest are often hard to distinguish from medically disparaged 'old wives' tales', and those based on scientific knowledge (e.g. thalidomide and DES) have not always been demonstrated to be either safe or effective (Raphael-Leff 1991; Garcia et al. 1990).

With childbirth, there are more treatments and interventions available. These include drugs and procedures such as episiotomies and caesarean sections to induce or accelerate labour and delivery, and ways of relieving pain such as epidurals. Their effectiveness and longer-term impacts are sometimes questioned by professionals and others who point to negative outcomes, as medical procedures developed to solve one problem can generate others which require further medical intervention. So, for example, forceps delivery are more common following epidurals, and postnatal discomfort and infections following episiotomies and caesarean sections (Cartwright 1979; Garcia et al. 1990; Rothman 1989). One woman points to the impact of stitches following an episiotomy:

> It was a normal delivery and everything. It was the pain I couldn't stand. I had stitches. They cut you because the head was big. . . . They cut so the head comes out easier. But another ten, fifteen minutes of hard work would save you a lot of trouble afterwards. The stitches are really bad afterwards. Three weeks after you can't walk, you can't get up, it hurts to sit up to breast-feed.

There is recognition of tension between biological–medical accounts and ones which attempt to engage with a broader notion of 'quality of experience' for women. The Department of Health report *Changing Childbirth* (1993: 9) argues that not only do interventions need to be evaluated in terms of traditional measures of risk assessment, but they also have to be set against considerations of the 'quality of experience' for women:

> There was strong emphasis on the need to ensure that care was designed around the needs of the individual woman and the choices she might wish to make. . . . Women want healthy babies and also to be healthy themselves after they have given birth. But this incorporates their desire to experience pregnancy, childbirth and the early days of parenthood as positive and fulfilling. . . . However the issue of safety used as an overriding principle, may become an excuse for unnecessary interventions and technological surveillance which detract from the experience of the mother.

This ideological shift in the management of pregnancy and childbirth is paralleled by some changes in the medical management of pregnancy (such as a reduction in the number of recommended antenatal clinic appointments), and postnatally (by the reduction in the time women spend on postnatal wards). These also draw on economic discourses and concerns with cutting costs (e.g. Hundley et al. 1995). However, these reductions in medical management of pregnancy and childbirth have to be set against the increasing use of scans and tests in pregnancy (such as amniocentesis) to monitor the normality of pregnancy and make decisions about interventions.

Taking a passive–patient role

There are a number of psychological consequences for women of the medical management of pregnancy and childbirth. One is that women are assigned to a passive–patient role, drawing on discourses of women as bodies to which pregnancy and childbirth happen (Raphael-Leff 1991) with decisions about delivery made largely by health professionals. However, there is increasing rhetoric about childbearing women as active consumers of maternity services and partners in decision-making. This can be seen in the following extracts:

> It is very important for you to feel in control of what is happening to you. So throughout your labour, don't hesitate to ask questions and to ask for whatever you want. You are working *with* [their emphasis] the midwife or doctor, and they with you.
>
> (*The Pregnancy Book* 1984: 49)

> The woman must be the focus of maternity care. She should be able to feel that she is in control of what is happening to her and able to make decisions about her care, based on her needs, having discussed matters fully with the professionals involved.
>
> (Department of Health 1993: 8)

Despite increasing reference to 'quality of experience' and to women as 'partners' in the childbearing process, there is still little evidence for substantive changes in biological–medical accounts. These draw on the scientific basis of obstetrics to claim precedence over other accounts and provide health professionals with a powerful rationale for regulating the child-bearing process (Schwarz 1990; Hewison 1993). In addition, they continue to marginalise other accounts through claiming a monopoly over concerns for safety and the health of the mother and child. Individual women (and groups such as the National Childbirth Trust) who question medical interventions are positioned as selfishly putting their own ideology before the 'safe delivery' of the child (Kitzinger 1990; Oakley 1980; Green et al. 1990). These tensions are articulated in *Changing Childbirth*:

Although a good outcome to a pregnancy is desired by the woman, her family, and the professionals who care for her, we found situations where there appears to be a conflict. We heard that some professionals appear to believe that occasionally women seem to care more about their own well-being than they do about the health of their unborn child. Some mothers, on the other hand, described unsympathetic doctors and midwives who used 'safety' as a reason to try to impose arrangements or interventions which the mothers found unhelpful and disturbing.

(Department of Health 1993: 9)

Women do resist the medical management of their pregnancies and deliveries and negative definitions of themselves and their wishes for more woman-centred approaches (Green et al. 1990) by, for example, disclaiming the radical nature of their views in terms such as 'I'm not a nature freak, but . . . ' (Griffin 1989). They also resist exclusively biological–medical accounts, as evidenced by their criticisms of practices and decisions which are made without reference to their psychological and social situations. This is illustrated in the following extract from an interview in which a woman resists the advice of health professionals as impractical in her circumstances:

I was told by the doctors to have plenty of bed rest. They wanted to admit me to hospital but I thought when I get there all I'll be doing is lying in bed all day, so why not rest at home and look after the first child too. If I went in, who would have looked after my other child because my husband goes to work? That's why I decided to stay at home and did less work and got bed rest.

However, women are also presented in biological–medical accounts as more active and as having an important role to play in ensuring their own and their babies' health and development – as, for example, in advice to women about what to eat during pregnancy. In the following extract from *The Pregnancy Book* (pp. 13–15), links are made explicitly between what a woman eats or takes into her body and the development of her baby:

A poor diet, some drugs, certain illnesses, smoking, alcohol, these and other things can hold back the baby's development or even cause abnormalities. . . . You need to make sure that from conception onwards you will be providing your baby with all the nutrients needed for healthy development. So eat a *variety* [their emphasis] of foods to get a range of nutrients. The best guide to healthy eating is to keep down the amount of sugar and fat you eat, and to step up the amount of fresh fruit, fresh vegetables and cereals.

Here women seem to be offered a more active role as partners with health professionals in ensuring an optimal outcome for their pregnancies. However, closer examination of the advice indicates the extent to which it draws on notions of 'good' patients as passive recipients of medical information and is used to regulate women by positioning them primarily as containers of the fetus (Raphael-Leff 1991). This is done through a lack of engagement with women as active decision-makers or with the implications of advice about what women eat. There is, for example, no discussion of the costs of 'healthy' foods, or how women might change their eating habits in the face of resistance to 'healthy' eating from other family members and advertising from the food manufacturers (Charles and Kerr 1988; Worcester 1994).

By concentrating on 'healthy' eating, biological–medical accounts avoid having to engage with evidence about the influences on the health of mothers and babies of factors such as poverty, inadequate housing, and chronic ill-health (not to mention the risks of medical interventions in pregnancy and childbirth). Ignoring the evidence that low birth weight is more common in poorer families individualises its causes, and encourages women to 'blame' themselves if their babies are small or ill (Rocherson 1988; Phoenix 1990; Oakley 1992).

PSYCHOLOGICAL DISCOURSES OF PREGNANCY AND CHILDBIRTH

Until this point our analysis has focused primarily on biological–medical discourses which serve to construct pregnancy and childbirth as a site for monitoring and intervening in the pursuit of the healthy delivery of a baby. It has been argued that women's accounts of their experiences and those of feminist and consumer groups draw on contrasting discourses and point to contradictions and omissions in the biological–medical discourse. These alternative accounts can be characterised as drawing on psychological discourses which position pregnancy and childbirth within the remit and experiences of individual women. They draw on a variety of theoretical positions within psychology (including psychoanalytic and social identity theories) to address women's psychological development, readings of their child-bearing bodies, women's identities as pregnant women and as mothers, and women's lives and relations with others.

Pregnancy is constructed within psychological accounts as an important transitional period and as a key life event as women acquire new identities and move from childlessness to motherhood (Wolkind and Zajicek 1980; Ussher 1989; Phoenix et al. 1991). Women make sense of, and impute meaning to, the bodily changes associated with pregnancy and childbirth. For example, *The Pregnancy Book* draws on psychological and social science discourses to examine women's readings of their pregnant bodies, as in the following extract (p. 22):

From the minute you know you are pregnant, things begin to change.

Your feelings change – feelings about yourself, about the baby, about your future. Your relationships change – with your partner and also with parents and friends. . . . But you are still yourself, and you still have to get on with your life, whether pregnant or not. For this reason adjusting to the changes that pregnancy brings isn't always easy.

Researchers within social science and feminist traditions, drawing on the perspective of women and their readings of their bodies, challenge the body–mind dualism and biological–medical discourses of pregnancy and childbirth as decontextualised bodily events (Oakley 1980; Marck 1994; Woollett et al. 1991; Ussher 1989). In their accounts, women draw on a variety of readings of the body and feelings and ideas about themselves – their desires for their pregnancies, increasing awareness of their bodies, whether pregnancies were wanted and planned, and the implications for their social relationships, as in many of the extracts given earlier, and in the following extract from an interview:

Interviewee   It went quite smoothly, I can't complain. I had morning sickness but I coped with it. It was just one of those things you have and you put up with.

Interviewer   Any things you did or didn't do because you were pregnant?

Interviewee   Just obvious things like not lifting heavy things and not pushing furniture around. Apart from that, no. I was very healthy throughout my pregnancy. But then again, I'm not one of those people who sit back and say 'Oh, I'm pregnant, I shouldn't do this and I shouldn't do that'. I did most of the things I would normally do. I would go dancing and would go out if I had a chance to. I didn't stop eating anything. I carried on working until I was seven-months pregnant. . . . I sometimes used to get depressed.

Interviewer   What made you feel like that?

Interviewee   At that time my husband and I were drifting apart. Just because of our different way of looking at things. . . . Maybe I wanted more attention from my husband . . . maybe I expected him to give me more attention.

Women's readings of the pregnant body are complex and often contradictory when, for example, their sense of their body-as-pregnant and the psychological reality do not match – such as when they find a wanted pregnancy difficult, as in the extract above, and an unplanned pregnancy enjoyable, as in the following extract:

This pregnancy was totally unexpected. Suddenly one day it started to move. I just cried and cried. It was a shock because I had started work. We couldn't afford another one. It was exciting. I like being pregnant. That doesn't mean I'm going to have more. It's nice being pregnant apart from the first four months. It's nice and a lovely feeling when the baby moves inside you. I think that's when the excitement starts. It's lovely to feel something inside you and it's yours. You get to know it.

Pregnancy and childbirth impact upon women's psychological development as they come to know themselves through their pregnant bodies and deal with new feelings and emotions, especially those around dependency and independence, autonomy and connection (Raphael-Leff 1991; Smith 1992; Michaels and Goldberg 1988; Ussher 1989). While women may be pleased to be pregnant and anticipate with pleasure their connectedness with, and nurturance of, a dependent child, others are concerned about the loss of independence and autonomy and how they will cope with the constraints and responsibilities of motherhood (Ussher 1989; Woollett et al. 1991; Wolkind and Zajicek 1980), as in the following interview extract:

> After we got married my husband and I used to go out and about together a lot, having a good time. If I had become pregnant just after I got married, I wouldn't have been able to have that fun and go out with friends.

Women deal with the emotional and psychological issues around pregnancy and childbirth in diverse ways. While some women discuss pregnancy and childbirth in highly charged emotional terms, others are very matter of fact suggesting that becoming pregnant and motherhood are assumed and expected and do not need elaboration (see Woollett 1996; Woollett et al. 1991). Women's feelings and concerns often change during the course of pregnancy, as their focus moves from getting pregnant, to being pregnant and then to looking ahead to having a baby and becoming a mother (Raphael-Leff 1991; Breen 1989; Marck 1994). Women's feelings and agendas may not coincide with medical timetables for scans and tests. Many women appreciate the information they receive from tests, but others prefer to recognise that they are pregnant at their own pace and to become close to their baby only once they are confident that the pregnancy is established (Raphael-Leff 1991), as is the case in the following extract:

> With this one I didn't mentally accept it and couldn't get to know it until near the end. I thought, 'Who is this inside me?' right up until the end. But with the others I loved them while they were inside. It's not that I don't love this one but it took me longer to adjust.

Pregnancy and childbirth as relations

Psychological accounts position the mother–child relationship as the *key* relationship for children and for mothers, which begins in pregnancy (Breen 1989; Marck 1994). Women's accounts draw on psychological and psychoanalytic discourses to examine the development of their relationship with the baby as a separate and independent being and their construction of the baby's subjectivity (Marck 1994; Everingham 1994). Women begin to think about making space in their lives – as well as in their bodies – for a baby, and what the child growing inside them is like, although their accounts focus largely on the child's gender (Breen 1989; Woollett and Dosanjh-Matwala 1990; Rothman 1989; Marck 1994). For some of the Asian women interviewed the gender of the child they were carrying was of considerable interest, as in the following extract:

> It went quite smoothly. It was quite interesting knowing that something is growing inside you and whether it is going to be a girl or a boy. It's all rather nice actually. It was OK and I wasn't worried.

Women's accounts of pregnancy as a relationship often take the baby's movements *in utero* as a signal that the pregnancy and the baby are real. The impact of these movements may be less significant now that ultrasound scanning has become routine. Scans provide women with a visual impression of their baby and may encourage women to begin to relate to their babies (Raphael-Leff 1991; Reid 1990), as in the following extracts from interviews:

> When I first found out I was pregnant I just cried because I thought it happened too soon, but when I had my first scan I was really happy. After that I felt good and enjoyed it because you start to develop a bond with the baby. So that was exciting.

> When I had my first scan the man explained everything, like this is his leg, this is his foot, little hands, little head. I couldn't see his other leg and asked 'Where's his other leg then?' Then they pushed him round and showed me his other leg. It was quite nice. That's when you realise you are having a baby, when you actually see it on the scan.

However, in the following extract from *The Pregnancy Book* (pp. 29–30), while the emotional and psychological salience of scans are recognised, the main focus is on the information they provide and their value as part of the process of 'monitoring normality' of the unborn baby:

> It can be very exciting to see a picture of your own baby before birth – often moving about inside your womb . . . an ultrasound scan can give a fairly accurate idea of the baby's age . . . can show the position of the baby and the placenta so both can be checked.

Fathers, pregnancy and childbirth

The birth of a child creates new relationships and requires women to renegotiate current relationships and, especially for women in stable heterosexual relationships, the relationship with the baby's father. Traditionally fatherhood was constructed largely in terms of financial support of woman and children, but increasingly it is assumed that fathers will be involved in pregnancy, childbirth and parenting. Biological–medical and psychological accounts emphasise the value of fathering for men themselves and their development, as well as for the baby, with the result that fathers are the preferred, and often the main, support for women in pregnancy and childbirth (e.g. Beail and McGuire 1982; Lewis and O'Brien 1987).

In biological–medical accounts, the value of the involvement of fathers is evidenced by their substantial inclusion in *The Pregnancy Book*. They are pictured supporting and assisting women in labour and holding their babies after delivery. They are discussed in terms of offering support, their excitement about becoming a parent, being close to their baby, and, as in the following extract (p. 25), their gendered experience of pregnancy:

> Adjusting to pregnancy and to the idea of a baby can be difficult when you don't feel any different. Men don't 'live with' their babies during pregnancy, so while they escape the nausea, the tiredness and the discomfort, they also miss that growing sense of the baby's real presence.

Psychological accounts also draw on discourses of the normality of sexual relations in pregnancy. Some women argue that bodily changes in pregnancy enhance their sexuality and sexual attractiveness but, as has already been suggested, this is by no means always the case (Antonis 1981). Sexual relations in pregnancy are sometimes affected by women's increasing size, and also by concerns about harming the baby, or by the 'presence' of the baby (Alder 1992). These concerns are addressed in *The Pregnancy Book* which seeks to reassure women that sexual relations are possible during pregnancy but also to point out that there are other ways of expressing intimacy and affection.

Women's accounts draw on psychological discourses about the value of the interest and involvement of fathers in pregnancy and childbirth. These may take the form of expressing feelings for the baby, interest in the pregnancy, and practical support in pregnancy and labour, as in the following extracts:

> We both read the pregnancy book we got from the hospital, together. When my back was hurting he would massage it for me. We did the breathing exercises together. Near the labour stage he used to help me relax if I got tense. He used to help me with relaxing.

> My husband was with me throughout labour and I found that he was a great help because I didn't get much support from the midwife. I'm glad my husband and I went through the breathing exercises together, he helped me a lot.

> My husband was so happy at the hospital. When he [baby] was about to

be born, his head started to show a little and my husband was so happy. He had tears in his eyes when he first saw [the baby].

Expectations about fathers' involvement and especially their presence at delivery are such that sometimes it is their absence, rather than their presence, which women comment upon, as in the following extract:

The second time my husband had to stay at home to look after [older child]. We couldn't leave her with anyone. I did feel I should have had someone with me but you have to look to your problems. My husband wanted to be there the second time but he couldn't leave her.

Other social relations

Increasingly the involvement of fathers is normalised, but the role of other social relations including those between a woman and her parents, friends, work and employment relations, are less acknowledged and explored. Many women give up paid employment outside the home in the late months of pregnancy. For some, this results in a loss of financial independence as well as a loss of identity and social support, as in the following extract in which a woman compares the support at work with that from her extended family:

I thought that nobody really helped me, taught me, told me to do this and do that, that will help your pregnancy, to eat this and that . . . I used to eat salads and fruit a lot. At work they did take good care of me: 'Don't do this, don't do that. Eat this and eat that'.

Most accounts draw on discourses of the benefits of fathers' involvement. Men in this culture–historical period are often contrasted with men in other cultures and/or at other times where pregnancy and childbirth are constructed as highly gendered, indicating the extent to which pregnancy and childbirth are socially and culturally constructed (e.g. Lozoff et al. 1988; Homans 1982), as Oakley (1980: 5) argues:

Having a baby is a biological and a cultural act. In bearing a child, a woman reproduces the species. . . . Yet human childbirth is accomplished in and shaped by culture. . . . How a culture defines reproduction is closely linked with its articulation of women's position: the connection between female citizenship and the procreative role are social, not biological.

Cultural context

However, in spite of Oakley's (1980) assertion of the cultural significance of pregnancy and childbirth, this is not often examined in biological–medical or psychological accounts. As we have already argued, psychological accounts draw on discourses about the intra- and interpersonal significance of pregnancy and childbirth, but the differing circumstances of women's lives and the cultural meanings of childbearing and parenthood tend to be addressed largely in stereotyped ways. So, for example, it is often assumed that 'Asian' fathers are not involved in childbearing and that 'Asian' women are supported by other women, although as the woman in the following extract argues, even when women live with their extended families, it cannot be assumed that they have the support of female relatives:

> When you're pregnant you still have to do the housework. Even though my mother-in-law lives with us, she can't do much because she can't see very well. If I decide not to do the housework, who's going to feed my children? So I have to do everything myself.

There is little consideration of the evidence about the social and economic position of many Asian women who live in poor housing and/or inner city areas, or their experience of racist practices which might discourage them from seeking contraceptive or antenatal care (Rocherson 1988; Bowler 1993). An exclusive focus on the differences between racial–cultural groups means that diversity *within* cultural groups and the meanings and practices of pregnancy and childbirth within both the dominant culture and minority social groups or cultures are rarely addressed (Woollett et al. 1995; Marshall 1992; Homans 1982).

NAUSEA AND SICKNESS AS EMBODIED EXPERIENCES

We have examined biological–medical and psychological accounts and the discourses on which they draw to point to similarities and tensions between those discourses and those on which child-bearing women draw. To contrast these different accounts and discourses a case study of one aspect of pregnancy, that of nausea and sickness, is examined.

Nausea and sickness are common experiences of pregnancy in this culture (Wolkind and Zajicek 1980). Biological–medical accounts construe them as 'normal/healthy' symptoms and experiences of pregnancy which are considered especially common in the early weeks and months of pregnancy, although they sometimes occur throughout pregnancy, and are explained in *The Pregnancy Book* (1984: 43) as follows:

> Nausea is very common in the early weeks of pregnancy. . . . The causes are not properly understood but the hormone changes taking place in early pregnancy are thought to be one cause.

There is, however, little discussion of how, given the universality of 'hormones changes . . . in early pregnancy' women's experiences of nausea and sickness vary so widely, why they are more common in first than in subsequent pregnancies, and in some cultures more than others.

Biological–medical accounts construct nausea and sickness as problems, and hence as 'illness', only when they continue after the early months and prevent women from gaining weight 'normally'. However, even when they seriously disrupt women's health and well-being, medical interventions are rarely offered, because of the vulnerability of the developing fetus. Instead, women are reassured that they are common symptoms of 'normal/healthy' pregnancy and are offered non-medical solutions and suggestions about diet to help them cope:

> It's worth trying tricks like eating a dry biscuit before you get up in the morning. . . . Some women find that keeping to bland foods like white bread and potatoes helps. . . . Ginger is supposed to help.
>
> (*The Baby Book* 1988: 26)

> Eat small amounts of food. . . . Avoid the smells and foods that make you feel worse. . . . Distract yourself as much as you can.
>
> (*The Pregnancy Book* 1984: 43)

In contrast, women's accounts indicate the extent to which nausea and sickness are positioned as part of women's embodied experiences of pregnancy. Over half of the women interviewed said they experienced nausea and sickness (Woollett et al. 1995), with some experiencing severe symptoms which restricted their activities, as in the following extracts from interviews:

> It was very bad. For nine months I was sick every day. For three, four months I went off food. I couldn't eat, couldn't stand the smell, and I kept bringing up everything . . . I used to get tired very easily. I was told to get as much rest as possible because of the [health] problem I had. . . . I started to eat apples for the first time in my life. I've never liked them before. We still met people as before, but I couldn't travel on long journeys because I felt sick.

> It was very bad. I couldn't do any work all day. I was vomiting a lot. This went on for five months. I couldn't get up. I just used to lie down all day. When I used to go to my GP and tell him about it, he'd say that's how it's supposed to be . . . I felt so weak . . . I couldn't eat anything. I couldn't keep down our Asian food . . . I usually keep busy with housework, like tidying. When I'm sick I can't do as much cleaning although it's on my mind that I must do it.

Because nausea and sickness were positioned as central to women's experiences of early pregnancy, women who did not experience them said they did not feel pregnant, as in the following extract:

> There were no problems. I've never had morning sickness. I didn't feel I was really pregnant.

Nausea and sickness were closely linked in women's accounts with food preferences, in terms of foods they could not eat, or those eaten as a way of alleviating nausea and sickness, in similar ways to biological–medical accounts. Asian women drew on somewhat different discourses of food: they explained their food preferences not merely in terms of nausea and sickness, but also in terms of hot and cold foods in the Ayurvedic system of medicine and their cultural context, in which older women reproduced cultural knowledge and traditional practices about foods to be eaten in pregnancy (Homans 1982; Woollett and Dosanjh-Matwala 1990).

Nausea and sickness are more common in early pregnancy and are often taken as an early indication of pregnancy (Wolkind and Zajicek 1980). Psychological accounts take nausea and sickness, not merely as embodied experiences of pregnancy, but as having symbolic significance and indicating – for example – a rejection of pregnancy, although there is little evidence to support this view (Raphael-Leff 1991; Macy 1986; Wolkind and Zajicek 1980). Even though they are unpleasant, nausea and sickness do focus the attention of women, and others, on the pregnancy and women's body-as-pregnant (Raphael-Leff 1991; Wolkind and Zajicek 1980).

Women's accounts of nausea and sickness are positioned largely in terms of women's lives, including their ability to cook for and feed their families. This is difficult when the food they are preparing makes them feel sick. Women had a number of ways of coping, such as a neighbour who cooked for them, or, as *The Pregnancy Book* suggests, trying to change family eating habits: 'If you are cooking for the family, choose menus that will suit *you* [their emphasis] as well as them' (p. 43). However, such advice is often of limited usefulness because it does not recognise the strength of social and cultural practices around food, and hence on the limits on women's ability to influence what their family will eat.

By positioning nausea and sickness as 'key' indicators of pregnancy, biological–medical and psychological accounts isolate them from other symptoms in pregnancy. This has the effect of negating the experiences of women who do not experience nausea and sickness and of giving less emphasis to other symptoms, in particular tiredness and symptoms associated with women's increasing weight and size. Unlike nausea and sickness, tiredness is experienced throughout pregnancy and has a significant overall impact on women's embodied experiences of pregnancy, as in the following extracts:

As this was my fourth I felt tired a lot. But I think that's because I was working . . . I tend not to feel ill, but other women feel as if they're ill. We [sister and self] weren't very big. I think if you are big it tends to slow you down.

It was all right. When you have two other children to look after the work becomes too much, but otherwise no problems. There was not much difference [in being pregnant], just that it seemed more hard work because of the other two: take them to school, bring them home. You still have to do the same for them. You do feel tired.

Tiredness is probably given less attention because it fits less easily into dominant biological–medical discourses and is less susceptible to medical intervention than other symptoms, rather than because of its lesser significance for women (Popay 1992).

Nausea and sickness are frequent physical symptoms of early pregnancy but are constructed somewhat differently in the various accounts. Women's accounts draw on biological–medical discourses and hormonal changes, and also on their impact on women's lives and their embodied experiences of pregnancy.

CONCLUDING COMMENTS

In this chapter we have used discursive methods to examine and compare biological–medical, psychological discourses of pregnancy and childbirth. In doing so we have drawn attention to disparate and at times contradictory constructions of the nature of pregnancy and childbirth and the regulatory role of discourses in defining 'normality/health' and the management of pregnancy and childbirth.

We have argued that in constructing pregnancy and childbirth in terms of universality, and predominantly biological and individualistic experiences, current discourses are inadequate for accounting for and explaining women's readings of their child-bearing bodies. They fail to take sufficient account of two key factors identified as central in women's accounts. The first is diversity in women's experiences and the meaning of the pregnant body (own/other, this pregnancy/an earlier pregnancy, early/late pregnancy). The second is the social, cultural and ideological context in which women are pregnant and become mothers and the impact of pregnancy on their emotions, identities, lives and relationships.

Positioning pregnancy and childbirth within the framework of health and illness and their management as if they are illnesses, and the omission of diversity and the wider cultural context of pregnancy and childbirth, means that women experience maternity care as narrowly focused and ineffective for dealing with key aspects of their experiences. Women draw on some biological–medical discourses in their accounts, but such discourses are also resisted. The language of 'health' and 'illness' are rarely used to describe women's pregnancies and childbirth, which are constructed rather as physical manifestations or symptoms (sometimes unpleasant and troubling) of a 'normal/healthy' state.

Women's accounts and feminist research position pregnancy and childbirth within the context of women's lived experiences and personal knowledge, emphasising the ways in which women manage the different (and often contradictory) demands of their pregnant bodies with domestic responsibilities and other relationships and responsibilities, and advice from health professionals. Their accounts contrast with biological–medical and psychological accounts which draw on narrower discourses of pregnancy and childbirth. These different discourses are of significance theoretically, and also practically in terms of the ways in which maternity care is managed.

Accounts and the discourses on which they draw are not mutually exclusive and change over time in response to cultural and ideological changes in the wider society. This can be seen in terms of changes in the provision of health care. With the emphasis on the patient as consumer and active participant in the decision-making processes, the management of pregnancy and childbirth are changing somewhat. However, for women the key task remains the negotiation of their readings of their pregnant bodies and the meanings of pregnancy and motherhood within the dominant framework of biological–medical discourses.

ACKNOWLEDGEMENTS

The authors would like to thank the women who participated in the studies reported here, and to acknowledge the contribution of Neelam Dosanjh, Averil Clegg and Patsy Fuller who carried out the interviews. The research was conducted with the support of an award from the Economic and Social Research Council (ESRC): Award Number R000232456.

REFERENCES

Alder, B. (1992) 'Postnatal sexuality', in P. Y. L. Choi and P. Nicolson (eds) *Female Sexuality: Psychology, Biology and Social Context*, London: Harvester Wheatsheaf.

Antonis, B. (1981) 'Motherhood and mothering', in Cambridge Women's Studies Group (eds) *Women in Society: Interdisciplinary Essays*, London: Virago.

The Baby Book (1988), London: The Newbourne Group.

Banister, P., Burman, E., Parker, I., Taylor, M. and Tinsdall, C. (1994) *Qualitative Methods in Psychology: A Research Guide*, Milton Keynes: Open University Press.

Beail, N. and McGuire, J. (eds) (1982) *Fathers: Psychological Perspectives*, London: Junction Books.

Bowler, I. (1993) ' "They're not the same as us": midwives' stereotypes of South Asian descent maternity patients', *Sociology of Health and Illness* 15(2): 157–178.

Breen, D. (1989) *Talking with Mothers*, London: Free Association (second edition).

Cartwright, A. (1979) *The Dignity of Labour*, London: Tavistock.

Charles, N. and Kerr, M. (1988) *Women, Food and Families*, Manchester: Manchester University Press.

Department of Health (1993) *Changing Childbirth*, report of the Expert Maternity Group, London: HMSO.

Everingham, C. (1994) *Motherhood and Modernity*, Milton Keynes: Open University Press.

Garcia, J., Kilpatrick, R. and Richards, M. (eds) (1990) *The Politics of Maternity Care: Services for Childbearing Women in Twentieth-century Britain*, Oxford: Clarendon Paperbacks.

Green, J. M., Coupland, V. A. and Kitzinger, J. V. (1990) 'Expectations, experiences and psychological outcomes of childbirth: a prospective study of 825 women', *Birth* 17: 15–24.

Griffin, C. (1989) ' "I'm not a women's libber, but . . . ": feminism, consciousness and identity', in S. Skevington and D. Baker (eds) *The Social Identity of Women*, London: Sage.

Hewison, A. (1993) 'The language of labour: an examination of the discourses of childbirth', *Midwifery* 9: 225–234.

Homans, H. (1982) 'Pregnancy and birth as rites of passage for two groups of women in Britain', in C. P. MacCormack (ed.) *Ethnography of Fertility and Birth*, London: Academic Press.

Hundley, V. A., Donaldson, C., Lang, G. D., Cruickshank, F. M., Glazener, C. M., Milne, J. M. and Mollison, J. (1995) 'Costs of intrapartum care in a midwife-managed delivery unit and a consultant-led labour ward', *Midwifery* 11: 103–9.

Kitzinger, J. (1990) 'Strategies of the early childbirth movement: a case study of the National Childbirth Trust', in J. Garcia, R. Kilpatrick and M. Richards (eds) *The Politics of Maternity Care: Services for Childbearing Women in Twentieth-century Britain*, Oxford: Clarendon Paperbacks.

Lewis, C. and O'Brien, M. (1987) *Reassessing Fatherhood: New Observations on Fathers and the Modern Family*, London: Sage.

Lozoff, B., Jordan, B. and Malone, S. (1988) 'Childbirth in cross-cultural perspective', *Marriage and Family Review* 12: 36–60.

Macy, C. (1986) 'Psychological factors in nausea and vomiting in pregnancy: a review', *Journal of Reproductive and Infant Psychology* 4: 23–56.

Marck, P. B. (1994) 'Unexpected pregnancy: the uncharted land of women's experiences', in P. A. Field and P. B. Marck (eds) *Uncertain Motherhood: Negotiating the Risks of the Childbearing Years*, Thousand Oakes: Sage.

Marshall, H. (1992) 'Talking about good maternity care in a multi-cultural context: a discourse analysis of the accounts of midwives and health visitors', in P. Nicolson and J. Ussher (eds) *The Psychology of Women's Health and Health Care*, Basingstoke: Macmillan.

Michaels, G. Y. and Goldberg, W. A. (eds) (1988) *Transition to Parenthood: Theory and Research*, Cambridge: Cambridge University Press.

Oakley, A. (1979) *Becoming a Mother*, Oxford: Martin Robertson.

—— (1980) *Women Confined: Toward a Sociology of Childbirth*, Oxford: Martin Robertson.

—— (1992) *Social Support and Motherhood: The Natural History of a Research Project*, Oxford: Basil Blackwell.

Phoenix, A. (1990) 'Black women and the maternity services', in J. Garcia, R. Kilpatrick and M. Richards (eds) *The Politics of Maternity Care: Services for Childbearing Women in Twentieth-century Britain*, Oxford: Clarendon Paperbacks.

Phoenix, A., Woollett, A. and Lloyd, E. (1991) *Motherhood: Meanings, Practices and Ideologies*, London: Sage.

Popay, J. (1992) ' "My health is alright, but I'm just tired all the time": women's experiences of illhealth', in H. Roberts (ed.) *Women's Health Matters*, London: Routledge.

Potter, J. and Wetherell, M. (1987) *Discourse and Social Psychology: Beyond Attitudes and Behaviour*, London: Sage.

The Pregnancy Book (1984), London: Health Education Council.

Raphael-Leff, J. (1991) *The Psychological Processes of Childbearing*, London: Chapman Hall.

Reid, M. (1990) 'Prenatal diagnosis and screening: a review', in J. Garcia, R. Kilpatrick and M. Richards (eds) *The Politics of Maternity Care: Services for Childbearing Women in Twentieth-century Britain*, Oxford: Clarendon Paperbacks.

Rocherson, Y. (1988) 'The Asian mother and baby campaign: the construction of ethnic minorities' health needs', *Critical Social Policy* 22: 4–23.

Rothman, B. K. (1989) *Recreating Motherhood: Ideology and Technology in a Patriarchal Society*, New York: W. W. Norton.

Schwarz, E. W. (1990) 'The engineering of childbirth: a new obstetric programme as reflected in British obstetric textbooks, 1960–1980', in J. Garcia, R. Kilpatrick and M. Richards (eds) *The Politics of Maternity Care: Services for Childbearing Women in Twentieth-century Britain*, Oxford: Clarendon Paperbacks.

Smith, J. (1992) 'Pregnancy and the transition to motherhood', in P. Nicolson and J. Ussher (eds) *The Psychology of Women's Health and Health Care*, Basingstoke: Macmillan.

Stoppard, J. M. (1995) 'Depression, women's bodies and women's lives: theorising distress in women', paper presented at BPS Conference, December 1995.

Ussher, J. (1989) *The Psychology of the Female Body*, London: Routledge.

Wiles, R. (1994) '"I'm not fat, I'm pregnant": the impact of pregnancy on fat women's body image', in S. Wilkinson and C. Kitzinger (eds) *Women and Health: Feminist Perspectives*, London: Taylor & Francis.

Wolkind, S. and Zajicek, E. (eds) (1980) *Pregnancy: A Psychological and Social Study*, London: Academic Press.

Woollett, A (1996) 'Reproductive decisions', in K. Niven and A. Walker (eds) *The Psychology of Reproduction. Vol. 2: Conception, Pregnancy and Birth*, Oxford: Butterworth Heinemann.

Woollett, A. and Clegg, A. (1989) 'Mother's experience of twin pregnancies and birth', in E. V. van Hall and W. Everaerd (eds) *The Free Woman: Women's Health in the 1990s* (papers presented at the 9th International Congress of Psychosomatic Obstetrics and Gynaecology), Amsterdam: Parthenon Publishing Group.

Woollett, A. and Dosanjh-Matwala, N. (1990) 'Pregnancy and antenatal care: the attitudes and experiences of Asian women', *Child: Health, Care and Development* 16: 63–78.

Woollett, A., Lyon, L. and White, D. (1983) 'The reactions of East London women to medical intervention in childbirth', *Journal of Reproductive and Infant Psychology* 1: 37–46.

Woollett, A., Dosanjh-Matwala, N. and Hadlow, J. (1991) 'Reproductive decision making: Asian women's ideas about family size, and the gender and spacing of children', *Journal of Reproductive and Infant Psychology* 9: 237–252.

Woollett, A., Dosanjh, N., Nicolson, P., Marshall, H., Djhanbakhch, O. and Hadlow, J. (1995) 'A comparison of the experiences of pregnancy and childbirth of Asian and non-Asian women in East London', *British Journal of Medical Psychology* 68: 65–84

Worcester, N. (1994) 'The obesity of the food industry', in N. Worcester and M. H. Whatley (eds) *Women's Health: Readings on Social, Economic, and Political Issues*, Dubuque, IA: Kendall/Hunt.

Chapter 10

Diet as a vehicle for self-control

Jane Ogden

INTRODUCTION

Dieting, overeating, anorexia and bulimia nervosa are in vogue in the late twentieth century. Research reports that everyone is dieting and that the prevalence and incidence of eating disorders are on the increase. Consequently, hospitals are opening specialist centres to accommodate this new clinical problem and self-help groups and those facilitated by professionals are proliferating. In parallel to these changes, experts have developed theories about the causes of these various forms of eating behaviour. Such theories are traditionally used to inform the reader about the nature of their object; theories are seen as unproblematic and as descriptions of 'reality'; theories of eating describe how eating 'really is'.

This chapter will examine primarily the status of theories about eating behaviour and suggest a more problematic concept of the relationship between theory and its object; such theoretical perspectives may not only be derived from data, but can themselves be used as data in order to examine changes in the way the object of theory is understood. From this perspective, theory no longer describes its object but begins to construct it. Therefore, as theory changes so its object changes in parallel.

In line with this premise, the chapter will then analyse changes in expert and lay theories about diet and eating behaviour over the past century. In particular, it will focus on changes in psychological and sociological approaches to diet, and suggest that the changing 'nature' of these theories reflects a shift in the concept of the object of these theories – the individual. Further, this analysis will outline the 'nature' of this changing individual and suggest that, whereas at the beginning of the century the individual was regarded as a passive responder to external events, in the middle of the century the individual became one who showed increasing agency and interacted with the outside world. The central proposition is that contemporary theories of eating behaviour describe and construct an individual who interacts with him or herself. Further, that this latter individual is characterised by self-control and a self to be controlled – an intra-active self.

Finally, this chapter will explore the implications of this shift in theory in terms of the relationship between theory and its object and the emergence of a new eating individual. It will be argued that contemporary theories on eating behaviour construct an individual who is characterised by both the absence and presence of self-control, and that eating disorders epitomise this self-controlling individual. The construction of this new individual through theory is reflected in the increasing interest in a range of eating-related problems and behaviours; the emphasis on such behaviours increases as eating becomes the ideal vehicle to control this new self-controlling body.

THEORY AS DATA

Traditionally, social scientists collect data from individuals and use these data to support and develop theories about human beings. Whether these data are collected using quantitative or qualitative methodologies, the relationship between theory, data and the subject of that theory (the individual) is considered to be relatively unproblematic. Theories are viewed as intentional constructs; they are 'about' the individual. Thus, the individual who is described by theory has an existence independent of that theory. Further, theoretical progress is understood in terms of an increasing approximation between the individual described by theory and the individual in reality: theory becomes more accurate. This model of science construes theory as a window through which the world is understood. However, such an unproblematic model of the relationship between theory and the individual ignores the capacity of this window to transform and distort the individual. Further, such a model also neglects the potential of the window to construct its subject.

Examination of theory within health psychology, through the twentieth century, suggests a pattern in terms of the description of the psychological individual (Ogden 1995a,b). If the relationship between theory and its object is conceptualised as more than a simple description, an examination of changes in these theoretical perspectives can provide insights into the way psychological models transform the individual. If, however, theory is conceptualised as constructing its object, perhaps such an examination can also reveal changes in psychology's construction and fabrication of its subject. In other words, theory can be treated as data, and such data can be analysed to explore their implications for the 'nature' of their object (the individual).

Changing models of the individual

The various theoretical perspectives within different areas of psychology are often viewed as distinct and unrelated. However, it has been argued that patterns can be seen in terms of the changing model of the individual (Ogden 1995a,b). During the early decades of the century psychological theory described its object as a passive responder to external events (Ogden 1995a,b). For example, early stress theories described stress as an automatic response to an external stressor (e.g. Cannon 1932). This stimulus response model can also be seen within the pain literature and early theories of classical and operant conditioning (Goldscheider 1920; Pavlov 1927; Skinner 1953). In short, the psychological individual in the early part of the twentieth century was characterised by an absence of agency, and environmental influences were seen as all important. However, in the latter half of the century, psychology attributed the individual with an increasingly active mind: the individual was analysed in terms of his or her ability to process and appraise external cues and events. Stress was viewed as a response to the individual's appraisal of the stressor, pain resulted from the individual's understanding of the painful stimuli, and behaviour was conceptualised in terms of representations, coding and information processing (Lazarus and Cohen 1977; Melzack and Wall 1965; Rescorla and Wagner 1972; Dickinson 1980). In effect, the individual became an interactive being who interacted with the environment (Ogden 1995a,b). The environment remained important but the individual no longer simply responded passively to this environment but selectively and actively processed environmental information.

In recent years, it is claimed, a new individual can be identified as emerging through psychological theory. Since the late 1970s, psychological theories describe an individual who no longer simply responds to the environment, nor one who interacts with the environment. Theories of behaviour now present behaviour as a product of self-control and in terms of Bandura's concept of self-efficacy (Bandura 1977, 1986; Rosenstock et al. 1988; Rogers 1983). Stress theorists discuss stress in terms of the individual's ability to control their own responses and to self-regulate, and pain is conceptualised in terms of pain self-efficacy (Lazarus and Folkman 1987; Wiedenfeld et al. 1990; Manning and Wright 1983; Dolce 1987). Psychological theory, therefore, has begun to describe an individual who is 'intra-active'. Further, parallels can also be seen between such intra-active models of the individual and contemporary models of the location of risk, with risks to health no longer conceptualised as coming from outside the individual, nor as resulting from an interaction with the environment, but as a consequence of the individual's self-control. For example, nowadays, the risk of cervical cancer is understood as coming from the individual's ability to have regular smear tests, the risk of heart disease is considered to be due to the individual's ability to control their smoking, diet and exercise behaviour, and the risk of HIV is conceptualised as a result of the confidence to practise safe sex. Accordingly, high risks to health relate to poor ability to have health checks and poor control over health-related behaviours. This contemporary model of risk has been called the 'risky self' (Ogden 1995a). In summary, the model of the 'intra-active' individual described by late twentieth-century theory regulates, controls and manages their own self

(Ogden 1995a,b). This new self is compartmentalised into the elements that are controlled and the aspects that do the controlling and behaviour results from the degree of success of this process.

Theories of eating behaviour

Psychological theories of eating behaviour can be seen to follow the same shift in individualisation. Early models of eating behaviour regarded the individual as passively responding to external food cues. Later theorists emphasised the processing and appraisal of these cues such that food intake resulted from an interaction between the individual and their environment (Schachter 1968; Schachter and Rodin 1974). Recent theories describe eating in terms of self-control, self-efficacy, and self-regulation (e.g. Herman and Mack 1975; Hibscher and Herman 1977; Herman and Polivy 1984). This is particularly salient in theories of overeating[1] in normal weight individuals and eating disorders.

Eating behaviour is therefore described using different language and different theory now than it was at the beginning of the century. This language and theory describes a different eating behaviour, a different set of eating-related cognitions and a different eating individual. Such changes would conventionally be explained in terms of an improving scientific sensibility: the model of a passive or interactive individual was 'mistaken' and the newer intra-active individual better fits the facts. However, this analysis of theoretical development presumes a great naïvety of early psychologists; but more important it treats the relationship between theory and fact as unproblematic. Perhaps contemporary theories that present an intra-active individual fit the facts better because those facts are themselves a product of the theory they sustain: an examination of the individual's self-control mechanisms already assumes the existence of a self that can control itself. In short, theory begins to constitute its own object. Is it only the descriptions of eating behaviour that are different, therefore, or is the individual who is eating also different? This chapter will explore this possibility using a more detailed examination of the changing psychological and sociological theories of eating behaviour over the past few decades and the emphasis on self-control in both expert and lay theoretical accounts.

PSYCHOLOGICAL THEORIES

Eating behaviour in normal weight individuals

Throughout the 1960s and 1970s psychological theories of eating behaviour emphasised the role of food intake in predicting weight. Both empirical and theoretical research aimed to examine the behavioural predictors of overweight and obesity, and evaluated the eating behaviour of the obese and the non-obese in order to develop theories of etiology. Schachter's externality hypothesis suggested that although all people were responsive to environmental stimuli such as the sight, taste and smell of food, and that such stimuli might cause overeating, the obese were highly and sometimes uncontrollably responsive to external cues (Schachter 1968; Schachter and Rodin 1974; Schachter and Gross 1968; Schachter et al. 1968). It was argued that this over-responsiveness was responsible for the development of obesity. In support of this, research examined the eating behaviour and eating style of the obese and non-obese in response to external cues such as time of day, sight, number and salience of food cues and taste. Within this framework, the object of the theories about eating behaviour was an interactive individual who interacted with and appraised cues in the environment.

However, during the late 1970s a new model of eating behaviour emerged from psychological theory. Spitzer and Rodin suggested that 'of twenty-nine studies examining the effects of body weight on amount eaten in laboratory studies . . . only nine reported that overweight subjects ate significantly more than their lean counterparts' (Spitzer and Rodin 1981) and contended that obesity may not be a product of over-responsiveness to external cues. Furthermore, Hibscher and Herman (1977) suggested that attempts at eating less (i.e. restrained eating) was a better predictor of food intake than weight *per se*. Restraint theory was developed as a means of predicting and evaluating eating behaviour and represented a shift from perceiving weight – a biological construct – as the main determinant of behaviour, and introduced restrained eating – a psychological construct – as a means to evaluate food intake (Herman and Mack 1975; Hibscher and Herman 1977). Restraint theory not only represented a shift in the theoretical perspectives of causes of food intake (from biology to psychology), but also represented a shift in the underlying psychological model of the individual. Restraint theory analysed food intake as resulting from the individual's self-regulation, self-control, self-efficacy and, in effect, described an individual who no longer interacted with their environment but was intra-active.

The intra-active overeater

Herman and Mack (1975) described overeating in the normal weight individual in terms of disinhibition and counter-regulatory behaviour. Using a laboratory-based paradigm, they suggested that whereas non-dieting individuals showed compensatory eating behaviour, dieters consumed more following a high calorie preload. This form of overeating has been shown in response to high calorie preloads, preloads only perceived to be high calorie, anxiety, depression, alcohol consumption, stressful situations and smoking abstinence (Herman and Mack 1975; Herman and Polivy 1975; Spencer and Fremouw 1979; Herman and Polivy 1989; Ogden 1992; Ogden 1994). As a means of understanding the mechanisms involved in disinhibition several theoretical perspectives have been developed. Originally, overeating in normal weight subjects was conceptualised in terms of compensation for the deprivation resulting from the dieters' maintenance of weight below their set point (Nisbett 1972). However, recent theories have shifted the focus from physiological mechanisms to psychological ones. Herman and Polivy (1984) developed the boundary model of food intake and claimed that the overeating found in dieters was a response to a transgression of the diet boundary. They suggested that preloading, lowered mood and stressors created a breakdown in the dieter's self-control. Within this framework, overeating reflected a 'motivational collapse' and indicated a state of giving in to the overpowering drives to eat. Such an emphasis described the individual as self-regulating and self-controlling and conceptualised overeating as a consequence of a failure of this self-control.

To support this model of overeating Glynn and Ruderman (1986) developed the eating self-efficacy questionnaire as a measure of the tendency to overeat. Again, this model of overeating placed the emphasis on self-regulation. Further, Ogden and Wardle (1991) analysed the cognitive set of the disinhibited dieter and suggested that such collapse in self-control reflected a passive model of overeating and that the 'what the hell effect' as described by Herman and Polivy (1984) may have contained elements of passivity in terms of factors such as 'giving in', 'resignation' and 'passivity'. The emphasis on the transgression of boundaries, motivational collapse and shifting cognitive states emphasised self-control and suggested that overeating was a consequence of the failure of this self-control.

The emphasis on self-control is also illustrated by an analysis of overeating in normal weight individuals in terms of an escape from self-awareness (Heatherton and Baumeister 1991). This model examined overeating in terms of both the overeating characteristic of dieters and the more extreme form of binge eating found in bulimics and suggested that overeating was a consequence of 'a motivated shift to low levels of self-awareness' (ibid.). Using escape theory, which suggests that there are multiple levels of meaning and multiple levels of self-awareness, it is suggested that individuals prone to overeating show comparisons with 'high standards and demanding ideals' (ibid.: 89) that result in low self-esteem, self-dislike and lowered mood. In addition, escape theory predicts that inhibitions exist primarily at high levels of awareness when the individual is aware of the meanings associated with certain behaviours. For example, cheating, unconventional sexual acts and suicide will be constructed with a set of meaning inhibiting their execution at a high level of awareness. In terms of the binge eater or overeater, a state of high self-awareness can become unpleasant as it results in self-criticism, anxiety and depression. However, such a state is accompanied by the existence of inhibitions. The individual is therefore motivated to escape from self-awareness to avoid the accompanying unpleasantness which is achieved through refocusing and cognitive narrowing. Such a shift in self-awareness may provide relief from self-criticism, but results in a reduction in inhibitions thereby causing overeating. Heatherton and Baumeister supported their model of overeating with evidence for the separate elements of the model: high standards, the aversiveness of the high awareness state, cognitive narrowing and overeating in response to lowered mood. The attempts at food restriction and the resulting overeating as described by restraint theory are indicative of a shift from high to low self-awareness.

The application of escape theory is a novel approach to the problem of overeating. However, central to this model remains the concept of self-control. The model characterises the individual's 'natural state' as one of disinhibition and indulgence, akin to a Freudian model of the id, or a biological model of instincts. The individual in this state has no self-control and does not respond to the inhibitions and constraints resulting from social and personal norms of acceptable behaviour. The state of high self-awareness, on the other hand, reflects an 'unnatural state' and the success of these social norms as the individual possesses self-control, as in a Freudian model of the ego or super ego. Therefore a shift to lower self-awareness results in reduced self-control and the drives to eat being released. Again, the escape theory of overeating emphasises self-monitoring, self-control and describes a psychological individual who is intra-active.

Theories of motivational collapse and the failure of inhibitions characterise the individual as passively responding to a breakdown in self-control. An alternative model of overeating in normal weight individuals contends that overeating may reflect an active decision to overeat. A series of studies indicated that dieters respond to preloads with an increase in an active state of mind characterised by a cognitive set reflected by items such as 'rebellious', 'challenging' and 'defiant' (Ogden and Wardle 1991; Ogden and Greville 1993), and that such a shift in cognitive set may result in overeating. It has been argued that rather than simply passively giving in to an overwhelming desire to eat, as suggested by other models, the overeater actively decides to overeat as a form of rebellion against self-imposed food restrictions. This rebellious state of mind has also been described in obese binge eaters who report bingeing as 'a way to unleash resentment' (Loro and Orleans 1981) and is implicit in the notion of 'what the hell' as described by Herman and Polivy (1984). It is also possible that eating as a form of rebellion may not only be a response to eating restrictions and food deprivation, but may at times indicate a rebellious statement against the deprivation of other substances such as cigarettes (Ogden 1994), and against deprivation of emotional support (Bruch 1974). However, although such a model of overeating reconceptualises the overeater as active rather than passive, central to this re-evaluation of overeating remains the concept of self-control. The individual does not eat as a passive response to the breakdown in self-control, but as an active defiance of self-imposed regulations. Self-control and self-regulation are central facets of the model – the individual is again characterised as intra-active.

The eating disorders

In parallel, theories of eating disorders show a similar pattern of change in their description of the individual. Throughout the 1960s and 1970s research into anorexia nervosa emphasised the role of cultural norms, social expectations and developmental influences, focusing on the individual's appraisal of these influences. Over recent years, however, although the role of environmental factors is still acknowledged, anorexia has been described in terms of self-control. Garfinkel and Garner (1986) suggested that the achievement of ever decreasing weight becomes a sign of mastery, control and virtue. Crisp, in 1984, compared the anorexic to the ascetic in terms of his or her 'discipline, frugality, abstinence and stifling of the passions' (p. 210), and analysed anorexia as resulting from a determination to keep 'the impulse to ingest at bay' and as a consequence of a 'never ending vigilance and denial'. Furthermore, Bruch describes the anorexic as having an 'aura of special power and super human discipline' (1985). In a similar vein, DSMIII-R presents a diagnostic criterion for anorexia as a 'refusal to maintain normal body weight', indicating individual will and control as central to the diagnosis (American Psychiatric Association 1987).

Similarly, bulimia nervosa has also become understood in terms of self-control but, in contrast to anorexia nervosa, the absence of this control is emphasised. Cooper and Taylor (1988) stated that 'episodes of excessive uncontrolled eating are a central feature' of bulimia. Bulimia was described as resulting from 'a profound and distressing loss of control over eating' (Cooper and Fairburn 1986) and 'irresistible cravings for food' was a central factor of the diagnostic criteria set by Russell (1979). Furthermore, binge eating is defined by Fairburn (1984: 235) as 'episodes of eating which are experienced as excessive and beyond the subject's control'.

Measures of eating behaviour

Self-control is also central to measures of disordered eating behaviour. For example, the Eating Attitudes Test (Garner and Garfinkel 1979) included items such as 'display self-control around food' and 'have the impulse to vomit after meals', both implicating self-control and self-regulation as important. A similar model of eating disorders can be seen in the Eating Disorder Examination (Cooper and Fairburn 1987) which included items such as 'attempting to obey dietary rules which relate to attempts to control body shape, weight or body composition' and 'fear of losing control over eating'. In addition, empirical studies have examined differences in self-control between eating disordered subjects and controls and have examined control in terms of eating self-efficacy, internal locus of control and perceived and actual control (Shisslak et al. 1990; Williams et al. 1990; Wagner et al. 1987). The emphasis on self-control is further illustrated by the proliferation of self-help groups and texts for both anorexia nervosa and bulimia nervosa in the UK and the USA. In summary, anorexia and bulimia have been analysed in terms of the individual's ability to control themselves.

WOMEN'S OWN REPORTS OF SELF-CONTROL

The data used so far in this chapter has taken the form of theoretical discourse. Such discourse is developed by 'experts' and is gradually transformed into the accepted truths about diet. Perhaps, however, the way in which non-experts understand diet and eating behaviour is different. It is possible that such expert accounts differ from those provided by the lay person, who may understand diet using a different model of the individual. An examination of women's own accounts of their eating behaviour suggests that this is not the case: parallel models of diet can be found in expert and lay accounts. The interview data from a study of twenty-five women who were attempting to lose weight suggests that the experts' discourse about diet and its focus on self-control finds reflection in women's own accounts (Ogden 1992). The results from this study indicated that the women described their dieting behaviour in terms of the impact on their family life, a preoccupation with food and weight, and changes in mood. However, the concept of self-control transcended these themes. For example, when describing how she had prepared a meal for her family, one woman said, 'I did not want to give in, but I felt that after preparing a three-course meal for everyone else, the least I could do was enjoy my efforts.' The sense of not giving in suggests an attempt to impose control over her eating. In terms of the preoccupation with food, a woman said, 'Why should I deprive myself of nice food?', and another said, 'Now that I've eaten that, I might as well give in to all the drives to eat.' Such statements again reflect a sense of self-control and a feeling that eating reflects a breakdown in this control. In terms of mood, one woman said that she was 'depressed that something as simple as eating cannot be controlled', and likewise this role of self-control was also apparent in the women's negative descriptions of themselves, with a woman saying, 'I'm just totally hopeless and weak, and though I hate being fat I just don't have the willpower to do anything about it.' Accordingly, theoretical discourses of diet describe eating behaviour in terms of self-control and conceptualise a late twentieth-century individual who is intra-active. In parallel, lay discourses illustrate a similar emphasis on self-control and describe a comparable model of the individual.

The lay–expert boundary

Models of communication within both psychological and sociological theory divide beliefs and theories into lay versus expert accounts. Lay accounts are regarded as varied and as corresponding to individuals' personal experiences, and expert theories are regarded as a product of study, knowledge and evidence. However, both lay and expert theories of diet describe a similar model of the individual who is self-controlling. Why are there such parallels between these two different types of data? One answer is to conceptualise expert accounts as the origin of models which permeate down to lay individuals. Alternatively, it could be argued that expert accounts are derived from an inductive analysis of lay theories. Accordingly, lay theories form the basis of expert knowledge. However, perhaps the boundary between lay and expert theories is itself constructed by theories of knowledge which differentiate between lay accounts (beliefs) and experts' accounts (knowledge). In line with this, rather than privileging either of these accounts, perhaps these two versions of knowledge are not only constructed as divided by knowledge, but are mutually constructive as knowledge. Accordingly, the lay–expert boundary becomes permeable and the problem of similarity is solved.

In summary, across a number of apparently distinct psychological discourses the eating individual of the late twentieth century is constructed as a divided, self-controlling and reflexive self. Sociological theories of eating and food illustrate a shift in their model of the individual to one who is intra-active.

SOCIOLOGICAL THEORIES

Early theories of food

Whereas early psychological theories focused on the mechanisms of food intake and described the individual as responding to his or her environment, the traditional (and minimal) place of food within sociological discourse has been as an illustration of social order. For example, early writers such as Engels and Marx regarded food as an essential component of human subsistence and its absence as an illustration of inequality (see Mennell et al. 1992). Accordingly, such an analysis focused on food as being located in the environment, and as an illustration of variations due to gender, class, culture or ethnicity. In line with this, Elias (1978, original 1939) used food as an illustration of the development of table manners and placed his discussion within the context of discrepancies between classes and changes over time. Likewise, Lévi-Strauss analysed cuisine in terms of the reflection and reproduction of differing social structures, and Douglas focused on food as an illustration of rules and boundaries, and in particular the delineation between the sacred and profane (e.g. Lévi Strauss 1965; Douglas 1966). Within these early sociological texts the emphasis was on food (not eating) as external to the individual and as a means of illustrating difference. Accordingly, food was given a symbolic role which has been developed in other texts focusing on the meaning of food in religion (e.g. Loveday and Chiba 1985), family relationships (Murcott 1983) and social rituals (Piette 1989). In parallel to early psychological theories of the individual as a passive responder, the individual within these sociological discourses was conceptualised as indistinct and in terms of an absence of agency.

Theories of self-control

Over recent years, however, there has been an increasing interest in food and eating within sociological theory, and such theories have suggested a more significant role for the individual.[2] In particular, contemporary theories illustrate an emphasis on an individual who has self-control. For example, Mennell argued that changing food preferences and cuisines should be understood in the light of social and political changes, and that the availability of plenty resulted in the need for individuals to impose control upon their food consumption (Mennell 1985, 1986). He further suggested that whereas to gorge was a sign of wealth in times when access to food differentiated between the classes, the rich now need to illustrate self-control as a means to separate themselves from the lower classes. In particular, he suggests that taste and appetite should be analysed within the 'broader shift in the balance between external constraints and self-constraints' and that 'more internalised control became valued more than the brute capacity to stuff' (Mennell et al. 1992; Mennell 1985). This emphasis on self-control can further be seen in van Otterloo's analysis of eating and appetite in the Netherlands as she suggested that 'the working class . . . is less successful than the middle class in restraining the problem of overweight' (Mennell et al. 1992; van Otterloo 1990). The use of the term 'restraining' suggests that overweight is a response to an internal desire to eat that needs to be controlled.

Recent sociological theories on diet and eating have also been developed by Turner (1982, 1992) and his work illustrates this contemporary model of the individual as self-controlling. For example, in his analysis of Cheyne's theory of dietary schema in the 1740s, Turner argues that 'Cheyne's dietary management involved a disciplining of the aristocratic, not the labouring body' (1992: 190) and suggests that Cheyne's work could be interpreted as similar to Methodism by 'subordinating the body'. He further focuses on Cheyne's belief that 'medical practice was seen to be secondary to sensible dieting in servicing this hydraulic apparatus' (1992: 184). Accordingly, Turner's analysis of these earlier texts emphasise the importance of self-regulation and self-control. Turner also analyses the work of Bruch and her writings on eating disorders. He suggests that Bruch argues that 'self-imposed starvation provides a form of personal control which is expressive of pseudo power' (1992: 221) and that 'not eating expresses autonomy from parental demands'. Therefore, Turner's analysis of the discourse of diet emphasises the role of self-control and suggests that in Cheyne's time control was important to resist temptation, and that in the late twentieth century a similar pattern of denial has emerged in the form of dieting and eating disorders. In fact, this shift to an intra-active model of the individual is also illustrated by the changing meaning of the word 'diet'. Early in the century, 'diet' was used predominantly as a noun to reflect the external availability of food, but now is used mainly as a verb – 'to diet' – emphasising the individual's ability to control food intake.

The status of text

Sociological texts on diet therefore illustrate a shift in their model of the individual similar to that found in psychological theories, with earlier texts describing an indistinct individual who responds to external factors and recent works attributing the individual with self-control. However, sociological texts present the problem of the status of texts and the relationship between primary and secondary sources. Whereas psychological texts have aimed to explore the mechanisms of food intake, recent sociological writings have resorted to analysing other sociological texts. Accordingly, in terms of an analysis of a changing model of the individual, does a late twentieth-century analysis of an eighteenth-century text belong now or then? Does the individual described within such an analysis reflect a modern model of the individual or a model contemporaneous to the original publication?

A further exploration of Turner's analysis of Cheyne's work illustrates this problem (Turner 1992). Turner argues that Cheyne was interested in the role of self-control and self-regulation. Accordingly, from this perspective, the quotes from the eighteenth century appear to have described a late twentieth-century self-controlling individual. However, an examination of Cheyne's text suggests that this may be a reflection of Turner's own explanatory framework. For example, Cheyne is quoted as saying 'the inventions of luxury, to force an unnatural appetite' and 'Since our wealth has increas'd. . . . The tables of the rich and the great . . . are furnish'd with provisions of Delicacy, Number and Plenty, sufficient to provoke, and even gorge the most large and Voluptuous appetite', and 'the richest foods and the most generous wines, such as can provoke the Appetites, Senses and Passions in the most exquisite and voluptuous manner'. Such quotes are analysed by Turner as reflecting a role for self-control. However, do these quotes really relate to self-control? An alternative analysis could suggest that Cheyne regarded eating as a response to the availability of plenty. Cheyne also remarks that the availability of 'fermented and distilled liquors [are the cause of] all or most of the painful and excruciating distempers that afflict Mankind'. His use of terms such as 'provoke' and 'force', and his emphasis on the impact of an increasing range and amount of food, suggest that eating is regarded as a response to external factors – that the individual has no choice but to eat because such a wealth of food has become available. Cheyne may be describing an eating individual who is in line with the passive responder as described by early psychological theories. However, as a late twentieth-century writer, Turner analyses this text in terms of self-control.[3]

Perhaps, as theoretical sociology has developed an interest in the body, in its status and regulation, and as constructionist models of surveillance have become increasingly recognised (Armstrong 1995), diet – as a means to control the body – has become a suitable area for sociological study. Accordingly, the sociological writings on diet have increased in number, and such works have emphasised the role of control and self-regulation in their understanding of diet, both in terms of its contemporary status and also in terms of its historical origins.

CONCLUDING COMMENTS

Examination of psychological theory suggests a consistent shift in its model of the individual – from a passive responder to external events, to one who interacts with these events, to a late twentieth-century individual who is intra-active. Examination of sociological theories of diet illustrate a parallel shift which is reflected in lay theories about eating behaviour. How have these changes happened? And what do they tell us about the relationship between theory and its object?

How have these changes happened? The problem of methodology

This chapter is based on the premise that theory can be used as data, and that an analysis of this data can enable an exploration of the relationship between theory and its object: the individual. If theory can be treated as data, then how are these data to be analysed? What methodology is to be used? Over the twentieth century, methodology can be divided into three dominant approaches. Each of these approaches has implications for understanding the theory–object relationship and for analysing theories as data.

First, an inductivist approach would involve collecting data and using these data to develop theories. An inductivist methodologist would observe the data and induce from this data its implications for developing a suitable theory. Accordingly, data collection would be seen as being an objective and theory-independent process. The inductivist researcher would be 'outside' the process of data analysis. Therefore, in terms of the data presented within this chapter, such an analyst would consider psychological and sociological theories of the twentieth century to speak for themselves: the theory of a changing individual identity emerges from the observations provided by the data – essentially a passive process. In line with this, the changes identified by methodological processes are therefore a product of progress and increasing accuracy. Such a methodological approach finds reflection in the concept of the individual (in this case the researcher) as a passive responder, and early theories of the eating individual as passively responding to their environment.

Perhaps, observations are not objective but theory-dependent. If individuals are subjective beings, then so are analysts. The second methodological approach, therefore, would involve collecting, analysing and interpreting data according to the theoretical perspective of the researcher. In terms of the data presented in this chapter, this methodological approach would regard psychological and sociological theories of diet as there to be examined, but would emphasise that the outcome of this examination process as influenced by the subjective state of the researcher. (In part, this has been recognised in terms of theories of experimenter bias and expectancy effects.) From this perspective, models of a changing eating individual over the past hundred years are a consequence of the interpretation and subjective analysis of data by the researcher. Data are transformed by the researcher through the use of methodology. This methodological approach describes a researcher who interacts with their data and finds reflection in mid twentieth-century theories of an eating individual who eats as a result of an interaction with his or her environment.

However, if the changing models of individual identity describe a contemporary eating individual who is intra-active, then perhaps the researcher is also intra-active. This third methodological approach, therefore, regards theory as linked to the object of that theory (the individual). Further, the researcher and the methodological approach used to explore that theory are also linked to the theory; methodology is as much part of theory as are individuals themselves. Experimenter bias is not, therefore, a contaminant of attempts at research which could and should be removed by understanding the transformation of the data, but 'what research is'. The individual being studied, the resulting theory and the researcher developing the theory are all part of the intra-active unit. This final methodological approach, with its emphasis on subjectivity, finds reflection in late twentieth-century theories of eating individuals who interact with themselves.

Accordingly, in answer to the question 'How are these changes analysed?', the method of analysis is itself a reflection of the contemporary model of the individual. Therefore, if this chapter had been written at the beginning of the century, the author could claim to be passively responding to the existing data – an inductivist approach. Psychological and sociological theory as data would be allowed to speak for itself and changes in this theory would be explained as progress. If it had been written in the middle of the century, however, the methodology used to analyse theories could be said to accept the theory dependency of these data and the subjectivity of the author. The data would be analysed according to an interaction between the researcher and his or her data – changes in theory would be a product of transformation of the data by a subjective researcher. However, if contemporary theory is a window which not only describes or transforms, but begins to constitute its subject, and if methodology is itself a facet of theory, then perhaps theory as data can only be analysed now using methodologies of its time – intra-active methodologies. Equally, this chapter, the data it describes, and the questions it addresses, cannot transcend the theoretical and methodological framework of the late twentieth century. Accordingly, the intra-active individual – as described by contemporary theories of diet – finds reflection in the contemporary interest in reflective, subjective and relativist methodologies (as illustrated by this book).

Theory and its object

Analysis of twentieth-century theories on eating and diet suggest a change in their descriptions of their object. Both psychological and sociological theories suggest that the contemporary individual is no longer described as either passively responding to their environment or as interacting with this environment but is characterised by either the presence or absence of self-control. Such an individual is considered intra-active.

This chapter began by examining the relationship between theory and the object of that theory. Accordingly, does this changing descriptive language simply indicate a reassessment of the individual, or a more radical reconstitution of the object itself? Does this shift in theoretical perspective simply reflect a new means to understand the same individual, or has a new individual emerged? Eating may now be described in different language from that used at the beginning of the century, but could the individuals who are eating also be different? If theories construct their object, then perhaps a new individual is being constructed through the new theories of eating, who not only appears different, but is different – a self-controlling individual. In addition, following Foucault, once constituted through theory, the individual may show resistance to the mechanisms which have provided the means for the origin of their identity (Foucault 1979). Accordingly, the resistance to self-control – as illustrated by the process of overeating and the cognitions of rebellion which precede such overeating – reflects the constitution of an intra-active individual existing through the theories on self-control. Further, the recent increasing interest in diet and food within psychological and sociological theories, the proliferation of hospital clinics and self-help groups to manage and treat eating disorders, and the generalised preoccupation with dieting, reflect the construction of a self-controlling and self-regulating body, with diet as the vehicle for this control and the anorexic as the ultimate self-controlling intra-active individual.

NOTES

1 The term 'overeating' can be seen as implicitly reflecting a sense of the absence of self-control.
2 It could be argued that over recent years the divisions between psychological and sociological perspectives have become less distinct as sociological theories have begun to create a role for the individual and psychological theories have emphasised a need to locate the individual within a social context.
3 This is not to privilege my own analysis of text, but to explore the problematic process of locating text within time.

REFERENCES

American Psychiatric Association (1987) *Diagnostic and Statistical Manual of Mental Disorders*, Washington, DC: American Psychiatric Association (revised 3rd edn).
Armstrong, D. (1995) 'The rise of surveillance medicine', *Sociology, Health and Illness* 17: 393–404.
Bandura, A. (1977) 'Self-efficacy: toward a unifying theory of behaviour change', *Psychological Review* 84: 191–215.
—— (1986) *Social Foundations of Thought and Action*, Englewood Cliffs, NJ: Prentice-Hall.
Bruch, H. (1974) *Eating Disorders: Anorexia, Obesity and the Person Within*, London: Routledge & Kegan Paul.
—— (1985) 'Four decades of eating disorders', in D. M. Garner and P. E. Garfinkel (eds) *Handbook of Psychotherapy for Anorexia Nervosa and Bulimia*, New York: The Guilford Press.
Cannon, W. B. (1932) *The Wisdom of the Body*, New York: Norton.
Cooper, P. J. and Fairburn, C. G. (1986) 'The depressive symptoms of bulimia nervosa', *British Journal of Psychiatry* 148: 268–274.
Cooper, P. J. and Taylor, M. J. (1988) 'Body image disturbance in Bulimia Nervosa', *British Journal of Psychiatry* 153: 32–36.
Cooper, Z. and Fairburn, C. G. (1987) 'The eating disorder examination: a semi-structured interview for the assessment of the specific psychopathology of eating disorders', *International Journal of Eating Disorders* 6: 1–8.
Crisp, A. H. (1984) 'The psychopathology of anorexia nervosa: getting the "heat" out of the system', in A. J. Stunkard and E. Stellar (eds) *Eating and its Disorders*, New York: Raven Press.
Dickinson, A. (1980) *Contemporary Animal Learning Theory*, Cambridge: Cambridge University Press.
Dolce, J. J. (1987) 'Self-efficacy and disability beliefs in the behavioural treatment of pain', *Behaviour Research and Therapy* 25: 289.
Douglas, M. (1966) *Purity and Danger: An Analysis of the Concepts of Pollution and Taboo*, London: Routledge & Kegan Paul.
Elias, N. (1978) *The Civilizing Process*, Oxford: Basil Blackwell.
Fairburn, C. (1984) 'Bulimia: its epidemiology and management', in A. J. Stunkard and E. Stellar (eds) *Eating and its Disorders*, New York: Raven Press.

Foucault, M. (1979) *The History of Sexuality: I. An Introduction*, London: Allen Lane.

Garfinkel, P. E. and Garner, D. M. (1986) *Anorexia Nervosa: A Multidimensional Perspective*, New York: Brunner-Mazel.

Garner, D. M. and Garfinkel, P. E, (1979) 'The eating attitudes test: an index of the symptoms of anorexia nervosa', *Psychological Medicine* 9: 272–279.

Glynn, S. M. and Ruderman, A. J. (1986) 'The development and validation of an eating self-efficacy scale', *Cognitive Therapy and Research* 10: 403–420.

Goldscheider, A. (1920) *Das Schmerz Problem*, Berlin: Springer.

Heatherton, T. F. and Baumeister, R. F. (1991) 'Binge eating as an escape from self-awareness', *Psychological Bulletin* 110: 86–108.

Herman, C. P. and Mack, D. (1975) 'Restrained and unrestrained eating', *Journal of Personality* 43: 646–660.

Herman, C. P. and Polivy, J. (1975) 'Anxiety, restraint and eating behaviour', *Journal of Abnormal Psychology* 84: 666–672.

—— (1984) 'A boundary model for the regulation of eating', in A. J. Stunkard and E. Stellar (eds) *Eating and its Disorders*, New York: Raven Press.

—— (1989) 'Restraint and excess in dieters and bulimics', in K. M. Pirke and D. Ploog (eds) *The Psychobiology of Bulimia*, Berlin: Springer Verlag.

Hibscher, J. A. and Herman, C. P. (1977) 'Obesity, dieting, and the expression of "obese" characteristics', *Journal of Comparative Physiological Psychology* 91: 374–380.

Latour, B. (1988) *Science in Action*, Cambridge, MA: Harvard University Press.

Lazarus, R. S. and Cohen, J. B. (1977) 'Environmental stress', in L. Altman and J. F. Wohlwill (eds) *Human Behaviour and the Environment: Current Theory and Research* (vol. 2), New York: Plenum Publishing.

Lazarus, R. S. and Folkman, S. (1987) 'Transactional theory and research on emotions and coping', *European Journal of Personality* 1: 141–170.

Lévi-Strauss, C. (1965) 'Le triangle culinaire', *L'Arc* 26: 19–29.

Loro, A. D. and Orleans, C. S. (1981) 'Binge eating in obesity: preliminary findings and guidelines for behavioural analysis and treatment', *Addictive Behaviours* 7: 155–166.

Loveday, L. and Chiba, S. (1985) 'Partaking with the divine and symbolizing the societal: the semiotics of Japanese food and drink', *Semiotics* 56: 115–131.

Manning, M. M. and Wright, T. L. (1983) 'Self-efficacy expectancies, outcome expectancies and the persistence of pain control in child birth', *Journal of Personality and Social Psychology* 45: 421–431.

Melzack, R. and Wall, P. D. (1965) 'Pain mechanisms: a new theory', *Science* 150: 971–979.

Mennell, S. (1985) *All Manners of Food: Eating and Taste in England and France from the Middle Ages to the Present*, Oxford: Basil Blackwell.

—— (1986) *Prospects for the History of Food*, Groniek: Gronings Historisch Tijdschrift 95: 7–21.

Mennell, S., Murcott, A. and van Otterloo, A. H. (1992) *The Sociology of Food: Eating Diet and Culture*, London: Sage.

Murcott, A. (1983) *The Sociology of Food and Eating*, Aldershot: Gower.

Nisbett, R. E. (1972) 'Hunger, obesity and the ventromedial hypothalamus', *Psychological Review* 79: 433–453.

Ogden, J. (1992) *Fat Chance! The Myth of Dieting Explained*, London: Routledge.

—— (1994) 'The effects of smoking cessation, restrained eating, and motivational states on food intake in the laboratory', *Health Psychology* 13: 114–121.

—— (1995a) 'Psychosocial theory and the creation of the risky self', *Social Science and Medicine* 40: 409–415.

—— (1995b) 'Changing the subject of health psychology', *Psychology and Health* 10: 257–265.

Ogden, J. and Greville, L. (1993) 'Cognitive changes to preloading in restrained and unrestrained eaters as measured by the Stroop task', *International Journal of Eating Disorders* 14: 185–196.

Ogden, J. and Wardle, J. (1991) 'Cognitive and emotional responses to food', *International Journal of Eating Disorders* 10: 297–311.

Pavlov, I. P. (1927) *Conditioned Reflexes*, Oxford: Oxford University Press.

Piette, A. (1989) 'Folklore ou esthétique du brouillage', *Recherches Sociologiques* 20: 177–90.

Rescorla, R. A. and Wagner, A. R. (1972) 'A theory of Pavlovian conditioning: variations in the effectiveness of reinforcement and non-reinforcement', in A. H. Black, and W. F. Prokasy (eds) *Classical Conditioning. II: Current Research and Theory*, New York: Appleton-Century-Crofts.

Rogers, R. W. (1983) 'Cognitive and physiological processes in fear appeals and attitude change: a revised theory of protection motivation', in J. R. Cacioppo and R. E. Petty (eds) *Social Psychology: A Source Book*, New York: Guilford.

Rosenstock, I. M., Strecher, V. J. and Becker, M. H. (1988) 'Social learning theory and the Health Belief Model', *Health Education Quarterly* 15: 175–183.

Russell, G. F. M. (1979) 'Bulimia nervosa: an ominous variant of anorexia nervosa', *Psychological Medicine* 9: 429–448.

Schachter, S. (1968) 'Obesity and eating', *Science* 161: 751–756.

Schachter, S. and Gross, L. (1968) 'Manipulated time and eating behaviour', *Journal of Personality and Social Psychology* 10: 98–106.

Schachter, S. and Rodin, J. (1974) *Obese Humans and Rats*, Potomac, MD: Erlbaum.

Schachter, S., Goldman, R. and Gordon, A. (1968) 'Effects of fear, food deprivation and obesity on eating', *Journal of Personality and Social Psychology* 10: 91–97.

Shisslak, C. M., Paxda, S. L. and Crago, M. (1990) 'Body weight and bulimia as discriminators of psychological characteristics among anorexic, bulimic and obese women', *Journal of Abnormal Psychology* 99: 380–384.

Skinner, B. F. (1953) *Science and Human Behaviour*, New York: Macmillan.

Spencer, J. A. and Fremouw, M. J. (1979) 'Binge eating as a function of restraint and weight classification', *Journal of Abnormal Psychology* 88: 262–267.

Spitzer, L. and Rodin, J. (1981) 'Human eating behaviour: a critical review of studies in normal weight and overweight individuals', *Appetite* 2: 293–329.

Turner, B. (1982) 'The discourse of diet', *Theory, Culture and Society* 1: 23–32.

—— (1992) *Regulating Bodies*, London: Routledge.

van Otterloo, A. H. (1990) *Eten en eetlust in Nederland 1940–1990. Een historisch-sociologische studie*, Amsterdam: Bert Bakker.

Wagner, S., Halmi, K. A. and Maguire, T. (1987) 'The sense of personal ineffectiveness in patients with eating disorders', *International Journal of Eating Disorders* 6: 495–505.

Wiedenfeld, S. A., O'Leary, A., Bandura, A., Brown, S., Levine, S. and Raska, K. (1990) 'Impact of perceived self-efficacy in coping with stressors on immune function', *Journal of Personality and Social Psychology* 59: 1082–1094.

Williams, G. J., Cahmove, A. and Millar, H. R. (1990) 'Eating disorders, perceived control, assertiveness and hostility', *British Journal of Clinical Psychology* 29: 327–335.

Chapter 11

Speaking the decorated body

John Soyland

INTRODUCTION

Summer 1995 – Edinburgh Festival – just after lunch. I am sitting at a table outside a pub. The weather is quite warm, and the pub is crowded; half a dozen tables are set up in front of the pub for the customers who want to watch people walk by. Lots of people drift past the open market stalls opposite the place where I sit. Because there are few empty table places, I am soon joined close at hand by a couple in their late twenties, a man and a woman; they act like a partnership. They might be students of some kind, but they clearly are not displaying any great deal of wealth, at least from the way they dress; their accents make me think they are from Newcastle, but I am often wrong about accents. She has a nose ring, and multiple ear piercing all the way up each side, more on one side than the other, and decorated with a variety of jewellery; just off the shoulder – on the upper arm – a visible tattoo, nothing very large or extravagant but in the all-black, slightly Celtic style that is becoming more popular now. Her companion is rather more decorated: apart from the pair of rings through one side of his nostril (is that one hole or two?), he has a ring through the skin on the bridge of his nose (that seems to be a novelty); I can see a couple of studs in the ear lobe, and also a stud through the tragus – I've never seen that cartilage in front of the earhole pierced except in pictures. 'If you can pinch it, you can pierce it', somebody told me in an interview once. He's got a long-sleeved shirt on – no visible tattoos. He has a pint of bitter, and she a half-pint of cola; they leave the table having talked and laughed for about twenty minutes. No one saw them as anything unusual or out of the ordinary – just another pair of decorated people, in the routine of everyday life. And perhaps there is no reason to see them as anything else.

Decoration and identity

The decorated body, whether tattooed, pierced or scarred, used to be something of a novelty: it signalled an exotic, non-white, or perhaps maritime identity. In *Moby Dick*, Melville (1851) combines both of these in the character of Queequeg, the tattooed sailor from a not very clearly specified tribe of head-shrinkers. Because of crowding at the inn where the narrator (Ishmael) is staying, the pair of them end up having to share a bed together (for the times a fairly common practice, even in hospitals), and that is how Queequeg is introduced. While Melville endows him with a range of strange views, and has him inspecting a clutch of scattered bones for messages of fate, he also shows him to be a true and trusted friend: loyal, honest, courageous; subversive to neither Christian morality nor ship's discipline. Queequeg's decorated body marks his identity as someone from an alien culture (the body being used as a visible sign of personhood), but Melville does not use it to undermine a belief in a common humanity. As the narrator has it: 'It's only his outside; a man can be honest in any sort of skin' (p. 37). The decorated body is a social marker of difference, but that difference can be undermined if the strategy is to show what is common to all people.

A similar strategy may be seen to function even earlier in the novel *Oroonoko* by Aphra Behn (1640–1689):

> those who are mostly from of that country (Coramantien [Ghana]) are so delicately cut and raced (slashed) all over the fore part of the trunk of their bodies, that it looks as if it were japanned; the works being raised like high point (lace) round the edges of the flowers. Some are carved with a little flower, or bird, at the sides of the temples . . . and those who are so carved over the body, resemble our ancient Picts, that are figured in the chronicles, but these carvings are more delicate.
>
> (1992: 112–113)

Here the exotic is described in terms of the (then) familiar – the flesh is black and glossy like japan varnish, parts of the flesh are raised like embroidered lace, the African body is more delicately worked than the carvings of the Picts of northern Britain (an ancient tribe with which the reader of the times could be familiar). Distance is combined with what the reader already knows. The emphasis is on the common element of human work: one range of practices is aligned with another, but the difference depends on the exotic work having been performed on human flesh, not on inanimate objects. Again, the body is used to mark an alien identity, and again a thread of common humanity is maintained – the social markers of the alien tribe are described here as beautiful, not grotesque, different, but not subversive of common understanding – the marks of the 'other' are not so strange.

Until recently, a novelist could easily have done the same things as Melville or Behn in order to mark the otherness of a character. But, in the 1990s, this could only be done with some difficulty – the degree (the position, the extent) of decoration would have to be stressed because the existence of body decoration alone would no longer be enough. For example, ear piercing is no longer regarded as strange, but is more typically to be expected as a routine part of the adorned body – normally on women, but the number of eyebrows raised on seeing a man with pierced ears would seem to be decreasing. Permanent, or semi-permanent, decorations of the body are no longer as exotic as the accounts of Melville and Behn imply may have been the case in former times. As the 'field notes' at the beginning of the chapter might suggest, the decorated body has begun to become a part of the mainstream social body – exotic identity markers have been made more ordinary. Of course, the scar, the tattoo, or the piercing can still be used to mark the social status of the prisoner, the sailor, the motor-cyclist, or the married woman from the Indian sub-continent, but these signs alone (without the forms of dress, the manner of walking, the types of ges-ture, and so on) are no longer sufficient ways of signalling such personal identity: far too many other individuals now also use these social markers for other purposes – to display social status, sexual preference, sub-culture allegiance or, most simply of all, an interest in personal adornment. And it is the last of these that I will be stressing later in the chapter.

Why, then, do normal, healthy individuals, from a range of different social classes, submit themselves to often uncomfortable procedures – the incision, the burn, the disposable stud gun, the mechanical needle – and risk bruising, infection, wounds going septic, or their body rejecting the pieces of foreign matter inserted into their skin? The answer to this question is bound up with issues concerning individual and group identity – with the body as a crucial material component in these operations. It was in order to investigate issues around this question, that I began a qualitative study which relies for the most part on data derived from semi-structured interviews. Thus far, very little work has been done on the everyday practices of the person who decorates their body (but see Vale and Juno 1989; Curry 1993), and the interview technique seemed appropriate as a method of documenting the ways in which it is possible to speak about the decorated body.

The discursive–material aspects of this research are important for several reasons. First, the decorated body is one that has been altered in fairly per-manent ways: piercings can heal over, but only if the punctures are not too large, or stretched or repeated; scars and tattoos can be altered by skin grafts or laser treatments, and may even fade over an extended period of time, but otherwise are sustained on the body. In this sense, the decorated body is unlike one that is altered by hair dye, nail polish or eyeliner; suntans and skin-lightening creams wear off in much shorter time periods; make-up, facial hair (side burns, moustaches, beards, hair-pieces) or permanent waves can be more easily removed or left to grow out. Therefore, the decision to decorate in the ways to be discussed here is to make a material change in the body. Second, such material changes are the result of discursive shifts: while the decoration may be used to change the identity of some body (in both senses), some of the accounts included in this chapter suggest that it is as if the changes to the surface of the body are the result of some inner, discursive sense of self, as if the decorations were pushed out from within, as if talk necessitated the changes to the material. Here the material and the discursive overlap and interweave: bodies cause talk, and talk causes new bodies (Soyland 1997). Thus, third, identity is both the consequence and the cause of the material. The task, then, is to understand how such talk can have material effects, and how such material effects are reconciled, justified and explained both in terms of identity, and in terms of the body.

Interviews as data

The original data in this chapter came from interviews conducted by the author at Lancaster University. Interviewees were self-selected in response to posters displayed around the campus and a general invitation issued during lectures (which were also concerned with the body, see Soyland 1997). Each respondent completed a short, informal questionnaire before the interview. Discussion time ranged between half an hour and an hour and the interviewees were paid for their time, using departmental funds for experimental subjects. Many of the interviewees expressed surprise at being paid to talk about their changed, but healthy, bodies: it was all just talk – no hooking up to some physiological machine or procedures involving measurement or even display. People could point to various parts of their body (which they did), but the object of the exercise was to get them to talk (and it is talk about bodies that is the issue here, not the bodies themselves, although the connections between the two are what is important). My impression was that these people wanted to talk, could see the point of the questions, and enjoyed being taken seriously – whilst not being seen as creatures from another planet (or simply just 'other'). All my work to date has been related to talk and writing about 'science' (where the certainties of truth are exactly those under scrutiny), but here the words of the body decorators are treated on the metonymic (part–whole) assumption that they refer beyond the given instance to some more general aspects of popular culture, that in some sense my interviewees were able to speak for other decorated bodies. (Later in the chapter, I give a discussion of problems arising from this assumption.)

On arrival, each interviewee was asked to fill out the questionnaire (the time for this was both paid for, and unlimited, but it only took a few minutes to complete): this was to provide general information (such as their age and gender, and what subjects they were studying), while also giving responses that would be used to generate discussion. (The questions are given as an appendix to this chapter.) In this way, comparisons could be made between answers on a similar range of issues across interviews (a standard technique in Discourse Analysis, see Potter and Wetherell 1987). It is the comparison between answers that is the basis for much of the following analysis. With permission, each interview was tape-recorded and much of the material transcribed, using standard discourse analysis conventions.

THEMES DERIVED FROM THE INTERVIEWS

Pain and decoration

Given the earlier mention of the fairly intrusive practices involved in decorating the body, and the question relating to pain that all of the interviewees answered before the interview commenced, pain would seem a good topic with which to start the analysis – and it was a question that was important to the respondents. All the interviewees discussed pain at some point in the interview, and some similarities show up by comparison. A typical example may be seen early on in the interview with a 39-year-old woman when the topic of tattoos was raised:

Interviewee   Mmm. Oh yeah, it's an ongoing thing, I will, (*laughs*) I think, I think I will, it's just the pain, yeah, I've got a few friends that have had them and it's quite painful because the areas where I'd probably have them, like I think I'd have one there, rather than on the actual arm . . .

Interviewer   Just off the shoulder?

Interviewee   Yeah, and you've not got much flesh, you know, it's bone and it's painful.

Interviewer   Right.

Interviewee   Yeah, and that is the only thing that really puts me off . . .

Interviewer   Yes?

Interviewee   . . . is the pain when you have it. I mean I've even decided I, I err, I think I'd probably have a dragon fly, I mean it's just actually having the bottle (*laughs*) to go.

Here, knowledge of the areas of the body that are both the desired site for future decoration, and those involving amounts of pain, is displayed. In general, all the interviewees intimated an understanding of their own bodily reactions. Pain, in these accounts, is seen as an obstacle to be overcome if the tattoo is to be done. The body, then, is something to be mastered or controlled if the ambition to decorate is to be realised; this can be taken as an overarching theme within many of the interviews. For instance, a 24-year-old man drew a distinction between the small amount of pain involved in getting his nose pierced, and the pain he expected to experience in getting the tattoo he wanted:

Interviewee   I think it will be painful, yeah, the one part that I'll least look forwards to, I think – actually sitting there with this needle going in and out of your arm several times.

Interviewer   Do you think that would put you off?

Interviewee   No, if I saw a design I liked I would have it done – if I had the chance I would drink half a bottle of whisky first, but

> (*laughs*) I think I would definitely go along and have it done 'cause the pain's not the main thing.

Here the 'main thing' is the decoration, and not the pain; it is a matter of finding the right design, and then submitting to the process. There is an obvious knowledge of the pain involved in the procedure – it is the part of the process that is 'least looked forward to' – but the pain is described as almost incidental to what can be had once the process is undergone. The laughter in this excerpt will be discussed later in the chapter. As it happens, professional tattoo artists will not work on the body of a person who is drunk – that is part of their code of correct decorating practice.

In both these accounts, pain is described as something that is feared, and it is the fear of the process of tattooing that needs to be overcome for an aesthetic goal. What both these descriptions allow then is the construction of the process of decoration as a kind of personal rite of passage: having the will to overcome the fear and the physical pain; to assert control over the body. So, although pain may be described as something negative, it can be used in other accounts as a positive way of separating those who decorate and those who do not. I will come back to this point in a later discussion of 'authenticity'.

Another interesting feature of the discussions of pain was the occasional reference to addiction. I will consider two examples, one rather more involved than the other. First, an excerpt from an interview with an 18-year-old woman: she is discussing her interest in getting additional piercings:

Interviewee . . . that's why I think people have started having their nose pierced twice 'cos that's going one step further.

Interviewer Is that why you're considering getting more, going one step further?

Interviewee Yeah, plus it's like a sort of addiction, it's really like fun when you're going to have it done. You can get loads more jewellery and have loads of studs and stuff.

Interviewer Why would it constitute an addiction?

Interviewee 'Cos it's just really enjoyable, I really like having it done, even though it hurts a bit.

Interviewer You like the process, sitting there and your eyes watering?

Interviewee Knowing I'm going to have it done, it's something to look forward to.

Here the interviewer attempts to reformulate what the interviewee is saying by drawing attention to the pain involved: it is not the pain that is part of the addiction (as the earlier part of the transcript might suggest), but the anticipation, and the post-piercing possibilities of gaining more 'studs' in order to adorn the expanded number of decorations. Perhaps this should be labelled as a form of *social* addiction, where the pain is not regarded as highly significant because it only 'hurts a bit'. But there is one example in my data in which the physical response to pain is related to a form of addiction.

> *Interviewee*   . . . umm, and I see that as the beginning of, umm, an addiction (*laughs*) to it. Umm, so that in the last, in the last three years, I've made roughly eighty to a hundred holes in my body.
>
> *Interviewer*   Are you using a local anaesthetic with this or . . . ?
>
> *Interviewee*   Oh no. Bad idea to use local anaesthetic. Well, you see, umm, when I first had them done I felt . . . I was glad that they hurt, but I felt I had cheated myself. Well, I had been wanting to get an earring in my left ear for a couple of years and I finally got around to doing it, started to get more, umm, but I felt I had cheated myself by getting someone else to do it.

In this extract, the speaker describes himself as physically addicted to the pain involved in receiving 'eighty to a hundred' piercings; more than that, anything which might reduce the intensity of the experience – the use of a local anaesthetic, or having someone else perform the decorating act – is described as cheating the self. Later in this interview, the speaker mentioned a physical sense of euphoria which he experienced for several days after having pierced his body, and expressed with regret that, as he continued this decorating practice, the sense of well-being extended over greatly reduced periods of time, as if the body had grown accustomed to the physical assault. The contrast between these two extracts is the difference between a psychological addiction, via anticipation and so on, and a physical addiction to the post-operative state of euphoria (much as a marathon runner may become addicted to the endorphins the body produces to counteract the pain of the activity).

Identity written on the body

At several points in the interviews, the issue of personal identity was mixed with that of authenticity. The authentic is that which is closest to the 'true' self, that which is part of the core of the person. The discursive problem, then, for the person who wants to decorate is to ensure that the decoration is genuinely regarded as part of their immutable selves, that the decoration springs from whom they 'really' are, that the practice by itself cannot bestow identity on its own. The problem of the 'authentic' becomes the discursive target. The following excerpt shows this in action:

> *Interviewer*   The nose is getting pretty common.
>
> *Interviewee*   Well, I don't really mind, it annoys me when conventional people want to have their noses done because I don't really see why

if they don't want to be part of the rest of the image that goes with it, I don't understand why they want that done, I don't know.

On this account, 'conventional' people are not authentic in their interests in decoration if they do not also make a commitment to the 'rest of the image' – in this case, an affiliation with a kind of counter-culture. This recurrent theme of authenticity will appear again in later discussions.

Attraction, not sexuality

The discursive tension between describing decoration as attractive and making it a mark of sexual preference is a complicated one to negotiate, not least in the interview situation. For the most part, attraction was given a premium. However, one lesbian respondent described herself as worried that further facial piercing would mark her out as someone interested in sadomasochistic practices, which she described herself as having no interest in. Too many decorations would be read as making her submissive in a lesbian relationship and, despite her expressed interest in further decoration, she claimed to want to abstain from further piercing because of the consequences she perceived. But a typical example of the alternative response is as follows:

Interviewer   So when you say you find it attractive . . .
Interviewee   Yeah, personally.
Interviewer   Attractive to you. What about seeing piercing or tattoos on other people?
Interviewee   I don't, I don't look at other people and find them attractive in that sense, do you know what I mean, but like on my partner, yeah, I'll say, get this done because that will look quite kinky, but it's not something that I'll go round to people and say, 'God he looks kinky', 'cos he's got a tattoo you know what I mean. It's nothing like that.
[. . .]
Interviewee   It's not like a thing where you go around, I don't like it on people that go round and display it, you know, show off, you know what I mean? To display it 'cos it looks nice, yeah, is one thing, but to show off and say, 'Look, I'm a hard man with tattoos and things', is another.

Here, there are several dichotomies working at once: first, personal versus public – attraction is discussed in terms of private interaction, something confined to talk between partners. Beyond that intimate situation, in the public arena, attraction is not part of the way this woman describes her experience of seeing other decorated bodies. In this way, a discursive boundary is drawn around finding something attractive in personal circumstances versus transposing that attraction to all other decorated bodies. This suggests the second dichotomy – the attraction of 'looking nice' versus 'showing off'. On this account, there are limits in the public arena to the display of decorations. Personal adornment for the sake of an aesthetic effect is being promoted, but the limit is imposed when adornment is merely for the sake of being seen as a 'hard man' – a kind of boast in the public setting that, on this account, has nothing to do with attraction. These two sets of dichotomies can be combined into a more general one – between the close and the distant. That is, the function of this excerpt is to create a distance between what is personal, aesthetic, an attractive effect, and what other people (not the speaker) do. I will label this a 'distancing strategy', a way of talking about one's own bodily practices that attempts to remove them from other associations, groups or practices. In particular, the distancing strategy is important because of the potential connections between decoration and sexual preference.

Not a subversive practice

In an essay called 'On doing being ordinary' (Sacks 1984), Sacks claims that we all know the practices and talk which form everyday life – that we know how to make ourselves appear to be nothing more than everyone else in the ways in which we interact with the world – and the same is true of the person who decorates their body. A common theme throughout the interviews conducted was that the decorated person wanted to make their practice relatively mundane – not the result of peer pressure, not the result of fashion, not the outcome of a rebellion against parents (for the most part) or against the party-political system (with one minor exception), but merely a personal desire, a whim, an interest in self and appearance. The spoken descriptions mirrored those given in the written answers to interview questions. To the question: Why did you decide to decorate your body? – twelve responses are typical:

1 To be different.
2 A statement of identity, to show that I did belong with a certain group of people.
3 I've always seen it as being fairly attractive, and maybe a sign of an interesting person.
4 Personally, I find it attractive.
5 It's part of an image I want to project, a form of self-expression. Partly to shock/annoy my parents.
6 Because I like tattoos.
7 They look nice.
8 Because we decorate it with clothes and so why not drawings and jewellery?

9   It was not so much a decision . . . had three ear piercing done, six months later I started and never stopped.
10 Fashion. Friendship gesture. To be different (at the time).
11 Aesthetically pleasing.
12 Became a means of characterising. I grew my hair at the same time; became an overall change.

The permanent decoration

From the interview data, a major part of the discourse was taken up with the theme of taking seriously the permanence of tattoos and piercings. Although some forms of decoration are only permanent in the medium term, subject to practices of removal or healing, the commitment to decorate is described as an important step in the creation of a personal identity. The discourse here centred around knowing when one 'is ready' for a commitment to the decoration of the body. For example, one television interview had a decorated person speaking about the pain he had experienced in his life, and wanting to show such a stage in his development in terms of marks on his body. He described wanting a tattoo of an Aztec sun on his shoulder, to represent light, truth, and passing into a better phase of life, and to incorporate into this the sign of the snake to represent the bad things in his life. He claimed that the combination of these symbols would show his commitment to earlier parts of his experience, through their permanent embodiment, whilst showing his personal readiness to change in making this experience part of his bodily appearance. Again, here is the claim to the mark of true authenticity: once the body has passed through a given stage, its passing can be marked on the body in good faith, as if to take the mark under other circumstances would be unauthentic. The permanent decoration needs to signal the body, and the self, as ready and able to take on images and decorations which would otherwise be inappropriate. In making (an albeit semi-) permanent corporeal image on the body, the personal identity of the decorator is paramount: permanence adds to this identity, making it a sign of commitment and authenticity. It is the extent of the affliction on the body which marks decoration discourse as something which can be used to manipulate the listener into thinking something has been achieved which is authentic and lasting.

Laughing about decoration

All of the interviews described here could generally be labelled as 'light-hearted', but that does not by itself explain the amount of laughter in evidence in the transcripts, nor the places in which it appears. While laughter is a form of non-verbal communication, a discourse–analytic perspective must regard it as part of the communicative act. It requires us to ask what function such laughter might fulfil – that is: what is the laughter being used for, when does it appear, and how does it alter an analysis that ignores its appearance? In this final section of the analysis, I will reconsider some of the material already quoted, paying attention to the laughter in terms of it being a rhetorical device in the speaking of the decorated body. The analysis started with a discussion of pain, and I will return to that now.

An excerpt about pain should be recalled first: the claim was that the anxiety of the experience of pain ought to be dulled (even though, under regulation, it could not be) with alcohol. The quotation suggested that the person would need to consume half a bottle of whisky before being brave enough to go through with the desired tattoo – the respondent laughs to show a lack of seriousness, but also an admission of the anxiety involved. Similarly, another excerpt from the section on pain stated: 'if I [*laughs*] had the bottle to go through with it'. Again, the admission of fear or anxiety is mitigated by the laughter which is part of the discursive act. In the same way, other examples of laughter in the transcripts showed the speakers placing a distance between themselves and others who criticise them for decorating practices (e.g. parents, students, employers, friends). But a slightly more complicated use of humour as a distancing device involves the recognition on the part of the listener that a sarcastic tone is being implied, as in the following example:

Interviewer   So, it's the reaction that you don't like?

Interviewee   Mmm, yes, I mean I get positive and negative reactions but to me they're all negative, someone coming up in a club and saying, 'Oh, you've got your eyebrows pierced,' and you think, 'Oh, I hadn't realised' (*sarcastic tone*) . . .

Interviewer   (*laughs*)

Interviewee   . . . or people going, 'Oh does that hurt?' and me going, 'No, it's totally painless.' Umm, to people going, 'Oh that disturbs me'. It's interesting to hear the reactions but I've heard so many, umm. And then people would take, tourists, would take pictures of me sticking my tongue out and I just started to realise what a freak I had become, and I don't like being a freak show . . .

Interviewer   Right.

Interviewee   . . . so now I want to be a normal person, but keep my hobby going.

Interviewer   (*laughs*)

Interviewee   (*laughs*)

Here, it is the response from the interviewer that recognises the humorous tone of the speaker, and allows the speaker to continue in this direction – to the point where a previously marginalised practice can be redescribed as merely a 'hobby', a recreational interest amongst many others. In this way, the speaker's description of his corporeal practices are rendered more mundane, less central to his definition of himself, and more distanced from the description of being a 'freak'. Humour is being used here to make more harmless the criticisms of others, to place a boundary between the speaker and other 'freaks' who lead a more liminal existence – humour both rules the speaker into the realm of the normal, whilst ruling others into a separate category.

CONCLUDING COMMENTS

Using interview material as data has advantages and disadvantages. Earlier, I mentioned that I would be treating this material on the metonymic assumption that the words spoken would refer to discursive practices beyond the particular discussions that were held – that interviewees who spoke about the decorated body could be seen as describing something in ways that could be used beyond the office setting in which their words were recorded. One way to argue against the analysis given here would be to hold that the interviews were atypical, that the respondents were unusual, and that the particular says little about the general (Billig (1996) calls this move 'particularisation'). But the grounds for making such a set of objections in this case are not all that firm: a range of interviews were undertaken with a variety of people from nineteen to thirty-nine years of age, with a variety of sexual preferences, and with very different degrees of decoration; the respondents were from a range of social classes, albeit with an educational background that distanced them from the average in the UK (where the number of people who are qualified to take up tertiary education do so in a percentage smaller than many countries in the Western world); even the interview situation should not be seen as one that generates responses that are beyond what these people would say in other similar circumstances.

The advantages of using interviews are rather more cheerful than the points on the disadvantages. The people interested in detailed conversation analysis (e.g. Atkinson and Heritage 1984; Boden and Zimmerman 1991) will object that these conversations are not 'naturally occurring', but that does not stop them being a part of the conversation on the decorated body. For many of my respondents, the interview was a chance to talk about something that they felt was important, but which was typically talked about in negative, or ironic, or unusual terms. The interview, as part of the battery of qualitative techniques, gave a space in which the respondents' talk could be heard. Second, the interview is a technique which allows for the researcher to engage with the respondent: unlike the questionnaire, it allows for follow-up questions, interventions, clarification (see Potter and Wetherell 1987: 163); the interviewer is able to attempt reformulations of what the interviewee has said, and then gauge the ways in which such formulations are accepted or rejected. In addition, the interview allows for the same questions and topics to be discussed with a number of different people, thereby allowing for comparisons and contrasts to be made. Even a fairly small sample of talk may be used to generate a number of conclusions, which can then be used to understand talk generated in other contexts (Wetherell and Potter 1988).

The themes within the discourse analysed here are not to be taken as stable components of the world, rather they should be seen as potential strategies for dealing with identity management on a moment-by-moment basis (Widdicombe 1993). A speaker is able to engage with different themes to cope with the conversational context: the themes are a set of discursive resources which may overlap or even contradict each other between or within discursive settings (Potter and Wetherell 1987). For example, the strategy of labelling other people as unauthentic in their decorating practices may lead to conflict in direct conversation, and therefore will perhaps be avoided. However, the same theme may be selected as highly appropriate when discussing other people's decorations in an interview setting, where the decorated speaker needs to maintain an authentic identity. In this way, different themes will emerge in various contexts, or at different times within a single setting, in accordance with the demands being made throughout the conversation.

On the basis of the material from the interview data covered here, it is possible to claim that the decorated body is no longer described as very important as a way of signalling group identity, but highly important for individual identity. On these accounts, given a desire to decorate, the healthy body will undergo any number of different quasi-medical procedures in order to attain an aesthetic effect, but they describe their actions in terms of personal attraction, as a way of gaining people's interest, and not as a political act or subversive practice. The body decorators that I talked to were all adept at making their own practices seem ordinary, distancing themselves from the perverse or perverted (Curry 1993), from particular sub-cultures or groups. Even the most decorated did not want to be seen as 'freaks', or to be rejected by their families and friends. No matter how adorned their bodies were in terms of fairly permanent decorations, these people stressed their sense of being ordinary – their bodies were all marked in different ways, but not in ways that made them seem or want to be unusual (to themselves, or to others). Whilst there was some talk of people wanting to overcome their body's reactions to various changes (to pain, septic wounds, or the body rejecting foreign matter), and there was some talk of being able to pass through the experience in order to gain the effect they desired, these operations were not described in ritualistic terms – a description which might be expected from speakers from other cultures. On the basis of this material, there is no commonly described ritual to which the body to be decorated must submit or fail. More than that, beyond personal desire, there is no common element in the interest in decoration. To speak of the decorated body is to speak an increasingly common and ordinary language, one that claims to be authentic in its interest, but no more so than any other aesthetic practice. The discourse of the decorated body has become incorporated into the social body.

APPENDIX: PRE-INTERVIEW QUESTIONNAIRE

Any information you give in answer to these questions will be treated in strict confidence. Please include whatever information you think is relevant.

1 Male/Female?
2 Age?
3 A student of: Humanities/Social Science/Science/Other.
4 Which parts of your body do you have pierced?
5 Which parts of your body, if any, do you have tattooed?
6 Why did you decide to decorate your body?
7 What other parts of your body have you considered having pierced?
8 What sorts of reactions have you received from other people?
9 What forms of employment are you intending after graduation?
10 Does it matter to you whether people can see the decorations on your body?
11 Did you find your piercing (or tattoos) painful?
12 If you did find there was pain involved, has that influenced any decisions about further decorations?
13 Please describe the way you normally dress.
14 What kinds of music do you normally listen to?
15 Do you see yourself as a member of a particular sub-culture?
16 (Optional question) How would you describe your sexuality?

REFERENCES

Atkinson, J. M. and Heritage, J. (eds) (1984) *Structures of Social Action*, Cambridge: Cambridge University Press.
Behn, A. (1992) 'Oroonoko', in J. Todd (ed.) *Aphra Behn: Oroonoko, The Rover and Other Works*, Harmondsworth: Penguin.
Billig, M. (1996) *Arguing and Thinking: A Rhetorical Approach to Social Psychology*, Cambridge: Cambridge University Press (2nd edn).
Boden, D. and Zimmerman, D. (eds) (1991) *Talk and Social Structure*, Cambridge: Polity.
Curry, D. (1993) 'Decorating the body politic', *New Formations* 19: 69–82.
Melville, H. (1851) *Moby Dick, or The Whale*, London: Oxford University Press.
Potter, J. and Wetherell, M. (1987) *Discourse and Social Psychology: Beyond Attitudes and Behaviuor*, London: Sage.
Sacks, H. (1984) 'On doing being ordinary', in J. M. Atkinson and J. Heritage (eds) *Structures of Social Action*, Cambridge: Cambridge University Press.
Soyland, A. J. (1997) *The Body in Culture: An Introduction*, London: Sage.
Vale, V. and Juno, A. (eds) (1989) *Modern Primitives: An Investigation of Contemporary Adornment and Ritual*, San Francisco: RE/Search Publications.
Wetherell, M. and Potter, J. (1988) 'Discourse analysis and the identification of

interpretive repertoires', in C. Antaki (ed.) *Analysing Everyday Explanations: A Casebook of Methods*, London: Sage.

Widdicombe, S. (1993) 'Autobiography and change: rhetoric and authenticity of "Gothic" style', in E. Burman and I. Parker (eds) *Discourse Analytic Research*, London: Routledge.

Index

Abraham, C. 72
Abrams, H.B. 104
Abramson, L. 76
accuracy 38
Addington, Lord 159
affordance 11
agoraphobia 110–11, 112–13; capitalist
    environments 124–6; cultural
    differences 123–4; *see also*
    disorientation
AIDS *see* HIV/AIDS
Alcorn, K. 133
Alder, B. 190
Allen, I. 159
Almeida, O.P. 101
Altheide, D. 41
Altmann, S.A. 94
anal sex 83–4
anchoring 132, 135, 144
Anderson, R. 31, 52, 73
Anderson, W.T. 34
anorexia nervosa 206
Antaki, C. 33, 34, 52, 162
anticipatory worrying 31–2
Antonis, B. 190
Apter, T. 164
Araujo, L. 39
Arcana, J. 164
Armstrong, D. 6, 211
Armstrong, D.F. 96
Aronoff, G. 77
arousal 127
arthritis: bodily impairment 60;
    social–biographical context 73
Ashbourne, Lord 162
Atkinson, J.M. 228
attribution theory 80

Baby Book, The 176, 193
back pain, chronic 77–81
Balint, M. 34
Bandura, A. 201
Banister, P. 28, 33, 39, 176
Barany, R. 111
Barber, H.O. 111
Barlow, D.H. 110
Barrenäs, M.-L. 102
Barrett, R.J. 8
Baszanger, I. 78
Baumeister, R.F. 204, 205
Beail, N. 190
Beck, A.T. 113
Beckmann, N.J. 99
Beharrell, P. 133
behavioural medicine 5
Behn, Aphra, 218–19
Benjamin, W. 124, 126
Benton, T. 4
Berger, P.L. 15–16, 96
Berman, P. 28
Berridge, V. 133
Bhide, A.V. 123
Billig, M. 53, 63, 151, 228
biological reductionism 4
biomedical model 3–4;
    pregnancy/childbirth 176–7, 177–86
biopsychosocial model 4–5; critics of
    5–7
Blaikie, N.W. 102
Blatch, Baroness 162
Blaxter, M. 34
Bles, W. 118
Bloor, D. 142
Bloor, M. 34
Boden, D. 228

body: awareness 16; diseased *see* illness; expressive of illness 59; non-conscious deployment as normality 57; as physical entity 53–4; role in chronic illness 61–2; as social construction 53–4

body decoration 217–30; addictional 222–3; and attraction 224–5; and identity 217–20, 223–4; interviews 220, 228–30; laughing about 226–8; pain 221–3; permanent 226; reasons for 225–6

Borges, J.L. 120

Borkan, J.M. 28

Bourdieu, P. 12

Bowler, I. 192

Brandt, T. 118

Breen, D. 188, 189

Brewin, C. 80

Britt, T. 35

Brodwin, P.E. 34

Bruch, H. 205, 206, 209, 210

Bruner, J. 43

Bryman, A. 70

bulimia nervosa 206

Burman, E. 35, 39, 41

Burrows, R. 16

Bury, M. 31, 52, 73, 78

Buunck, B.P. 81

Byrne, D. 105

Cahmove, A. 207

Campion, P.D. 33

cancer: coping strategies 73; social meanings 33

Cannon, W.B. 201

capitalism 124–5

care, professional 32–3

Carney, A.E. 97

Cartwright, A. 183

case-study approach 36

castration complex 113

Chambers, J. 123

Chambless, D.L. 110, 113

Changing Childbirth 183, 184–5

Charles, N. 186

Charmaz, K. 32, 36, 39

Chase, S.E. 35

Cheyne, 209–11

Chiba, S. 209

childbirth *see* pregnancy/childbirth

Children of a Lesser God 95

Chirimuuta, R. 142

cholera 136

Christensen, A. 72

chronic illness 60; adjustment to 62–5; health psychology 72–4; independence of action 61–2; interpretative phenomenological analysis 72–4; loss of control 74–7, 80; medical sociology 72–4; social perceptions 61; stigmatisation 61; uncertainty 80–81

chronic pain: inability to communicate experience 115; lower back pain 77–81; *see also* pain

Clabber Moffat, J. 77

Clark, D.B. 114

Clark, D.M. 113

Clark, M.R. 112

Clegg, A. 176

closed questions 33

cochlear implants 95–6, 97, 98–9

coding schemes 28–9, 37–9

Cohen, J.B. 52, 201

coitus interruptus 112

Collie, F. 33

Collins, H.M. 142

Comaroff, J. 136, 145

communication 12–13

comprehensiveness 38

condoms 84–6

Conrad, P. 31, 52, 69, 72

Conrad, R. 96

consciousness, intersubjective (shared meaning) 30–31

containment 55–6

control: locus of 76–7; loss of *see* loss of control; self-control *see* self-control; sexual health 157; stress-control relationships 76–7; Western preoccupation with 121–3

conversation *see* discourse

Cooper, P. 157

Cooper, P.T. 206

Cooper, Z. 206

coping: cancer 73; concept of 8; discursive analyses 7–8

Corbin, J.M. 31–2, 36, 38

coronary artery disease: activity as demonstration of health 61, 63–4; falling ill 55; research material 50–51

Coulter, J. 11, 92, 93

Cox, R.M. 99

Crabtree, B.F. 36

Crago, M. 207

Crampton, G.H. 118
Crisp, A.H. 206
Csordas, T.J. 12, 13
Cullum-Swan, B. 14
Curry, D. 219, 229
cyborgs 16

Daroff, R.B. 118
Darrow, W. 82
Davidson, I. 93
Davis, A. 99, 100
Davis, K. 20
de Swaan, A. 123
deafness *see* hearing impairment
deconstruction 17, 34–5
Deleuze, G. 16
Denzin, N. 70
depersonalisation 119–20
Derrida, J. 17
DeVellis, R.F. 81
Dewey, J. 70
diagnostic process 8–9
Dickinson, A. 201
dieting *see* eating behaviour
Dillon, H. 100, 105
disability: ecological analysis 11; WHO
    definition 101
discourse: analysis *see* discourse
    analysis; approaches to 33–5;
    deconstruction 34–5
discourse analysis (DA) 32–5, 37, 52–3;
    coping 7–8; development 5–9;
    diagnostic process 8–9; professional
    care 32–3; research methods *see*
    discursive methods; versus
    interpretative phenomenological
    analysis 70–71; versus
    phenomenology 52–3
discursive methods 25–44; discourse
    analysis 32–5; hermeneutics 29–32,
    36–7; material consequences 44;
    phenomenology 29–32;
    quantitative/semi-quantitative 27–9;
    representativeness 36–7; validity
    35–41
disease *see* illness
disorder, WHO definition 101
disorientation 109–28; authentication of
    physical diagnosis 115–16; context
    121–6; depersonalisation 119–20;
    dualist/individualist approaches
    111–17; ecological–constructionist
    analysis 109, 117–26; loss of control

109, 121–6; *nervios* syndrome 123–4;
    perceptual 118–19; phenomenology
    117–20; psychic model 112–14;
    psychological therapies 113–14;
    psychosomatic versus somatopsychic
    debate 114–17; role of arousal 127;
    somatic model 111–12; stigma 121–2;
    therapeutic interventions 127–8;
    vestibular dysfunction 110, 118–19
dizziness: agoraphobia *see* agoraphobia;
    panic disorder 111; psychogenic
    diagnosis 111–12; *see also*
    disorientation
doctor–patient interactions 6–7, 33–4
Dolce, J.J. 201
Dolnick, E. 95
Dosanjh-Matwala, N. 176, 189, 194
Douglas, M. 122, 124, 208, 209
Duveen, G. 135
dysfunction, signs of *see* symptoms

Eagger, S. 114
Eating Attitudes Test 206
eating behaviour 199–214; disorders 206;
    early theories 208–9; lay–expert
    boundary 208; measures 206–7;
    methodology problems 211–13;
    normal weight individuals 202–3;
    obesity 202–3; object of theory
    213–14; overeating 203–6;
    psychological theories 202–7;
    restraint theory 203; self-control
    theories 209–10; sociological theories
    208–11
Eating Disorders Examination 206
Eaton, W.W. 110
Eatwell, Lord 160
Eccleston, C. 27
ecological psychology 11; disability 11;
    disorientation 109, 117–26; hearing
    impairment 92; *see also*
    self–environment relationship
Economic and Social Research Council
    (ESRC) project 151, 164–5, 170
education policy 158–64
Edwards, D. 52, 70
Elias, N. 208
Elles, Baroness 162
embodied existence 10–13, 17, 18, 54;
    and material discourse 13–17; nausea
    and sickness of pregnancy 192–5
end-stage renal disease 74–7
Engel, G.L. 5, 6, 51

Engels, F. 208
escape theory 204–5
ethnomethodology 31
Evans, D. 163
Everingham, C. 189
experience of illness approach 31, 52
experiential realism 17
expertise 40–41

Fairburn, C.G. 206
Family Planning Clinics 157
Farmer, P. 133, 141
Farrior, J.B. 105
Featherstone, M. 16, 124
Feldman, M.S. 31, 35, 41
feminist standpoint 26
Festinger, L.A. 80
Fewtrell, D. 29, 119
Fitzpatrick, R.M. 4
Flowers, P. 19, 82, 84, 86
focus groups 34
Folkman, S. 52, 201
Foster, S. 96
Foucault, M. 7, 15, 16, 95, 151, 154, 213
Fox, N.J. 9, 32
Frank, A.W. 2, 34
Frank, M.A. 121
Franks, J.R. 99
Fraser, C. 137
Freeman, M. 34
Freeman, S.H. 34
Fremouw, M.J. 203
Freud, S. 111, 112
Freund, P.E.S. 10
Friday, N. 164
Frisby, D. 124
functionalist analysis 14, 17, 40–41

Gagnon, J.H. 82
Gallagher, S. 11
Garcia, J. 183
Garfinkel, H. 143
Garfinkel, P.E. 206
Garner, D.M. 206
gay men: as health problems 157;
    HIV/AIDS see HIV/AIDS; sexual
    behaviour 81–6
Geodert, J.J. 141
Gergen, K.J. 5, 6, 7, 41
Gibson, J.J. 11, 92, 102, 103
Gibson, W. 120
Gillett, G. 7, 37

Gilman, S. 136
Gilmore, C. 99
Giorgi, A. 30, 70
Glaser, B.G. 31, 72
Glynn, S.M. 204
Goffman, E. 31, 56, 72, 92, 101, 125
Goldberg, W.A. 188
Goldscheider, A. 201
Goldstein, A.J. 113
Goldstein, D.P. 100
Gordon, D.R. 4, 111, 121
Gorman, J.M. 113
Gracely, E.J. 113
Green, J.M. 181, 182, 184, 185
Gresty, M.A. 125
Greville, L. 205
Griffin, C. 27, 185
Grisby, J.P. 119
Groce, N.E. 97
Gross, L. 203
grounded theory approach 31–2, 36
Guattari, F. 16
Guba, E.G. 25, 40
Gubrium, J.F. 31
Guildford, Bishop of 160
Guthrie, R.V. 102
Guye, A. 111

haemodialysis 74–7
Hallam, R. 127
Hallberg, L.R.-M. 102
Halmi, K.A. 207
Halsbury, Earl 161
Hampson, S. 72
handicap 101–2
Haraway, D. 15, 16
Harper, D.J. 2
Harré, R. 7, 14, 37
Hart, G.J. 82
health: health/disease dichotomy 18;
    metaphorical concepts 15; risk 201;
    see also illness
Health Belief Model 156
Health Education Authority (HEA)
    project 151–2, 154–8
Health of the Nation, The 154
health psychology 5; chronic illness
    72–4; critics of 5–7; disorientation
    112–17; eating behaviour 202–7;
    hearing impairment 106; and
    interpretative phenomenological
    analysis 69–72; pregnancy/childbirth
    177, 186–92; theory as data 200–202

hearing aids 95–6, 98–9; audiological
    rehabilitation 100, 104; avoidance of
    use 99–100; use patterns 100–101
hearing impairment 92–106; capital-D
    deafness/small-D deafness 94–7;
    clinics 104–5; cochlear implants 95–6,
    97, 98–9; concepts of 92;
    connotations 97–9; corrective
    perspective 96; culture perspective
    96–7; deaf communities 96, 97;
    deficiency perspective 96–7;
    dumbness 97–8; ecological approach
    92; hearing health 103–5; role of
    psychology 106; social
    constructionist approach 92–3; and
    social ecology 102; as a status
    99–101; stigma 101–3
Heatherton, T.F. 204, 205
Hegel, G.W.H. 10
Heidegger, M. 10, 30, 120
Hemphill, K.J. 81
Henriques, J. 6, 15
Henwood, K. 32
Herbst, K.G. 101
Heritage, J. 228
Herman, C.P. 202, 203, 204, 205
Hermans, H.J.M. 43
hermeneutics 29–32, 36–7
Heron, J. 87
Herzlich, C. 15, 58, 133, 135
Hétu, R. 31, 102
Hewison, A. 180, 184
Hewstone, M. 33, 135
Hibscher, J.A. 202, 203
Hirsch, H.G. 99
HIV/AIDS 132–48; alien practices
    139–40; anchoring 132, 135, 144;
    education policy 158; and gay
    identity 140–41; Green monkey
    theory 141–2; Haitian links 141;
    health campaigns 140; interpretative
    phenomenological analysis 81–6; lay
    representations 132–3, 138–40,144–5;
    material-representational debate
    133–4; medical/scientific
    representations 132–3, 140–45;
    objectifications, 135–6; otherness
    137–45; out-groups 138–9, 140–41,
    144; school-based education 158–64;
    social construction 143; social
    representations theory 134–48; study
    rationale 137–8
Hockett, C.F. 94

Holland, J. 154
Hollinger, R. 41
Hollway, W. 5, 14, 34, 152, 153, 171
Holstein, J.A. 31
Homans, H. 191, 192, 194
homosexual men see gay men
Houghton, Lord 160
House of Lords debate 152, 159–64
Huberman, A.M. 28, 38, 39
Humphrey, C. 101
Humphries, T. 95
Hundley, V.A. 184
Hurt, William 95
Husserl, E.G.A. 10, 70

Ibanez, T. 16
identity: and body decoration 217–20,
    223–4; see also otherness
Idler, E.L. 80
illness: being ill 59–62; body's role 50–66;
    causes, psychological/social 51–2;
    chronic see chronic illness; diseased
    body 51–2; experiences of 31, 52;
    falling ill 54–9; grounded theory
    analysis 31–2, 36; ideas about 51–4;
    inactivity as threshold 58–9; mass
    incurable illness 136–7; mechanistic
    concepts 17; narrative accounts 34;
    recovery 59–62; as social status 54,
    56–7; see also health
impairment: hearing see hearing
    impairment; WHO definition 101
inactivity 58–9
independence of action 61–2
individual, changing models of 200–202
Ingham, R. 20, 42, 151, 152, 166
inter-rater reliability 28, 37–8
interpretative phenomenological analysis
    (IPA) 68–88; chronic illness 72–4;
    chronic lower back pain 77–81; and
    health psychology 69–72; HIV/AIDS
    81–6; interviews 86–7; preventative
    health interventions 88; psychological
    therapeutic interventions 88; renal
    dialysis 74–7; sexual health 81–6; and
    social-cognitive approach 70–72,
    76–7; versus discourse analysis 70–71
interviews 34; body decoration 228–30;
    interpretative phenomenological
    analysis 86–7; parents 167–8

Jackson, J.E. 8, 11, 115
Jacob, R.G. 110, 114
Jacobson, G.P. 111
Jaspers, J.M. 137
Jensen, M.P. 81
Jodelet, D. 134
Joffe, H. 19, 42, 43, 133, 134, 144
John, I.D. 27
Johnson, A.M. 166
Johnson, J.L. 31
Johnson, M. 17, 121
Johnston, C.L. 119
Johnston, J.M. 41
Jones, E.F. 166
Jones, L. 102
Jost, J.J. 17
Juno, A. 219

Kaes, R. 137, 144
Kant, I. 10, 29
Kaplan de Nour, A. 76
Kardy, P. 81
Karpas, A. 141, 142, 144
Kasden, S.D. 100
Katan, A. 113
Kelle, U. 38
Kenna, M.A. 105
Kerr, M. 186
Keyl, P.M. 110
Kingsley, L.A. 82
Kirby, D. 158
Kirkland, D. 20, 42, 152, 166, 167
Kirkpatrick, B. 121
Kirmayer, L.J. 8
Kitzinger, J. 34, 133, 180, 184
Klein, D.F. 113
Kleinman, A.M. 52
knowledge: assimilation by mass media
    135; construction by scientists 142–3;
    construction, validity 37–40; of
    illness 135; realist theories 25–6, 35–6
Kvale, S. 27, 30, 39, 126

Lacey, C.J.N. 141
Lakoff, G. 17, 121
Lane, H. 95
Langman, L. 124
language: deconstruction 17, 34–5;
    functionalist theory 14, 17, 40–41;
    linguistic processes 26; meaning *see*
    meaning; and practice 17;
    representationalist theory 13;

structuralist/post-structuralist
    analyses 13–17
Lather, E.P. 41
Latour, B. 142, 143
Lau, R. 72
Lazarus, R.S. 52, 201
learned helplessness 76
Lee, C. 168
Lehman, D.R. 81
Leininger, M. 40
leprosy 136
Leudar, I. 33, 34
Lévi-Strauss, C. 133, 208, 209
Levin, D.M. 12, 30, 121
Lewis, C. 190
Lewontin, R.C. 4
Lichtman, R. 76
life-story research 26
Lincoln, Y.S. 25, 40
Lings, A. 12
Linstrom, C.J. 111
Litton, I. 137
Lloyd, B. 135
Lobel, M. 81
Lock, M.M. 121
Locker, D. 80, 112
locus of control 76–7
Lonkila, M. 32
Lorenz, M. 113
Loro, A.D. 205
loss of control: chronic illness 74–7, 80;
    disorientation 109, 121–6; youth
    culture 122–3
Loveday, L. 209
Lovegrove, R. 100
Low, S.M. 123
lower back pain, chronic 77–81
Lozoff, B. 191
Luckmann, T. 15–16, 96
Lupton, D. 8, 53
Luxon, L.M. 127
Lyotard, J.-F. 41, 120, 124

McCormick, B. 96
McCormick, M.S. 111, 112
McGuire, J. 190
McGuire, W. 137
McIntosh, J. 34
Mack, D. 202, 203
McKenna, T. 122
McLean, J. 83
McNally, R.J. 113
McNamee, S. 6

Macy, C. 194
Mahoney, M.J. 6
Manning, M.M. 201
Manning, P.K. 14
Marck, P.B. 187, 188, 189
Marks, D. 41
Marks, D.F. 7
Marks, G. 72
Marshall, H. 20, 42, 43, 192
Martha's Vineyard 97, 98
Marx, K. 208
Masham, Baroness 160
mass media 135
masturbation 112
material–discursive approaches 1–3,
    9–17, 18–21;see also discourse
    analysis
material ecology 93
Matlin, Marlee 95
Mauss, M. 12
Mays, N. 28
Mead, G.H. 92
meaning: and context 13–15; discourse
    analysis 32–5; shared (intersubjective
    consciousness) 30–31; of statements
    about pain 14
medical model 51
medical sociology 72–4
Meltzoff, A.N. 12
Melville, H. 218–19
Melzack, R. 201
Mennell, S. 208, 209
Merleau-Ponty, M. 10, 11–12
metaphor 17; cancer 33; information-
    processing metaphor 15
Michael, M. 41, 124
Michaels, G.Y. 188
Miles, M.B. 28, 38, 39
Millar, H.R. 207
Millar, T. 207
Miller, D. 133
Miller, W.L. 36
mind–body dualism 109, 111–17;
    pregnancy/childbirth 187
Mishler, E.G. 8, 33, 34, 37, 40
Moir, J. 41
Molleman, E. 80
Monks, J. 60
Moore, M.K. 12
Morris, R.J. 136
Moscovici, S. 33, 134, 135, 137, 144
multiple sclerosis: bodily impairment 60;
    phenomenological analysis 12–13

Murcott, A. 209
Mylanus, E.A. 105

narrative analysis see discourse analysis
National Childbirth Trust (NCT) 177,
    180, 184
National Curriculum 158
Neuland, C.Y. 141
Nisbett, R.E. 204
Noble, W. 19, 42, 43, 93, 102
Noyes, R. 110

Oakley, A. 179, 180, 184, 186, 187, 191
obesity 202–3; see also eating behaviour
objectification 12, 135–6
O'Brien, M. 190
O'Connor, K. 29, 119
Ogden, J. 8, 20, 42, 43, 200–205, 207
Oliver, M. 41
Orleans, C.S. 205
Osborn, M. 19, 78
otherness 136–7; dehumanisation 146;
    and HIV/AIDS 137–45

Padden, C. 95
Page, N.G.R. 125
pain: body decoration 221–3; chronic see
    chronic pain; meaning of statements
    about 14; relief in childbirth 181–2
panic disorder 111
parents' interviews 152, 167–8
Parker, I. 35
Parkinson's disease 61
Pavlov, I.P. 201
Paxda, S.L. 207
Pearson, Lord 161
perception: disorientation 118–19;
    ecological approach 92
phenomenology 10–13, 18, 26, 70;
    discursive methods 29–32;
    disorientation 117–20; interpretative
    see interpretative phenomenological
    analysis; multiple sclerosis 12–13;
    socio-cultural processes 30–31;
    transcendental 30; versus discourse
    analysis 52–3
Phillips, M.J. 2
Phoenix, A. 27, 179, 186
Pidgeon, N. 32
Pierret, J. 15, 133, 135
Piette, A. 209
Pilgrim, D. 2

Pinder, R. 52, 61
Plomp, R. 99
pluralism 41
poliomyelitis 136
Polivy, J. 202, 203, 204, 205
Poll, I. 76
Pollard, C.A. 121
Pollock, K. 8, 112, 115
Popay, J. 195
Pope, C. 28
postmodernism: concepts of validity 41;
    and disorientation 124–6
post-structuralism: concepts of validity
    41; language analysis 13–17
Potter, J. 5, 14, 33–4, 38, 32–3, 37, 52,
    70–71, 137, 176, 220, 228–9
power 32, 40–41; negotiated 33–4;
    preconceptions 30; sexual health 157
Pregnancy Book, The 176–8, 180, 182,
    184–7, 189–90, 192–4
pregnancy/childbirth 176–96; Asian
    women's experiences 177–8, 182, 189,
    192, 194; biological–medical
    discourses 176–7, 177–86; body–mind
    dualism 187; cultural context 191–2;
    detection of abnormality 182–4;
    episiotomy 183; fathers 189–91;
    health and illness 180–82; medical
    intervention 182–4; monitoring
    normality 177–8;
    mother–child relationship 188–9;
    nausea and sickness 192–5; pain relief
    181–2; passive-patient role 184–6;
    psychological discourses 177, 186–92;
    regulating normality 178–80; scans
    189; sexuality 190; social
    relationships 191; weight gain 178–80
psychology: ecological *see* ecological
    psychology; health *see* health
    psychology
public health initiatives 8
Pursell, C. 126

qualitative research 27–9; grounded
    theory approach 31–2, 36;
    hermeneutic principle 29–32, 36–7;
    validity 35
quantitative research 27–9
Quirk, M. 28

radical relativism 2

Radley, A. 3, 10, 19, 42–3, 52–3, 55,
    61–4, 80, 121
Raguram, R. 123
Raphael-Leff, J. 179, 183–4, 186, 188–9,
    194
Ray, M.A. 30
realist theories 25–6, 35–6
Reason, P. 87
recovery 59–62
reflexivity 28, 39
Reid, M. 178, 179, 189
renal dialysis 74–7
representationalist theory 13
representativeness 36–7
Rescorla, R.A. 201
research: discursive *see* discursive
    methods; numerical coding 28–9;
    qualitative *see* qualitative research;
    quantitative 27–9; realist versus
    discursive 35–6; reflexivity 28, 39;
    traditional methods 25–6
restraint theory 203
Ricoeur, P. 13, 30
Riessman, C.K. 2, 34, 37, 40, 41
Riger, S. 26
risk 201
Robinson, M. 100
Rocherson, Y. 186, 192
Rodin, J. 202, 203
Rogers, N. 136
Rogers, R.W. 201
Ronell, A. 120
Roosevelt, Franklin D. 136
Rosenstock, I.M. 201
Ross, M. 96
Rothman, B.K. 183, 189
Rotter, J. 76
Ruderman, A.J. 204
Russell, Earl 160
Russell, G.F.M. 206
Rutherford, S.D. 95

Sacks, H. 93, 225
Salomon, G. 100
Sampson, E.E. 41, 124
Sarbin, T.R. 34, 37
Sartre, J.-P. 11, 120
Schachter, S. 53, 202, 203
Scheper-Hughes, N. 121
Schneier, F.R. 110
Schwandt, T.A. 39
Schwartz, G.E. 5
Schwarz, E.W. 182, 184

Seidel, J. 38
self-awareness 204–5
self-control: eating behaviour theories
    209–10; eating disorders 206;
    overeating 204–6; society's demands
    for 124; women's reports of dieting
    207–8
self-efficacy 201
self–environment relationship 10–13;
    information-processing metaphor 15;
    man and machine 16–17; see also
    ecological psychology
Seligman, M. 76
Selover, P.J. 97
sex education 158–64
Sex Education Forum 163
sexual health: education policy 158–64;
    empowerment versus damage
    limitation 157; family discourses
    164–8; gay men 81–6; healthy
    alliances 155; interpretative
    phenomenological analysis 81–6;
    outcomes 152, 168–71; policy 154–8;
    power/control 157; young people
    150–73
sexuality: discourses and policy 154;
    discourses in society 152–4; dyadic
    discourse 168–71; female as health
    problem 157; have–hold (romantic)
    discourse 152–3; health workers'
    attitudes 154–8; male sexual drive
    (predatory) discourse 152–3;
    medicalisation 82; not interested
    discourse 153; permissive discourse
    153; and pregnancy 190
Shaffer, M. 120
shamans 122
Sharpe, J.A. 111
Sheeran, P. 72
Shilling, C. 71
Shisslak, C.M. 207
Shotter, J. 6, 7, 9, 17
Shulman, I.D. 110
sign languages (Sign) 94, 95, 97, 98
Silverman, D. 7, 34, 39, 72
Simmel, G. 124, 125
Simon, W. 82
Singer, J.E. 53
Skinner, B.F. 201
Smith, J. 188
Smith, J.A. 10, 19, 42, 70, 71, 74, 78, 86,
    87
Smith, M.B. 124

Snaith, R.P. 113
social comparison 80–81
social constructionism 15–16, 53–4;
    eating behaviour 208–11; hearing
    impairment 92–3; HIV/AIDS 143
social ecology 102; see also ecological
    psychology; self–environment
    relationship
social engagement 93
social medicine 4–5
social representations theory 15, 33,
    134–6; HIV/AIDS 134–48
social rules 31
socio-cultural context 7; diagnostic
    process 9; phenomenology 30–31;
    pregnancy/childbirth 191–2
socio-linguistic analysis 2–3
Sontag, S. 33, 136
Soyland, A.J. 2, 20, 42, 43, 220
Spencer, J.A. 203
Spitzer, L. 203
Stacey, M. 112
Stainton-Rogers, W. 6, 7, 9
Stallard, Lord 162
Stam, H.J. 6
Steckler, A. 27
Steele, R.S. 35
Steier, F. 28
Stenner, K. 151
Stenner, P. 27, 41
Stephens, S.D.G. 100
stereotypic public discourses
    (interpretive repertoires) 37
Stern, P.N. 31
Stevens, D. 152, 159
stigmatisation: anticipated 31; chronic
    pain 61; disorientation 121–2;
    hearing impairment 101–3
Stiles, W.B. 39
Stokoe, W.C. 95
Stoppard, J.M. 180
Strauss, A. 31–2, 36, 38
Strauss, A.L. 31, 72
stress-control relationships 76–7
stress theories 201
structuralism 13–17
Sullivan, M. 28, 111, 114
symbolic interactionism 31, 70
symbols 33
symptoms: accommodation, breakdown
    of 56, 58; containment 55–6; early
    54–9; response to 57–8
syphilis 136

Tajfel, H. 144
Taussig, M.T. 8
Taylor, K. 104
Taylor, M.J. 206
Taylor, S. 73, 76
Taylor, S.E. 81
Teasdale, J. 76
Telch, M.J. 121
Tesch, R. 31
Theory of Reasoned Action 156
Thomas, A.J. 101
Thompson, S. 76, 166
Thorn, B.E. 80
Toombs, S.K. 12, 65
triangulation 39–40
Tuckett, D. 33
Turner, B.S. 4, 9, 13, 209–11
Turner, J. 144
typhus 136
typicality 37

uncertainty: chronic pain 80–81;
    disorientation 109, 115–17
Ussher, J. 186, 187, 188

Vale, V. 219
validity 35–41; forms of validation
    40–41; of knowledge construction
    37–40; persuasive 40–41
Van den Berg, J.H. 11
Van der Merwe, W.L. 17
Vanderzee, K.I. 81
van Otterloo, A.H. 209
van Zessen, G. 165
Vass, A. 141
vertigo 111, 112, 119–20; see also
    disorientation
Vesterager, V. 101
vestibular dysfunction 110, 118–19
Ville, I. 8
Voestermans, P.P. 17
Voysey, M. 53

Wacquant, L.J.D. 12
Waddell, G. 77
Wagner, A.R. 201

Wagner, S. 207
Wagner, W. 135
Waitzkin, H. 6, 8, 35
Walden, B.E. 99
Wall, P.D. 201
Wallen, W.C. 141
Wang, A. 9
Wardle, J. 204, 205
Waridel, S. 100
Waugh, M.A. 141
Weeks, J. 154
Weiss, E. 113
Wellings, K. 133, 141
Wetherell, M. 5, 14, 33–4, 38, 52, 70–71,
    176, 220, 228–9
White, D. 9
Widdicombe, S. 229
Wiedenfeld, S.A. 201
Wiener, C.L. 60
Wight, D. 153, 171
Wiles, R. 180
Williams, D.A. 80
Williams, G. 73
Williams, G.J. 207
Wittgenstein, L. 14
Wolkind, S. 179, 186, 188, 192, 194
Wood, J. 76
Woodcock, A.J. 151, 163
Woolgar, S. 142, 143
Woollett, A. 20, 42–3, 176, 182, 187–9,
    192–4
Worcester, N. 186
Wright, T.L. 201
Wynne, A. 28

Yardley, L. 10, 13, 31, 42–3, 52, 61, 93,
    110, 114, 118–19, 121, 127
young people: contraception advice
    (Drop-in Centres) 157; loss of control
    122–3; sexual health 150–73

Zajicek, E. 179, 186, 188, 192, 194
Zijlmans, W. 165
Zilbergeld, B. 170
Zimmermann, D. 228
Zola, I.K. 54, 56